Liturgical-Missional

Liturgical-Missional
Perspectives on a Reformed Ecclesiology

Edited by
NEAL D. PRESA

Foreword by
OLAV FYKSE TVEIT

◆PICKWICK *Publications* · Eugene, Oregon

LITURGICAL-MISSIONAL
Perspectives on a Reformed Ecclesiology

Copyright © 2016 Wipf and Stock Publishers. All rights reserved. Except for brief quotations in critical publications or reviews, no part of this book may be reproduced in any manner without prior written permission from the publisher. Write: Permissions, Wipf and Stock Publishers, 199 W. 8th Ave., Suite 3, Eugene, OR 97401.

Pickwick Publications
An Imprint of Wipf and Stock Publishers
199 W. 8th Ave., Suite 3
Eugene, OR 97401

www.wipfandstock.com

PAPERBACK ISBN 13: 978-1-62564-702-3
HARDCOVER ISBN 13: 978-1-4982-8799-9

Cataloguing-in-Publication Data

Liturgical-Missional : perspectives on a reformed ecclesiology / edited by Neal D. Presa ; foreword by Olav Fykse Tveit.

xvi + 278 p. ; 23 cm. Includes bibliographical references.

ISBN: 978-1-62564-702-3 (paperback) | ISBN: 978-1-62564-702-3 (hardback)

1. Reformed Church—Doctrines. 2. Mission of the church. 3. Missions—Theory. I. Tveit, Olav Fykse. II. Presa, Neal D. III. Title.

BX9422.3 .L55 2016

Manufactured in the U.S.A.   02/08/2016

In honor of the 500th anniversary of the
Protestant Reformation

Contents

List of Contributors | ix
Editor's Preface | xi
Foreword by Olav Fykse Tveit | xv

Part I: Gathering

1. A Call-and-Response Ecclesiology | 3
   —*Joseph D. Small*

2. Locating the Liturgical-Missional Church in the Bible's Story | 15
   —*David Stubbs*

3. Worship as the Missional Church's Whence and Wither | 33
   —*Teresa Stricklen Eisenlohr*

4. Opening the Doors of the Church: Identity and Mission at the Thresholds of Christian Worship | 47
   —*David Gambrell*

5. Ecclesiology Without Metaphor | 64
   —*Jerry Andrews*

Part II: Hearing, Proclaiming, Sealing

6. The Church as Missional Community | 77
   —*Darrell Guder*

7. Preaching for Liturgical-Missional Congregations | 83
   —*Jennifer Lord*

8. Baptism: The Already and the Not Yet | 94
   —*Martha Moore-Keish*

9. Is There Any Reason to Join a Church? Baptism as Commissioning to Life Together | 104
   —*John Burgess*

10 The Centrality of the Eucharist | 119
    —Thomas E. Smith

11 Missional Eucharist | 133
    —Marney Wasserman

12 The Space Between Acts 2 and Acts 10: An Ecclesiology of Text, Time, and the Holy Spirit | 139
    —Frank Yamada

Part III: Sending and Serving

13 Worship and Justice: The Church's Identity and Calling | 155
    —Mark Labberton

14 Mutual Transformation in Mission | 167
    —Heidi Worthen Gamble

15 A Praxis of Worship and Witness | 177
    —Allen Permar Smith

16 Newbigin House of Studies: An Experiment in Missional Theological Education | 184
    —Scot Sherman

17 From the Palace to the Streets | 197
    —Steven Toshio Yamaguchi

18 Testificar: A Call to the Presbyterian Church (USA) | 212
    —Ruth-Aimée Belonni-Rosario

19 From Blueprint to Foretaste: Worship, Mission, and Multiculturalism in Reformed Congregations | 222
    —Corey Widmer

20 A PC(USA) Reflection on an Ecumenical Understanding of Ecclesiology | 232
    —Robina Winbush

Epilogue: Outside the (United) Church Is No Salvation | 244
    —Edwin Chr. van Driel

Contributors

Jerry Andrews is Senior Pastor/Head of Staff of the First Presbyterian Church in San Diego, California.

Ruth-Aimée Belonni-Rosario is Dean of Admissions at Lancaster Theological Seminary in Lancaster, Pennsylvania.

John Burgess is the James Henry Snowden Professor of Systematic Theology at Pittsburgh Theological Seminary in Pittsburgh, Pennsylvania.

Teresa Stricklen Eisenlohr was previously Associate for Worship for the Presbyterian Mission Agency in Louisville, Kentucky.

Heidi Worthen Gamble is Mission Advocate for Hunger, Poverty, and Peacemaking Concerns with the Presbytery of the Pacific in Los Angeles, California.

David Gambrell is Associate for Worship at the Presbyterian Mission Agency of the Presbyterian Church (USA) in Louisville, Kentucky.

Darrell Guder is the inaugural Henry Winters Luce Professor Emeritus of Missional and Ecumenical Theology at Princeton Theological Seminary in Princeton, New Jersey.

Mark Labberton is President and Lloyd John Ogilvie Professor of Preaching at Fuller Theological Seminary in Pasadena, California.

Jennifer Lord is the Dorothy B. Vickery Professor of Homiletical and Liturgical Studies at Austin Presbyterian Theological Seminary in Austin, Texas.

Martha Moore-Keish is Associate Professor of Theology at Columbia Theological Seminary, California, and cochair of the global dialogue between the World Communion of Reformed Churches and the Pontifical Council for Promoting Christian Unity.

Scot Sherman is the Executive Director of the Newbigin House in San Francisco, California.

Joseph D. Small is church relations consultant with the Presbyterian Church (USA) Foundation, and served as the Director of Theology, Worship, and Education with the Presbyterian Mission Agency in Louisville, Kentucky for more than two decades.

Allen Permar Smith is Pastor of the Kenilworth Presbyterian Church in Asheville, North Carolina.

Thomas E. Smith is Pastor of Presbyterian Chapel of the Lakes in Angola, Indiana.

David Stubbs is Professor of Theology and Ethics at Western Theological Seminary in Holland, Michigan.

Olav Fykse Tveit is the General Secretary of the World Council of Churches based in Geneva, Switzerland.

Edwin Chr. van Driel is the Directors' Bicentennial Associate Professor of Theology at Pittsburgh Theological Seminary in Pittsburgh, Pennsylvania.

Marney Wasserman is an honorably retired teaching elder of the Presbyterian Church (USA) who lives in Rockport, Texas. She chaired the General Assembly Sacraments Work Group.

Corey Widmer is Senior Pastor/Head of Staff of Third Presbyterian Church and copastor of East End Fellowship in Richmond, Virginia.

Robina Winbush is Associate Stated Clerk and Director of Ecumenical and Agency Relations with the Office of the General Assembly of the Presbyterian Church (USA), and President of Churches Uniting in Christ.

Frank Yamada is President and Cyrus McCormick Professor of Bible and Culture at McCormick Theological Seminary in Chicago, Illinois.

Steven Toshio Yamaguchi is Dean of Students and Assistant Professor of Pastoral Theology at Fuller Theological Seminary in Pasadena, California.

Editor's Preface

The whole is not greater than nor equal to the sum of its parts. While we affirm that adage, when applied to the Church, the Reformed theological tradition in the Presbyterian Church (USA), specifically, asserts the following: "The congregation is the basic form of the church, but it is not of itself a sufficient form of the church" (section G-1.0101 of *The Book of Order*).

What we find in the local expression of the Church called the congregation is the characteristics of the Church described in the third article of the Nicene Creed: one, holy, catholic, apostolic. But, even then, in a congregation, we don't have the fullness of the one, holy, catholic, apostolic Church. The Church is expressed in regional, national, and global contexts.

In the sixteenth-century continental Reformation, the churches who find their theological roots in John Calvin identified three markers that signaled the presence of the Church of Jesus Christ:

> the Word of God is truly preached and heard,
> the Sacraments are rightly administered, and
> ecclesiastical discipline is uprightly ministered.
> (section F-1.0303 of *The Book of Order*)

The multiplicity of ecclesiastical polities, worship practices, mission endeavors, and theological engagements shows that it is not simply a matter of finding these marks or even doing the marks to be the Church. When the Church seeks to be a faithful witness of the Gospel in a given context, the Church—in its global, national, regional, local expression—acts in a variety of ways. Sometimes, what the Church does can look more like a bureaucracy than a beloved community. Or in another season of the Church's life, the community of believers can be more involved in seeking the betterment of society and world and less inwardly focused on its own survival.

Four hundred years after the Protestant Reformation, it became clear to many Christians that the divided household of faith of the one holy catholic apostolic Church was no longer tenable; that given the realities of the first World War, followed by the Second World War, division and brokenness in the body of Christ needed to be overcome. But it proved to be easier said as a hoped-for goal than undertaken.

As the modern ecumenical movement took shape in the latter part of the nineteenth century, burgeoned in the early to mid-twentieth century with the birth of the World Council of Churches in 1948 and the convening of the Second Vatican Council in 1962, the liturgical movement also took shape. This was an effort to bring ecumenism and the Church's worship within a framework for dialogue, study, and, in some cases, shared practice, or at the least, to seek to understand the worship practices and life of separated communities and theological traditions. The merger of the international missionary conferences with that of the faith and works movements into the World Council of Churches and its Faith and Order Commission were, likewise, attempts to continue the related and necessary conversation between mission and the theology of the Church's faith. The question is asked: whose mission is it? God's mission? The Church's mission?

In the late 1990s, the pioneering scholarship of the Gospel and Culture Network, with leading theologians such as Darrell Guder and George Hunsberger, led to the coining of the term, "missional," to speak of the necessity of the Church to recalibrate its identity and being in the mission of God.

The realities and challenges of the first decade of the twenty-first century are enormous. Globalization, social media, terrorism, religious fanaticism, rising inequality and inequity among the world's rich and poor, climate change and environmental degradation that threatens the integrity of creation, just to name a few. What should the Church of Jesus Christ be about in the twenty-first century? What has it always been about but which Christendom and the power and politics that accompany that erstwhile position obscured or stifled? What does faithful Gospel witness look like in our contexts, in our generation?

When I was elected to serve a two-year term as Moderator of the 220th General Assembly of the Presbyterian Church (USA) in 2012, I set out to convene conversations that sought to reflect carefully on the Church's identity, desiring to put liturgical theology and missional theology into conversation. I was inspired by two groups I belonged to and whose discussions were formative in my understanding of our faith and common mission: the General Assembly's Sacraments Work Group and the Re-Forming Ministry Core Cluster. The former was constituted as an official study group given a specific task to examine the historical, ecumenical, and liturgical relationship of the baptismal font and the Lord's Table. The latter was a project funded by the Lilly Endowment that involved a six-year conversation in a

21-member small group consisting of pastors, seminary professors, and judicatory officials, seeking to exegete American Presbyterianism, Reformed theology, and a Church that is missional, or ought to be missional, at its core.

What resulted were three moderatorial colloquia. With the support of my moderatorial partner, the Rev. Dr. Tom Trinidad, pastor of Faith Presbyterian Church in Colorado Springs, CO and who served ably as Vice Moderator of the 220th General Assembly, we convened three gatherings in April 2013, December 2013, and March 2014, in order to catalyze conversations on the liturgical-missional nature of the Church.

Billed as the Moderator's Colloquium on Ecclesiology, the three colloquia were hosted by three theological seminaries. Each colloquium featured seven invited presenters who engaged worship and mission from different angles. The seven presenters were pastors, seminary professors and judicatory officials. Three respondents (a local pastor or ruling elder, a seminary student from the host seminary, and a seminary professor from the host seminary) engaged each presenter.

We augmented this with the use of a live Web stream, a Twitter feed (#ModCE) and a live teleconference to allow for maximal participation in the conversation. This book compiles those presentations.

I am grateful to Vice Moderator Tom Trinidad for his partnership as we co-convened the three colloquia. My special thanks go to the three host seminaries, their presidents, faculty, staff and students: Austin Presbyterian Theological Seminary led by President Ted Wardlaw who hosted the first colloquium in April 2013; Princeton Theological Seminary led by President Craig Barnes who hosted the second colloquium in December 2013; and Fuller Theological Seminary led by President Mark Labberton who hosted the final colloquium in March 2014. I thank the support of the General Assembly Committee on Theological Education for officially endorsing this initiative and encouraging the theological institutions related to the General Assembly to support this project. My thanks also go to the Presbyterian Church (USA) Foundation and its president Tom Taylor and his staff for their support and providing a mechanism for promotion and financial support. Key to the success of the colloquia were the staff of the Office of the General Assembly who provided magnanimous support during my moderatorial service, generally, and the three colloquia, specifically: Stated Clerk Gradye Parsons, former Associate Stated Clerk Loyda Aja, Manager for the Stated Clerk and Moderator Angie Stevens and her predecessor Molly Williams, Manager of Web Services Randy Hobson, and Communications Director Toya Richards and her predecessor Sharon Youngs.

On the publication of this book, my thanks go to all the contributors who presented their essays in the colloquia, all of whom are faithful pastors, professors, judicatory officials, ecumenists, and theologians. Many thanks to WCC General Secretary Olav Fykse Tveit for offering the foreword in the midst of his busy travel and speaking schedule, and his assistants, Garland Pierce and Diana Chabloz. Although space limitations prevented the publication of the 63 prepared responses, the richness of these papers offer important perspectives as we discern the distinctiveness of Reformed worshipping-witnessing communities in a twenty-first-century world. Special thanks to the staff at Wipf and Stock Publishers, especially Assistant Managing Editor Matthew Wimer and his predecessor Christian Amondson, and Editorial Administrator Laura Poncy, for guiding this process with patience and perseverance. Additional thanks to Mark Caton and Dictate Express for the *pro bono* transcription of the oral presentations given by Mark Labberton and Darrell Guder. I am grateful to three communities who supported my service as General Assembly Moderator and who demonstrate being liturgical-missional: Middlesex (NJ) Presbyterian Church, New Brunswick Theological Seminary, and Village Community Presbyterian Church. My church in miniature, our home, demonstrate everyday what it means to be gathered in God's grace and sent to live it out. My love and thanks to my wife, Grace, and sons, Daniel and Andrew, for supporting this project, the colloquia, and the moderatorial journey we took together.

My hope and prayer is that these perspectives on a Reformed ecclesiology will catalyze conversation on "Why the Church," inspire the Church to creative and faithful ministry, and, on the cusp of the 500th anniversary of the Protestant Reformation, contribute several Reformed theological insights on the essential character of and continual calling to the Church. It is in honor of and celebration of the quincentenary of the Protestant Reformation that this volume is dedicated.

Soli Deo Gloria
Neal D. Presa
Rancho Santa Fe, CA
Palm Sunday 2015

Foreword

The reader may find it paradoxical that this foreword to a book on aspects of "Reformed ecclesiology" is authored by a Norwegian Lutheran pastor and theologian who serves as the General Secretary of the World Council of Churches. After all, this book is not only clearly anchored in the Reformed tradition, but it has been developed primarily in the context of Reformed communities in North America.

And yet the paradox is superficial. *Liturgical-Missional* is a book firmly rooted in a confessional tradition that has always insisted on its own catholicity and the essential unity of the one Church. Among the first Reformed theological journals was a publication called *The Catholic Presbyterian*. The founders of the World Alliance of Reformed Churches, a predecessor of today's World Communion of Reformed Churches (WCRC), saw it as an "ecumenical" endeavor, a first step toward a wider alliance of Reformation (rather than just Reformed) churches.

The outstanding Presbyterian missiologist and ecumenist John Mackay, a native of Scotland and scholar of Spanish and Latin American cultures as well as chairman of the International Missionary Council and president of Princeton Theological Seminary, led the World Alliance of Reformed Churches in the twentieth century to state officially that Presbyterianism should never be seen merely as an end in itself, for the highest glory of the Reformed tradition is "to maintain the vision and viewpoint of the church universal, seeking continually its welfare and unity."

Bishop Lesslie Newbigin, a Reformed and "Uniting and United" pioneer of "missional" thinking and at one time Associate General Secretary of the WCC, wrote in *The Open Secret* of "mission as hope in action" and described the churches' part in that journey: "The reign of God that the church proclaims is indeed present in the life of the church, but it is not the church's possession. It goes before us, summoning us to follow." This is one description of our pilgrimage together.

It is no wonder that some twenty united and uniting churches hold membership in the WCRC today, and that the WCRC distinguished itself in the second half of the twentieth century by its remarkable engagement in bilateral ecumenical dialogues with Catholic, Orthodox, Pentecostal and African Independent churches as well as more conventional conversations among Western Protestants.

It is no wonder that in the first pages of this present work, theologian Joseph Small, very much a *catholic Presbyterian*, insists on the fact that in Reformed ecclesiology the local gathering around Word, sacraments and obedience is fully the Church—and yet the local church is not the whole Church: the local presupposes the universal, and the universal is manifest in the local. There is movement within the whole church—a missional movement, and an ecumenical movement.

The gathered-and-sent, call-and-response, liturgical-and-missional dynamic of this book is quintessentially ecumenical. The missional focus is historically inseparable from a focus on Christian unity "so that the world may believe" (John 17:21). Christian unity provides the horizon of this book, as indicated particularly by the contributions of Robina Winbush and Edwin Chr. van Driel.

As world Christianity observes the anniversary of events centered on Wittenberg in 1517, a peculiarly Lutheran moment in church history, we may ask in which ways the Reformation churches best honor Luther, Calvin and their heirs? In response, we embark on a fresh rediscovery of God's design for what Calvin, following the church fathers, called "the mother of all believers"—the Church. This collection of essays contributes to a renewed sense of what it means to be "*semper reformanda* (always being reformed) according to the Word of God"—and according to our response to current challenges.

The renewal of the Church by the Word and the Spirit "so that the world may believe" is a central insight of the modern ecumenical movement. Unity becomes visible in liturgy and fellowship, and this leads many churches to recognize our sin of division.

But if Christ is not only the head of the Body but also the head of the new creation, the struggle for us to manifest the unity of the Church is inseparable from the struggle to overcome everything that prevents the unity of humanity (as the 2013 WCC Assembly in Busan made clear in its statement on Unity). The renewal of the Church is inseparable from following Christ throughout the whole world, in a common pilgrimage of justice and peace.

Olav Fykse Tveit, General Secretary
World Council of Churches
Geneva, Switzerland

PART I

Gathering

I

A Call-and-Response Ecclesiology

Joseph D. Small

> A company of believers is like a prisonful of criminals: their intimacy and solidarity are based on what about themselves they can least justify.
>
> —John Updike, *In the Beauty of the Lillies*[1]

What do we mean when we speak the word "church"? In everyday speech the word evokes a variety of images that are maintained kaleidoscopically, with ever-shifting changes in pattern and hue: buildings, people, congregations, organizations, denominations, communions, and more. The situation is only marginally better when the word is used theologically, thus the necessity for qualifiers such as "local" and "universal," "visible and invisible," and alternates such as "ecclesial communities" and "faith communities" to specify what we mean by our use of "church." Luther detested the word. "This . . . meaningless and obscure . . . word *kirche* [church] is not German," he said, "and does not convey the sense or meaning that should be taken."[2]

What we mean by the word is important because the church is central in the reception, preservation, and transmission of Christian truth. And yet ecclesiology—the doctrine of the church—is usually a theological afterthought. Who, what, when, where, why, how is the church? To the extent that

---

1. Updike, *In the Beauty*, 416.
2. Luther, "On the Councils and the Church," 363.

these questions are asked, they are too often left to the sociologists or, God help us, the branders, marketers, and funds developers. When theologians get around to the church, having dealt with all of the really important and interesting theological loci, they usually present an abstraction, a picture of the church that bears only a vague resemblance to what we experience in actual congregations, judicatories, and denominations. We are presented with lovely portraits of the church, ideal paradigms meant to show us that there is more than meets the eye when we look at actual churches. On the other hand, sociologists—both academic and amateur—generally show us a documentary film of the flawed church, sometimes designed merely to deconstruct, but often meant to suggest strategies that can produce the church that *could be*. The problem, of course, is that both are instances of what Nicholas Healy calls "blueprint ecclesiologies,"[3] two-dimensional templates that outline either normative construals in the guise of description, or description as the backdrop for normative prescription. In both cases, ecclesiology is about what should or could be rather than theological engagement with what is.

Dietrich Bonhoeffer put the matter plainly more than eighty years ago: "There are basically two ways to misunderstand the church," he said, "one historicizing and the other religious; the former confuses the church with the religious community, the latter with the Realm of God."[4] Neither sociology nor theology alone is adequate to understand the reality of the church, which is simultaneously a historical-sociological phenomenon and a Christ/Spirit-created communion of faith. Theological talk apart from the concrete reality of actual churches easily becomes irrelevant to *lived* faith; sociological examination apart from faithful attention to the one holy catholic apostolic church easily becomes irrelevant to lived *faith*.

It is a fundamental conviction of classic Reformed ecclesiology that the gathered congregation is the basic form of church. More precisely, Reformed ecclesiology understands that the gathered congregation is most truly itself when it is gathered around word, water, bread and wine in worship of the one God who is Emmanuel—God with us—and whose active Word is spoken: "I will be your God and you shall be my people" (Jer 7:23 passim). It is also a fundamental conviction of Reformed ecclesiology that the gathered congregation is not a sufficient form of church. The congregation gathered by Word and Sacrament *is* the one holy catholic apostolic church, but not of itself alone—as if it were a solitary, self-sufficient ecclesia. The gathered congregation is the one holy catholic and apostolic church

---

3. Healy, *Church, World*, 25–51.

4. Bonhoeffer, *Sanctorum Communio*, 125.

only in its essential communion with the Lord and therefore its communion with other gathered congregations.

Both of those convictions require considerable unpacking because they are not manifest in the self-understanding of contemporary Reformed churches. However, all I can offer now is a sketch of the church's communion with Christ that I hope will be suggestive.

A Church of the Word and Sacrament

The Swiss reformation had a particular approach to the nature and purpose of the church that began, not with the church itself, but with Christ. In the words of the *Ten Theses of Berne* (1528), "The holy Christian Church, whose only head is Christ, is born of the Word of God, and abides in the same, and listens not to the voice of a stranger."[5] This declaration is more than a self-evident bromide, for the Word of God sounds in the midst of many other voices—cultural, societal, political, and religious—and so the church must always be called back to its true self, to its Lord. Centuries after Berne, the Theological Declaration of Barmen sought to recall the church to the evangelical truth that "Jesus Christ, as he is attested for us in Holy Scripture, is the one Word of God which we have to hear and which we have to trust and obey in life and in death." Barmen went on to "reject the false doctrine, as though the church could and would have to acknowledge as a source of its proclamation, apart from and beside this one Word of God, still other events and powers, figures and truths, as God's revelation."[6] What the Reformed tradition means by "church" begins with the Word of God, Jesus Christ, revealed to us through the word of God, Scripture. As the creation of the Word in the power of the Holy Spirit, the church comes into being continuously through the real presence of Christ in Word and Sacrament—the *real* presence of the *living* Christ in proclamation, Baptism, and Eucharist.

How do we know this creature of the Word when we see it? It is in Word and Sacrament, said Calvin, that, "the church comes forth and becomes visible to our eyes. Wherever we see the Word of God purely preached and heard, and the sacraments administered according to Christ's institution, there, it is not to be doubted, a church of God exists"[7] The Word of God rightly proclaimed and heard . . . Baptism and the Lord's Supper celebrated in fidelity to Christ . . . these are the clear indicators of the one holy catholic

---

5. Leith, "Ten Conclusions of Berne," 129.
6. Theological Declaration of Barmen, in *The Book of Confessions*, 249.
7. Calvin, *Institutes*, 1023.

and apostolic church. Where we see faithful proclamation and reception, and faithful sacramental life, we see the church.

Calvin's two marks of the church center on lived faith within congregations. Clearly, proclamation and enactment of the gospel are not the only things that congregations do. Churches engage in many other forms of ministry and mission, and organize numerous programs. But at the heart of it all, animating and shaping everything else, must be God's Word, most audibly and visibly present in preaching and teaching, Baptism and Eucharist. So central are these two marks, Calvin continued, that we must embrace any church that has them, "even if it otherwise swarms with many faults."[8]

Three features of Calvin's formulation must be emphasized, one explicit and the others implicit. First, notice that Calvin adds the two little words, "and heard" to the preaching of the Word. A faithful congregation is where the proclaimed Word is heard, not in a merely auditory manner of course, but rather received, believed, and lived. Similarly, the sacraments are to be "administered"—carried out, conducted—within and by the whole assembly in accordance with Christ. The marks are not simply functions of what ministers do, but characteristics of the whole people of God who are called to faithful living under the Word, not listening to the siren voices of strangers.

Second, Calvin was certain that proclaiming the Word of God—the living, present Christ—and being united with the living, present Christ through Baptism and the Lord's Supper, formed faithful disciples in a faithful community equipped for faithful living in the world. Calvin was confident that Word and Sacrament are effective: they give to us precisely what they portray. Preaching God's word imparts Christ himself to us, disclosing Christ's living presence among us ("The word is near you, on your lips and in your heart," Rom 10:8). The sacraments re-present the person and work of Christ, making real among us the very presence of Christ ("We were buried therefore with him by baptism into [his] death, so that as Christ was raised from the dead by the glory of the Father, we too might walk in newness of life," Rom 6:4; "The cup of blessing which we bless, is it not a communion in the blood of Christ? The bread which we break, is it not a communion in the body of Christ?" 1 Cor 10:16). Calvin takes it as "a settled principle that the sacraments have the same office as the Word of God: to offer and set forth Christ to us, and in him the treasures of heavenly grace."[9] The church, born of the Word made flesh, abides in union with the crucified and risen Christ through proclamation and sacraments, for they

---

8. Ibid., 1025.
9. Ibid., 1292.

are more than liturgical activities, and certainly more than the memory of a long-ago and far-away Jesus; they are the principal means by which we come to life as the body of Christ.

Third, neither Word nor Sacraments is limited to the church's liturgy. The Word proclaimed and heard, the Word enacted in Baptism and Eucharist, Christ present with us, thrust the congregation into the world where it is called to bear witness to Christ 'in Jerusalem and in all Judea and to the end of the earth" (Acts 1:8). The church's witness takes primary shape in the lives and words of its individual members as they live out their calling in homes, neighborhoods, and occupations. Corporate witness is also found in missional initiatives of the congregation, often in concert with other congregations and judicatories. Just as Jesus "suffered outside the gate in order to sanctify the people through his own blood," so the church is called to "go forth to him outside the camp, bearing abuse for him" (Heb 13:12f.). Jesus Christ, present in Word and Sacrament, is the same Jesus Christ, present with his disciples in the world.

Contemporary application of Word and Sacraments as marks of the church is not mere nostalgia for Reformation clarity, for Word and Sacraments provide the churches with foundational identifiers of ecclesial faithfulness. The question to be asked of any congregation (or denomination) is whether Word and Sacraments are found at the heart of common life. When we look at a Christian community, at *our* Christian community, do we see—at the center of its life—spoken and enacted proclamation of the gospel? Although congregations and denominations engage in a wide variety of activities that grow from preaching, teaching, and celebrating the sacraments, programs and initiatives and services must not bury Word and Sacrament, or push them to the periphery of church life. The whole range of church life must remain subject to authentication by Word and Sacrament, the embodiment of the gospel in the life of Christ's women and men.

If Word and Sacrament together are the heart of the church's true and faithful life, neglect of one leads inexorably to deformation of the other, for when either Word or Sacrament exists alone it soon becomes a parody of itself. Reformed Christians are aware of how the sacraments can become objects of eccentric piety in churches where sacraments are exalted and preaching is minimized. But we may be less aware of how easily preaching and teaching can deteriorate into idiosyncratic monologues, institutional marketing, human potential promotion, ideological advocacy, or bourgeois conformity, in churches that magnify preaching while marginalizing Baptism and Eucharist. The real and present danger of sacramental minimalism is that a church of the word *alone* will degenerate into a church of mere words.

Two Natures Ecclesiology?

Jürgen Moltmann sets forth a crucial ecclesiological axiom: "The way one thinks about Christ is also the way one thinks about the church. . . . Thus ecclesiology can only be developed from Christology, as its consequence and in correspondence with it."[10] One can think about Christ in myriad ways, of course, some of which lead to odd ecclesiological notions. A particularly damaging ecclesiological trajectory emerges from a flawed appropriation of Chalcedonian Christology. Chalcedon is always understood wrongly when it is removed from the context of the ecumenical councils that preceded it (Nicaea, Constantinople, and Ephesus), and from the theological ferment that surrounded the conciliar trajectory. Such disengagement leads to an appropriation of Chalcedon that separates what the Definition holds together. Chalcedon declares "One and the same Son" who is "truly God and truly human," at once "*homoousias* with the Father and *homoousias* with us." Chalcedonian Christology speaks of the *one* Jesus Christ, and it does this inductively, grounding its judgments in the visible, tangible reality of the Word of God in human flesh. And yet this unity is often distorted into an abstract distinction between two conceptual natures. Thinking of the one Jesus Christ in terms of two different, nonconcrete substances—divinity and humanity—inspires a "two natures ecclesiology." The way one thinks about Christ is also the way one thinks about the church, and so the church is also said to have a divine nature and a human nature, each conceptually distinct.

A familiar "two natures ecclesiology" is found in the invisible-visible church distinction, particularly in its popular version. With apologies to the bishops at Chalcedon, the church is understood as "invisible and visible, essential and empirical, internal and external, ideal and real, one holy catholic and apostolic as regards its true nature and like other societies and institutions as regards its human nature." The preferred Protestant version of the two-natures, invisible-visible ecclesiology is thought to be especially useful when faced with the obvious proliferation of separated and fragmenting churches, for it enables recourse to the essential unity of the capital C Church, a universal reality that transcends all of the disconnected churches we experience. This authorizes us to claim that we remain united in the body of Christ even in the midst of our obvious churchly divisions.

Distinctions between the visible and invisible church have been made at least since Augustine, although he did not use the terms. In the classical version of the distinction, the invisible church consists of the communion of saints throughout time and space, while the visible church is perceived

---

10. Moltmann, *Church in the Power*, 66.

in actual Christian communities that are evident at any given time. Calvin noted that Scripture sometimes speaks of the church as all the living and dead who are elect in Christ, and sometimes with reference to living people who now profess the one true God. But since the elect who are in God's presence are known only to God, Calvin immediately turned his attention to the only church that is humanly knowable, the visible church. "Just as we must believe, therefore, that the former church, invisible to us, is visible to the eyes of God alone," wrote Calvin, "so we are commanded to revere and keep communion with the latter, which is called 'church' in respect to men."[11] Calvin understood that, unlike the invisible church, the visible church is a *corpus permixtum*, a body in which not all who profess Christ are actually in communion with Christ. Nevertheless, Calvin insisted that we are called to keep communion with this all too visibly mixed body because we are unable to know what God alone knows—who is elect in Christ and who is not. Because of the obvious limitation of human knowledge and judgment, Calvin notes that God has given us a "certain charitable judgment" whereby we recognize as members of the church *all* who "profess the same God and Christ with us."[12]

Calvin's charitable judgment did not hold, however. A line of thought soon developed and became prevalent among ministers and members alike, in which the invisible church is understood as the true church, the body of Christ, while the visible churches are merely human constructions, genuine churches only to the extent that they conform faith and life to the presumed standard of the invisible church. The predictable result is a denigration of all institutional embodiments of the visible church, together with a view of their dispensability. Too often, this leads to justification for easy exit from particular denominations and the multiplication of separated churches. Effortless confidence in the intangible unity of the invisible church opens the revolving door to endlessly repeated church ruptures, separations, splits, and schisms. The invisible church is presented as the real thing whose spiritual unity remains untouched by any and every division.

Call-and-Response Ecclesiology

Clearly, there are numerous angles of approach to a christological ecclesiology. A particularly suggestive tack, focusing on the real presence of Christ, is suggested by Dietrich Ritschl's inquiry in *Memory and Hope*. Ritschl begins by noting with approval Bonhoeffer's critique of scholastic theology

11. Calvin, *Institutes*, 1022.
12. Ibid., 1022f.

that asks "what is Jesus Christ?" rather than "who is Jesus Christ?" Only by asking "*who* is?" do we avoid a separation between Christ's being and work, between his person and his benefits. Answering the "*who?*" question turns attention to the whole Christ's present actions. Hans Frei makes the same point in his discussion of the identity of Jesus Christ: "A person *is* what he *does* centrally and most significantly. He is the unity of a significant project or intention passing over into its own enactment."[13] The person and work of Jesus Christ are not two separate topics; it is in Christ's "work" that his "person" is realized and revealed.

So Ritschl asks *who* Christ *is* by asking *what* Christ *does*. His inquiry incorporates a synopsis of New Testament passages that speak of Christ's actions, what Christ does, as a way of understanding who he is. After all, neither gospels nor epistles sets out a self-contained Christ apart from his acts within Israel, with disciples, and for the world. And, neither gospels nor epistles separates Christ's acts from his being. In the New Testament witness, Jesus acts as God to humans and as a human being to God. Karl Barth makes the point vividly: "[Jesus Christ's] divine authority has also the form of human authority. What this one man does . . . is really done for God and really done for us. . . . The grace addressed to human essence in Jesus Christ is thus the authority to attest and serve and accomplish the 'for God and for us' of the eternal Son."[14] Ritschl summarizes the representative actions of Christ in a call-and-response schema: Jesus Christ is *simultaneously*:

YAHWEH'S	MAN'S
call	response
demand	fulfillment
invitation	prayer
will	obedience
revelation	understanding
word	reply
command	following
anointed	servant
help	cry
etc.	etc.[15]

The list is deliberately incomplete, and the specific terminology is not the main point. Ritschl's basic contention is that "Jesus should not

---

13. Frei, *Identity of Jesus Christ*, 92.
14. Barth, *Church Dogmatics* IV/2, 98.
15. Ritschl, *Memory and Hope*, 208.

be described in terms of being, location, or relation of natures, but of functions."[16] He sets out a call-and-response Christology in terms of Christ's priestly actions as the One who does both the initiating works of God and the fittingly responsive human works. In these priestly actions, the human response is no less astonishing and no less salvific than the divine call. In sum, *how* Jesus Christ *acts* reveals *who* Jesus Christ *is*. He is "for us and our salvation," the One who is both "the living and active Word of God" (Heb 4:12) *and* the One "who in every respect has been tempted as we are, yet without sinning" (Heb 4:15). In Ritschl's view the creedal formula—"truly God and truly human"—is not a static description of substances, but a dynamic condensation of God's faithful call and humanity's faithful response embodied in the one person, Jesus Christ.

Ritschl's aim is to inquire into the *presence* of Christ, so his call-and-response Christology is not restricted to long ago and far away Galilee and Jerusalem. The risen, living Christ remains present to us and with us as the mediator, as our "great high priest" (Heb 4:14, passim) who continues to be God's call to us and who continues to be faithful human response on our behalf. Christ *is* the righteousness of God, whose call generates knowledge of God's covenantal will to be our God and to form us as his people. Christ *is* the righteousness of God whose call, once heard, elicits our response.

"The way one thinks about Christ is the way one thinks about the church" (Moltmann). Just as we have asked *who* Christ is rather than *what* Christ is, and just as we have answered who Christ *is* by what Christ *does*, so we can ask *who* the church is by observing what the church *does*. Like Christology, ecclesiology can be approached dynamically rather than statically by looking theologically at the life of the actual church rather than distilling a "nature" of the abstract church. Looking theologically at the life of the church requires cutting through the myriad activities of countless congregations in order to perceive the actions that lie behind them. With apologies to Dietrich Ritschl, then, what we see in the life of churches is:

GOD'S	*CHURCH'S*
call	response and indifference
demand	fulfillment and obstinacy
invitation	prayer and curse
will	obedience and disobedience
revelation	understanding and ignorance
word	reply and silence
command	following and defiance

16. Ibid., 215.

anointing	service and selfishness
help	cry and boast
etc.	etc.

A call-and-response Christology embodies dynamic movement rather than static categories, it focuses on particular actions rather than abstract natures, and it preserves the humanness of Christ against docetic distortions. Similarly, a call-and-response ecclesiology focuses on the church's actual life rather than an ideal nature, and casts the relationship between the Triune God and the church in dynamic reality within history. The way we think about Christ is the way we think about the church. But the church is not Christ, for unlike its Lord, the church's response to God's call is always mixed, ambiguous, equivocal: *ecclesia simil iustus et peccator*.

Each gathered congregation consists of people who have responded to God's gracious call in Jesus Christ. Responses are never perfect; they may not even be intentional. Yet the people who are there are there! The congregation gathered around pulpit, font, and table is a strange blend of faithfulness and faithlessness, ebbing and flowing in time. But the One who calls is the ever-faithful, ever-present living Christ, whose invitation comes in a gracious multitude of ways. The people are not gathered by virtue of their devotion, but in their ambiguous yet actual response to the call—some in gratitude and others in hope, some in service and others in need, some in anticipation and others out of habit. The call of Christ cannot be limited and response cannot be divided into pure and tainted. God knows our hearts, but all we know is that the church is the *ekklēsia*, the called ones whose responses remain mixed. Karl Barth is certainly right when he deplores every attempt to distinguish between "real Christians" and Christians only in appearance. "The truth," says Barth, "is that not merely some or many but all members of the Christian community stand under the sad possibility that they might not be real Christians, and yet that all and not merely some or many are called from death to life and therefore to the active life of service."[17] The company of Christians is bound together, not by its faithfulness, but by what in its life it can least justify.

What You See Is What You Get

So, when we look at the church that is before our eyes, what we see is what we get: rural churches and suburban churches and mega-churches . . . Catholic and Protestant, Orthodox and Pentecostal . . . old mainline and new immigrant . . . congregational and episcopal and synodical . . . all are churches

---

17. Barth, *Church Dogmatics*, III.4, 489.

and together they are the church because all have come to be by the call of the Lord to which they have given (mixed) response, and because all are sustained by the continued speaking of the Lord, proclaimed and enacted. Some of these churches hear more clearly and respond more faithfully while others turn a deaf ear and mumble in reply, yet all are churches as surely as the churches in Ephesus, Smyrna, Pergamum, Thyatira, Philadelphia, and Laodicea. God's speaking does not return empty.

The continuing call of God may be that "the time is fulfilled and the kingdom of God is at hand, repent and believe the gospel" (Mark 1:15). And the unresponsiveness of a church may lead to "a famine of hearing the words of the Lord" (Amos 8:11). Yet as the Word of God is preached, however equivocally, and the sacraments are celebrated, however vaguely, the Lord's speaking will not return empty. There is no pure church above or beyond or in parallel to the flawed churches we see around us, the defective churches we view from the inside out. There is no haven from the stench of grand and petty infidelities.

The church is a group, a society, an institution that can be seen, studied, and analyzed just like any other human community. The church is open and accessible to historians and sociologists. But the church is a particular group, society, institution. What may only be visible, however dimly, and audible, however faintly, from *inside* the church is the presence of Christ. The church is not left on its own, reduced to self-deceptive marketing of its achievements or self-defeating despair over its failings. Our response to Christ's call is always ambiguous, but Christ's call remains his faithful call to communion with him, a call to be joined to him in doing the will of God on earth as it is in heaven. The church is the place where Christ's call is heard most clearly, even over the din of preaching that may be more about the preacher than the gospel, and even in the midst of sacramental celebrations that may be more about congregational camaraderie than union with Christ. Through it all, Christ is present as God's word, invitation, revelation, command, and help. And through it all Christ is present as faithful human reply, prayer, understanding, obedience, and cry. Present with us in Word and Sacrament, Christ's call is not a distant summons, but an intimate disclosure that we are his friends, his sisters and brothers, his body. The gathered congregation in all of its ambiguity is most truly itself in Christ-initiated communion with its Savior and Lord.

There is considerable Presbyterian talk these days about turning our gaze away from the dismal reality of our declining and fractured present, toward "the future that God has for us." Rarely is it acknowledged that the future God has in store may be one of judgment. The ever-present grace of the Lord Jesus Christ is not cheap grace. His ever-present call is demand as well as invitation, command as certainly as help. And so the church is called to move from obstinacy to fulfillment, defiance to following, boast to cry for help. The church is simply, sometimes for better and sometimes for worse, the community of people who respond to God's call.

Reformed liturgies are well-known for their prayers for illumination before the reading of Scripture, and for the epiclesis in their Eucharistic prayers. This calling upon the Holy Spirit to give us ears to hear, eyes to see, tongues to taste, and wills to obey is not mere liturgical window dressing, but an acknowledgement that we are deaf and blind and mute, and that no "one can say 'Jesus is Lord' except by the Holy Spirit" (1 Cor 12:3).

Bibliography

Barth, Karl. *Church Dogmatics: The Doctrine of Creation*, III/4. Edinburgh: T. & T. Clark, 1961.

———. *Church Dogmatics: The Doctrine of Reconciliation*, IV/2. Translated by G. W. Bromiley. Edinburgh: T. & T. Clark, 1958.

Bonhoeffer, Dietrich. *Sanctorum Communio: A Theological Study of the Sociology of the Church*. Trans. Reinhard Krauss and Nancy Lukens. Minneapolis: Fortress, 1998.

Calvin, John. *Institutes of the Christian Religion*. Vol. XXI, *Calvin: Institutes of the Christian Religion*. Edited by John T. McNeill. Translated by Ford Lewis Battles. The Library of Christian Classics. Philadelphia: Westminster, 1960.

Frei, Hans W. *The Identity of Jesus Christ*. Philadelphia: Fortress, 1975.

Healy, Nicholas. *Church, World and the Christian Life: Practical-Prophetic Ecclesiology*. Cambridge: Cambridge University Press, 2000.

Leith, John A. "The Ten Conclusions of Berne." In *Creeds of the Churches: A Reader in Christian Doctrine from the Bible to the Present*, edited by John A. Leith, 129–30. 3rd ed. Louisville: John Knox, 1982.

Luther, Martin. "On the Councils and the Church" in *Martin Luther's Basic Theological Writings*. 2nd ed. Edited by Timothy F. Lull. Minneapolis: Fortress, 2005.

Moltmann, Jürgen. *The Church in the Power of the Spirit*. New York: Harper & Row, 1977.

Ritschl, Dietrich. *Memory and Hope*. New York: Macmillan, 1967.

The Constitution of the Presbyterian Church (U.S.A.), Part I, Book of Confessions. Louisville: The Office of the General Assembly, 1999.

Updike, John. *In the Beauty of the Lilies*. New York: Knopf, 1996.

2

Locating the Liturgical-Missional Church in the Bible's Story

DAVID STUBBS

Stories, Tornados, and the Liturgical-Missional Church

I originally learned about the power of stories and tornados in Texas. Even though I spent most of my boyhood years in the megapolis of Los Angeles, every summer my parents, sister and I would pack up the station wagon and drive to Alice, Texas, near Corpus Christi. Every summer we would spend several weeks there in Alice surrounded by my extended family and the Texas countryside.

During those Texas times, my sister and I heard many stories. Uncle Ed, Aunt Zel, Uncle Kronke, Aunt Ole, Grandpa and Gramma would tell my sister and me story after story about our family and its history. Those stories rooted us. They surrounded us with meaning in such a way we better understood who we were and where we might or should be going. Because of those stories, our lives made better sense to us.

What I learned in my bones in Texas, I learned to appreciate more fully when I read Alasdair MacIntyre's important book, *After Virtue*. In that book, MacIntyre argues stories are powerful and important. Our personal identities, the intelligibility of our actions, and our sense of accountability all depend upon the larger stories or narratives in which our selves are located.¹ MacIntyre writes, "Deprive children of stories and you leave them unscripted, anxious stutters in their actions as in their words."²

What is true for persons like you and me is also true for the church. Given the importance of narratives for identity, a good way to begin our discussion about the church is to locate and identify the church by telling a good, fitting story about it.³

But what story should we tell? There are many stories that are told about the Church and various churches, but the most authoritative one is the Bible's story about it.⁴ But telling that story is no simple task.⁵ In this

---

1. "The concepts of narrative, intelligibility and accountability presuppose the applicability of the concept of personal identity, just as it presupposes their applicability and just as indeed each of these three presupposes the applicability of the two others" (MacIntyre, *After Virture*, 218).

2. Ibid., 216.

3. By doing so, I hope to raise the stakes of our conversation. I would like to argue that the "liturgical-missional" ecclesiology under discussion is not merely one good idea among many for how the church might think of itself in our cultural situation, but rather it is a way of understanding the church that helps us drill down to the core vision of who we are called by God to be, a vision borne out by the biblical witness. Such a unified and concrete vision of what the church is, should be, and should do is absolutely crucial for the health of the church in our context.

4. There are similarities between different accounts of the church and the varieties of stories that are told about Jesus. Using a variety of methodologies, scholars and writers have constructed many accounts of Jesus Christ. For a brief history of these histories, and an argument for how "historical" accounts might be related to the gospel accounts, see Wright, *Jesus and the Victory of God*, 3–144.

5. Whether or not the Bible does tell an overarching story is debated. I agree, however, with those such as Richard Bauckham who argue that there is such an overarching story. The Bible tells a sweeping story, one that starts with the creation of the world and ends with the new creation. As Richard Bauckham notes, "Christianity and Islam are among the world religions that tell a story about the meaning of the whole of reality. The Bible . . . tells a story that in some sense encompasses all other human stories, draws them into the meaning that God's story with the world gives them" (Bauckham, *Bible and Mission*, 5). And within this story, a central "character" is the people of God, the children of Abraham, Israel of the Old Testament whose most important extension is identified in the New Testament as the Church.

We in the church often fail to tell that story in coherent manner. Peter Liethart points out this problem in his wonderful book, *A House For My Name: A Survey of the Old Testament*. Based on his experience as a professor, but also a teacher in his local church, he finds Christians rarely teach or preach the full story in a thematically coherent way. He writes that especially with the Old Testament, "Christians teaching the Old Testament are constantly tempted to treat it as a collection of moral fables" (14). In this book, he gives a thematically coherent reading of the Old Testament.

While I do think there is a single, coherent story that we can tell, I do not want to discount the complexity of it. For example, I am convinced by David Kelsey's *Eccentric*

presentation, I will try. But before doing so, I will start with an initial claim about the central characteristics, roles, and purposes of the people of God. In other words, I will start with a basic ecclesiology. Here it is: I think the people of God are intended by God to be a "liturgical-missional" people. After I explain what that means, I will step through seven select parts of the biblical story in order to test that vision, to see if indeed a "liturgical-missional" vision of the people of God easily fits with and emerges out of the larger biblical story.[6]

So, what is this "liturgical-missional" vision or picture of the church? In this vision of the church, I think the church looks a bit like an upside-down tornado.

Going back to my childhood trips to Texas, I have a vivid memory of a tornado. It wasn't a full-blown Wizard of Oz tornado, but it was big enough. One time when my family was driving toward Corpus, we saw a twister, a small tornado, form not too far from us, move across the ground, and

---

Existence that there are three basic, yet intertwining plots about how God relates to all that is not God that can be found in the scriptural canon: "Instead, this project proceeds on the basis of a construal of the movement of the canon-unifying narrative as plotted by three distinct but complexly and inseparably interrelated plots of stories of, respectively, God relating creatively, to draw to eschatological consummation, and to reconcile" (476). For the purposes of this paper, I do not feel the need to call attention to those complexities, but hope you will hear echoes of all three of those intertwining plots in my comments on the biblical story below.

6. Such a task has been done using a "missional" vision of the people of God in recent works by Christopher Wright and Richard Bauckham. Christopher Wright, in his sweeping book, *The Mission of God* does precisely this task for the "missional" aspect of God's plan. Bauckham, in *Bible and Mission,* provides another shorter example of relating a "missional" vision of God's people to the larger narrative of the Bible. Peter Leithart and G. K. Beale have recently attempted a similar yet different task, telling the sweeping narrative of the Bible (for Leithart, mainly the Old Testament) by relating the people of God to the temple. See Beale, *The Temple and the Church's Mission.* As Leithart puts it, God's mission is building of a house in which God's "name" can dwell. I hope to point to the possibility of combining these two themes that guide these narrations around the idea of a "liturgical-missional" nature of God's people—these storylines must be combined in order to fully understand both who Jesus is and what the Church is called to be and do.

Theologically, I understand my ecclesiological vision to be very similar to what one finds in, for example, Torrance, *Worship, Community, and the Triune God of Grace,* or Hans Urs von Balthasar's trinitarian vision of how the "form" of the Son is enfleshed in Christ and then mediated to the church through Word and Sacrament which in turn mediates it to the world through the power of the Holy Spirit. See von Balthasar, *Seeing the Form.* He and Torrance ultimately draw from the theology of the early church; in von Balthasar's case, from the Alexandrian trope of the three bodies of Christ. I merely am drawing lines of connection between such a theological vision of the church back to the biblical text.

then totally destroy a small wooden building in its path. When it touched the building, the building almost instantly exploded. Its pieces were taken high up toward the top of the funnel and then tossed out horizontally in all directions. It was an awesome sight.

So, picture that tornado, and then turn it upside down. I think the liturgical-missional church is a bit like an upside-down tornado. The church is a place in the world where the bottom-now-top of the "tornado" comes into contact with God and God's Kingdom, the ways of the Kingdom are funneled down into the worship and life of the church and then they are spun out into the world. I hope that image works for you!

For a more precise definition, however, let me first unpack the word, "missional." To call the church "missional" is to claim that the church is a people who participate in the "the present reign of Christ" in such a way that "the coming completed reign of God . . . is revealed and becomes effective in the present."[7] The word "missional" involves a series of claims about the church's relationship to the reign or Kingdom of God. First, the reign or Kingdom of God is at the center of Jesus's gospel. Second, the reign of God is not a kind of individual spiritual state, but rather a renewed state of the created world in which all relationships between God and humanity, humans and humans and humans and the creation are set right. Third, the church is called to represent the coming reign of God to the world by partially embodying it and also proclaiming the good news that in and through Christ, the reign of God has been inaugurated. And finally, the "mission," "calling," or "vocation" of the church is this task of representing the reign of God to the world in this way—this "mission" is the core of what the church is. The church does not do its thing as a vendor of religious goods and then, when it has time and extra money, send people usually overseas to do "missions"—instead, the church in its very being is "missional."

A good summary of this vision of the church, using words from the title of chapter 4 of the book *Missional Church*, is this: the church is a visible community called and sent to represent the Kingdom of God in and to the world.[8]

---

7. Küng, *The Church*, 126.

8. "Missional Vocation: Called and Sent to Represent the Reign of God," chapter 4 of *Missional Church*, 77–109, originally drafted by George Hunsberger. Christopher Wright defines the church's mission as "our committed participation as God's people, at God's invitation and command, in God's own mission within the history of God's world for the redemption of God's creation" (see Wright, *Mission of God*, 23). In defining this redemption, he will often substitute the phrase, "God's intention of blessing the nations" (Wright, *Mission of God*, 24–25). He also stresses that the state of blessed existence includes a full set of relationships and states, including the worship of

So, as we turn to the story of the Bible, we will want to notice places in the larger story of the Bible where this vision of a visible community called and sent to represent the reign of God in and to the world is made apparent.

What about the term "liturgical"? This term is a bit harder to define because people mean so many different things when they use it. When I use it, however, I am not pointing towards a ritualistic or old-fashioned way of conducting a Sunday service. Rather the vision of worship behind my and others' use of the word "liturgical" also relates to the Kingdom of God. This "liturgical" vision is that as the church gathers in worship, it encounters God and the patterns of the Kingdom of God in a unique and powerful way.[9] The church gathers together to perform a kind of patterned "service" or "work" centered on God and God's presence in Word and Sacrament. In that gathering, God is present to God's people, molding and shaping them into the patterns of activity of the Kingdom of God. Worship is a kind of thin place between heaven and earth. God's presence in worship molds and shapes the gathered church into representatives of the Kingdom of God. Put another way, God is present in worship to bless the gathered assembly towards *shalom*. This use of the word can be summarized well using words from the website of the Association for Reformed and Liturgical Worship: liturgical worship is worship that "offers a foretaste of the fullness of God's Reign."[10] A liturgical church is a church centered on this kind of worship.

It follows then, that people who are liturgical in this way would be concerned that what we do in worship fits well with the patterns of the Kingdom of God. More precisely, our actions and everything else about it should be typical of things that happen when God and the ways of God's reign intersect with a community of sinful but faith-filled people. Given this, we should expect praise of God, confession of sin, movements of reconciliation with God and one another, listening to God's word, offering ourselves and our possessions to God, communing with God, prayer for the world and being blessed and sent into a life of service and witness. The word "liturgical" thus makes the claim that life of the people of God should be centered around such encounters with God in which the patterns of the God's reign press down and shape and mold the people of God into the ways of God's Kingdom.

YHWH vs. idolatry, and the fruitfulness and full enjoyment of creatures in the world. This full picture of right relationships and existence can be summed up with the words "blessing," "the Kingdom of God," or "*shalom*."

9. In my chapter in *A More Profound Alleluia*, I paint this vision of the Church's worship, drawing from writers in the Reformed, Orthodox, and Anabaptist traditions. Stubbs, "Ending of Worship—Ethics," 133–55.

10. See www.arlw.org.

So, as we turn to the story of the Bible looking for a "liturgical" vision of the people of God, we will want to notice places in the larger story of the Bible where we find a visible community gathered around the presence of God, and in that encounter they are shaped and molded into the patterns and ways of God's Kingdom.

Putting the terms together, a "liturgical-missional" vision of the people of God is one in which God regularly gathers God's people as a body around places where God is particularly present, and in this encounter with God's mediated presence, the people of God are shaped, trained, and molded into the patterns of God's reign, into the ways of *shalom*. After this shaping encounter, they are sent into the world to represent and partially embody the coming Reign of God in their life together and in their life in and towards the surrounding world. In this way, the liturgical-missional people of God look a bit like an upside-down tornado.

Locating the "Liturgical-Missional" People of God in the Story

So, to the biblical story itself. I hope to show this "liturgical-missional" vision of the people of God is central to the story of the Bible. I will point to seven important moments in that larger story, highlighting a few of the key themes and details of those moments in which we see that "upside-down tornado." I doing so, I aim to both lend credence to and help us understand the significance of what I am calling a liturgical-missional vision of the church.

a. The Garden

While there are many aspects of the creation stories relevant for our purposes, let me simply point to two.

The first, related especially to our missional theme, is that in these stories God intends a life of blessing and *shalom* for his creation and his people. In the first Genesis account of creation, over and over God pronounces blessing on his creation (1:22, 28; 2:3) and declares its goodness. In the continuation of the story in Gen 2:4 and following, the garden in Eden is pictured as a place in which God walks and in which God "made to grow every tree that is pleasant to the sight and good for food. . ." The garden is a good, beautiful, healthy place. These details suggest, given protology is some indication of eschatology, that God's final end for all of creation is a similar state of *shalom*, the fullness of a good and beautiful creation in proper relationship to God, rather than the salvation of individual souls out of God's creation.[11] As God's reign extends from heaven to earth, the created order is made fruitful and blessed. Missional literature rightly picks up on this theme and argues our salvation and mission involves living into these patterns of *shalom* as a people.

But there is another crucial dimension. In the creation stories, there are strong allusions back and forth between the details of Adam and Eve's life of *shalom* in the garden and Israel's worship at the temple.[12] I'll point to just a few. First, the garden is a specific place in Eden (Gen 2:8)—it was not the entire "pre-fall" world. Like the temple's holy of holies and holy place, it was a place set aside where God dwelt with humanity. God in the garden was intimately present with his people. God is described as "walking" (Gen 3:8) in the garden; the same word is used in Leviticus, Deuteronomy, and 2 Samuel to describe God's presence in the temple and among his people (Lev 26:11–12; Deut 23:14; 2 Sam 7:6–7). In addition, at creation, one of God's primary actions is to "bless" (Gen 1:22, 28; 2:3). Similarly, at the end of most liturgical services at the temple, the priest, using the words of the familiar Aaronic blessing—"the Lord bless you and keep you . . ."—places "the Name" of God on the Israelites, and in this way they are "blessed" (Num 6:27). Finally, notice the details of Adam's vocation. Adam, the archetype of humanity, is called to "till and keep" or "serve and protect" (*abad/shamar*) the garden (Gen 2:15). The same words are used to describe what the Levites are called to do at the temple (Num 18:3–7, when they are commissioned).

These parallels suggest the garden, like the temple, was to be a place where God's presence and reign was specially present. Using New Testament language, it was a place where the Kingdom of God was breaking into the world. It was the place where the funnel of the heavenly tornado coming down from on high first encounters the world. In the space of the garden as in the temple, the patterns and ways of God's kingdom were being made present on earth as they already were in heaven. God was present to dwell with and bless priest-like humanity, and humanity communed with God in joyful obedience.

This vision of God's intentions for humanity—a life of shalom and a "priestly" calling—are rightly highlighted as we read and teach and preach about the creation stories.

---

11. *Shalom* is best understood as life in which the relationships between humanity and God, humans and each other, humans and themselves, and humans and the earth are all rightly ordered. See Wolterstorff, "For Justice in Shalom," 109.

12. For example, see Beale, *Temple and the Church's Mission*, 66–80.

b. *The Patriarchs: Abraham, Jacob, and Joseph*

The stories of Abraham, Jacob, and Joseph also have many details related to our liturgical and missional themes. Let me suggest a few.

Genesis 12:1–3 is a foundational text. In that passage God tells Abraham first to leave his "father's house" and go to the "land" that God will show him. In that land, in that particular place, God promises to bless Abraham, and through the people or house that God will build through Abraham, all people will be blessed. In the stories to follow God keeps God's promise to Abraham. And, in Abraham, Jacob, and Joseph, the primal sins of humanity outlined in Gen 3–11—those of Adam and Eve, Cain and Abel, and the sons of God—begin to be reversed. Instead of the disobedience of Adam and Eve, Abraham obeys God in the famous passage of the near sacrifice of Isaac. The relationship between God and humanity begins to be repaired in Abraham. And then, from that altar of sacrifice, that renewal seems to spread into more "horizontal" relationships. In the Jacob stories, unlike the fratricide of Cain and Abel, the problems that Jacob has with his brother Esau and his relative Laban are resolved. And then in the Joseph stories, the sin of the intermarriage of the sons of God with the other parts of humanity in Gen 6, a sin that results in the loss of their special calling, seems to be reversed. We see in Joseph a model of a better way the people of God are to act toward the nations. Joseph resists the seduction of Potiphar's wife and instead provides wise leadership to the nation of Egypt—by living into his special calling, he brings blessing even beyond the people the God. As in the missional theme, God calls this people, this family or house to represent the ways of God. In this way they are blessed and bring blessing to others. Reflecting the intended shalom of the garden, in the stories of the patriarchs, we see relationships between humanity and God, humanity and humanity, and in this case the people of God and their special calling as a people being made right.

But we also get greater glimpses of the "liturgical" aspect of the people of God in two very important stories. The stories about the problems and reconciliation of Jacob with both Esau and Laban (Gen 25–36) are interrupted by the story of the ladder of Jacob (Gen 28) and the story of Jacob wrestling with the angel at Peniel (Gen 32). Jacob mysteriously sees that angels are ascending and descending in the land where his reconciliations between Esau and Laban take place—that place is called "the house of God," and marked with a stone that rabbinic tradition tells us is the very stone that provided the central stone for the holy of holies of the second temple. The name "Israel"—meaning one who wrestles with God—comes from the second story. What might this intercalation of stories mean? It suggests God is building a house, a people in whom the ways and patterns of heaven are beginning to take shape on earth. God's mediated presence wrestles with this people, blesses them, begins to reshape them into a people in whom God's reign and blessing is specially present and represented, and then God shoots them out into the nation of Egypt to bless it as well (Gen 45:5; 47:7–10).

c. The Covenant at Sinai

A few years ago, I was invited to write a commentary on the book of Numbers—not a typical task for a theologian. Through my research and writing I grew to absolutely love the book, in part because of the rich vision of the calling of the people of God contained in the Sinai covenant. It is a vision of their life that includes both their ethics as well as their worship. As Protestants, we tend to see view the Sinai covenant strictly as "law," and perhaps guided by our confessional heritage, we often sum up that law through an exposition of the Ten Commandments. This makes good sense, but it can also obscure the rich texture of the vision of who the people of God are to be that emerges from an imaginative reading of the covenant. The covenant paints a "liturgical-missional" portrait of who Israel is to be. One can even spot that twofold vision in Exod 19:6, the introduction to the covenant that clearly states God's purposes for Israel: God says them, "Indeed the whole earth is mine, but you are to be for me a priestly people and a holy nation."

The "missional" component of this vision is plain to see. God, in and through the covenant, is structuring Israel's life by setting up institutions, practices, and laws with the goal of creating a holy nation, a city on a hill, a people in whose life together the nations get a glimpse of the Kingdom of God. God called these people out of the slavery of Egypt not only to save them from oppression, not only to save their souls when they die, but to mold them into a special kind of community, and to place this people in the center of great empires of the Ancient Near East so they could shine. Just as God is holy, they too are to be holy. This is the emphasis of what is arguably the very center of the Sinai material in the book of Leviticus, the so-called "holiness code." Just as God is just, just as God is merciful, Israel too is to be just and merciful. In the Sinai covenant, from the laws that treat forgiveness of debts in the Sabbath and Jubilee years to laws of reconciliation between people, to laws on how to justly and mercifully treat aliens and foreigners in their midst, the patterns of a renewed shalom are pictured. God intends these patterns to be embodied in the life of the people: "You shall be holy, for I the Lord your God am holy" (Lev 19:2).

But notice how this "missional" aspect flows out of the "liturgical" aspect of who they were called to be. They are also to be a "priestly people." Israel is to be a people structured around their worship of God who dwells in their midst. The placement of the tabernacle at the very center of their camp, like an upside-down tornado funnel, like a pillar of cloud and fire—is a living symbol of the centrality of God and worship for God's people.[13] While the covenant of Sinai does contain an ethical vision of the kingdom life of the Israel, an even larger portion of the Sinai covenant gives specific details about the shape of Israel's worship life. In the symbolic structure of the tabernacle, in the details of their worship life together, both their daily worship and their yearly cycles of feasts and festivals, a pattern of worship—a "liturgy"—is given which is intended to shape and train them to be that holy people. In their acts of confession, their offerings, their music, their celebratory meals in which God was an invited guest, their prayers and other practices, God was forming and molding them to be a people in which God's intended patterns for human life were to be represented.

d. *The Prophets*

But what about the prophetic literature? The prophetic literature is often understood to undercut or oppose the vision of the worship life of Israel seen in the covenant at Sinai. Especially in modern biblical studies, the "good" prophets are often seen to be opposed to the "bad" or "petty" priestly writers.[14] However, a strong opposition of the two is not the best way to interpret the message of the prophets. Many contemporary biblical scholars are trying to undo this opposition that is deeply ingrained in the modern Protestant imagination.[15]

Certainly the writings of the prophets fit well with a "missional" vision of the people of God. The people of God, according to the prophets, are to

---

13. Stubbs, *Numbers*, 29–51.

14. Wellhausen's characterization of the priestly tradition as having "a petty scheme of salvation" is representative and influential. See Wellhausen, *Prolegomena*. It was originally published in 1878 and set the stage for investigations into the literary evolution of the Pentateuch.

15. For example, Gorman, *The Ideology of Ritual*; Balentine, *The Torah's Vision*. Brueggemann, *The Theology of the Old Testament*, 651–53, discusses how Christian supersessionism, classical Protestant reactions to Roman Catholicism, History-of-Religions approaches, and Wellhausian approaches have combined to create an acute prejudice against the priestly writings and worship at the temple. I would add to that list of culprits our modern scientific worldview (i.e., Bultmann's "closed causal nexus"), which has little conceptual space for God's sacramental activity.

be a people in whom the patterns of the Kingdom shine forth. The people of God are called to act righteously and justly toward one another, toward the alien in their midst, toward the poor, and they are to walk humbly with God.

But is there also a "liturgical" aspect of the prophets' vision of who the people of God are to be? Can we spot the upside-down tornado in their writings? Amos cries, "I hate, I despise your festivals . . ." (5:21). Is this because God no longer wants the worship he commanded on Mount Sinai? I do not think so. Instead, I believe that Amos and the other prophets are critical of aspects of Israel's worship because Israel has become blind to their true meanings. We see in these familiar prophetic critiques of false worship an underlying understanding of true worship. In true worship the concerns and character of God should be mirrored in the patterns of Israel's worship and then flow out into, roll down and outward into, Kingdom-like patterns in the life of Israel. "Let justice roll down like waters and righteousness like an overflowing stream" (5:24), Amos cries. The ways of heaven should shape the patterns of Israel's worship and these patterns of God seen in their worship should flow down like waters from the temple mount into the ethical practices of their life together as a people. The "liturgical" should flow into the "missional." What is arguably implied in Amos is made clear in the vision and prophecies of Zechariah. Zechariah, in his vision of the day of the Lord, does not see the abolition but rather the fulfillment of the liturgical. On the great day of the Lord, all the nations will go up to Mount Zion and celebrate the festival of booths. But Zechariah clearly sees the liturgical must be deeply intertwined with the ethical: "On that day . . . there shall no longer be traders in the house of the Lord," Zechariah prophesies. On that day, the holiness of the temple and its worship will flow out into the lives of the entire city of Jerusalem. Even the bells of horses will be inscribed with "holy to the Lord." Every cooking pot in Jerusalem will be just as holy as the pots and vessels used at the worship of the altar in the Temple (Zech 14:16–21). Instead of "farm to table," Zechariah prophesies about an even more profoundly ethical movement, "altar to table"!

e. Christ and the New Covenant

This liturgical-missional vision of God's people is at the core of gospel. The good news announced in the Gospels is that what God has always intended for humanity and the people of God is finally brought into being in Christ. Because of Christ's work, we are not only forgiven for our failure to achieve God's intentions for us, but also invited into the fulfillment of those intentions through our connection to Christ through the Spirit.

In the gospels, Christ fulfills the "liturgical" theme. He is the tornado come down from heaven. He is the new temple. "Destroy this temple, and in three days I will raise it up," Jesus mysteriously claims (John 2:19; cf. Matt 26:61; 27:40; Mark 14:58; 15:29; Acts 6:14). As New Testament scholar N. T. Wright argues, Jesus' relationship to the temple is the deepest clue to the Christology of the gospels.[16] What the temple symbolically represented—the place on earth where heaven and earth come together, where the ways of patterns of God in "heaven" become enfleshed on earth in human life—is fulfilled in the two-natured person of Christ. The Word, Wisdom, or Way of God is united with humanity in the person of Jesus Christ. He in his person is the fulfillment of Jacob's vision of the ladder that stretches between heaven and earth. As Jesus tells Nathaniel at the beginning of John's Gospel: "Very truly, I tell you, you will see heaven opened and the angels of God ascending and descending upon the Son of Man" (John 1:51). And like the temple, those patterns of heaven embodied in the very person of Christ flow out into Jesus' actions of love, justice, care, healing, forgiveness, teaching and proclamation throughout his ministry.

In that way Christ in his person also fulfills the "missional" theme. He is the kingdom of God in himself. Unlike the covenant of Sinai, which was a blueprint for what the people of God was to be and do but was never completely put into practice by the people of Israel, in Jesus Christ this vision of human life under God's rule is fulfilled. In Jesus' own person, God in Christ heals and renews the humanity of Christ to be the proper covenant partner of God. He fulfills the vocation of Israel.

f. The Church as the New Temple, the Body of Christ, and Partial Embodiment of the Kingdom of God

But this new temple of Christ, in which humanity and divinity are joined in harmony, was not intended to have closed doors. Switching metaphors, Jesus invites us into the tornado. Jesus calls the twelve disciples to not only to be with him and to learn from him and imitate him, but to share the reality of his renewed humanity with them. As Jesus tells them in John 8, "I am the bread of life . . . unless you eat the flesh of the Son of Man and drink his blood, you have no life in you" (vv. 48, 53). The salvation Christ offers involves participating in him, like branches joined to a vine or like parts of a body joined to its head, or even, in the imagery of 1 Peter, like stones build upon a foundation stone into a new temple. Peter writes, "Come to him, a living stone, though rejected by mortals yet chosen and precious in God's

---

16. Wright, *Jesus and the Victory of God*, 653.

sight, and like living stones, let yourselves be built into a spiritual house, to be a holy priesthood, to offer spiritual sacrifices acceptable to God through Jesus Christ" (1 Pet 2:4–5).

In the book of Acts, at Pentecost and its aftermath, we see the beginning of this new spiritual temple of the renewed people of God beginning to form. The Spirit is poured out, and in the new community of disciples, the hoped for "liturgical-missional" patterns seen on Mount Sinai begin to be fulfilled in a new way.[17]

Throughout the New Testament the imagery of the temple come to be applied both to the individual Christian and to the entire corporate body of the Church. For example, the church for Paul is a "spiritual temple." The church is a temple not made with stones, but rather it is a visible temple of the gathered people of God constructed by the Spirit. Paul writes in 2 Corinthians, "For we are the temple of the living God; as God said, 'I will live in them and walk among them, and I will be their God, and they shall be my people'" (2 Cor 6:16). In keeping with this "liturgical" vision, Peter also writes that we are called to be a new "spiritual house" (1 Pet 2:5; Eph 2:19–22) built on the cornerstone of Christ through the Spirit that offers "spiritual sacrifices" (1 Pet 2:5; cf. Rom 12:1–2) to God.

But, this new community joined to Christ through the Spirit gathered in worship also begins to live into the patterns of the Kingdom due to God's presence among them. The "blessings" of the Old Covenant start to be fulfilled in a "now-but-not-yet" way in their lives together. Not only is the Word is preached, bread broken, and people baptized as they gather together. In addition, the ways of the coming Kingdom, its ways of love and justice begin to be embodied in their life together: walls are broken down between Jew and Greek, masters and slaves begin to see each other as brothers and sisters, women are treated with dignity and even take roles of leadership, and we are told that "there was not a needy person among them"—a direct fulfillment of the covenant blessings foretold in Deut 15:4 (ex. Acts 2:42–47; 4:32–37; Gal 3:25–29; Phlm 1:16; Phil 4:2–4). The patterns of their worship flow out into their discipleship, evangelism and mission (Rom 12:1f.; 1 Pet 2:1f.). Through their practices "the wisdom of God . . . might now be made known" (Eph 3:10). So, while the mission of the church starts with the "church being the church" in its worship, its mission spirals out through words and witness into the world so that the church might be "a city on a hill" (Matt 5:14), visible to all.

---

17. Johnson, *The Acts of the Apostles*, 45–47, points out ways in which the experience of Pentecost mirrors and fulfills the experience of the people of God at Mount Sinai, as noted by the many literary allusions between the two events.

g. New Creation

God's good future involves all things made being made new (Rev 21:5), not the creation of all new things. In the visions of the renewed creation in Revelation, when Christ returns, we see the "liturgical" and "missional" aspects of the people of God finally reach their goal.

The point of the liturgy of the temple will be finally fulfilled. Through the presence of "the Lord God the Almighty and the Lamb" in and among us (Rev 21:3, 22), life and blessing will be extended to all (Rev 19:9; 22:1–2, 14). And in this fulfillment, the walls of the temple explode as the particularity of God's dwelling is now expanded to include the whole earth.

It is in this way that God's mission will also be fulfilled. The practices, patterns and reality of the Kingdom of God seen in a provisional way in God's people will be fully extended throughout the whole earth. As it is written, "And I heard a loud voice from the throne saying, 'See, the tabernacle of God is among mortals. He will dwell with them; they will be his peoples, and God himself will be with them; he will wipe every tear from their eyes. Death will be no more; mourning and crying and pain will be no more, for the first things have passed away'" (Rev 21:3–4).

Implications for Theology, Worship, and Mission

I hope you are convinced by this brief presentation that a liturgical-missional vision of the people of God is at the center of the biblical story. I am. I am also convinced this vision of the identity and vocation of the people of God fits quite well with the theology of the great theologians of Christianity (including Irenaeus, Athanasius, Augustine, Aquinas, Luther, Calvin, and Barth). I also think it fits quite well with the theological vision that guided the seven great ecumenical councils of the church. In this closing section, I will first point out two strands of Christianity that this vision does not fit so well with, and then highlight a few basic implications of this liturgical-missional vision of the church for the church's worship and mission.

a. How This Story Differs from Protestant Liberalism and Moralistic Therapeutic Deism

This understanding of the larger sweep of the biblical story and the role of the church in it is different in important ways from the theology of Protestant liberalism. By Protestant liberalism, I mean in part the lines of thinking from Friedrich Schleiermacher, Adolph Harnack, Ritschl, and others through people like Paul Tillich up to the present day.

One hallmark of Protestant liberalism is discomfort with the particularity of God's work in a specific people. The particularity of the tornado image is disturbing. Instead, Protestant liberalism highlights the universal accessibility of God to all people; God is accessible through some kind of universal religious feeling or experience so that the particularity of Christ and church is to a greater or lesser extent undercut.[18]

While some sources say Protestant liberalism now makes up only 12 percent of American Christianity, it seems to me that much of the lived spirituality of many young people today, a spirituality often labeled "moralistic therapeutic Deism," shares many features with classical Protestant liberalism.[19] When classic Protestant liberals and those with a theology of "moralistic therapeutic deism" read these same biblical stories, they are interpreted not as a description of God's actual plan of salvation in which a particular people of God play an important role. Instead, they are read as stories of people's faith that point to larger patterns of universally accessible religious experience. They are read as moral fables. The story of Abraham would be read merely as a story meant to call us to a deeper faith and openness to God in general.

As opposed to this, this "liturgical-missional" reading of Scripture emphasizes the particular work God is doing in a through a particular people. God meets the church in Word and Sacrament, forming us into the patterns of the Kingdom and then sends us out to represent God's reign before and to the world.

b. How This Story Differs from the Story Certain Evangelicals Tell

This understanding of the larger sweep of the biblical story and the role of the Church in it is also different from certain ways that Protestant evangelicals and fundamentalists have often read and told the story of the Bible. The liturgical-missional story emphasizes that "blessing" and the renewal of creation is the final end of God's purposes, rather than simply forgiveness of one's own individual sins and the salvation of our disembodied souls, which

---

18. While many in this tradition maintain a special or even unique role for Christ and the Church, the lack of Nicene-Chalcedonian Christology seems to press most liberal thinkers towards a non-particular view of divine action in the world.

19. Smith, *Soul Searching*, see 162ff for a summary interpretation of Moralistic Therapeutic Deism.

go to heaven and remain there. In addition, in the liturgical-missional story, the church as a visible body of people matters deeply. The church represents the Kingdom of God to the world through both its proclamation and its life together and in the world. And finally, this liturgical-missional vision contains a high view of the Old Testament, the law, and the worship of Israel. This understanding is in concert with the Reformed tradition's "third use of the law." It, however, does not fit quite so well with certain ways of talking about the relationship between faith and works or the Old and New Covenants that I find to be still quite prevalent in some evangelical circles.

c. *Implications for Worship and Liturgy*

One important implication of those differences involves the way that we think about worship. As I contemplate this movement of God's saving work in history and the way the church is located in that story, the most basic observation I would make about worship is that as Protestants we would do well to rediscover the basic meanings of the temple as they are presented throughout the Bible. We need to rediscover how these meanings are related to the images of the Kingdom of God and body of Christ, and then, based on this, re-imagine what we are doing in worship. Such a re-imagining will push us to see that our gathered worship centered on Word and Sacrament, we are coming into contact in a special way with God and God's reign, and through God's presence we are being shaped into a community that embodies the patterns of the Kingdom of God.

Given that basic imagination about what our gathered worship is or should be, our most important discussions about worship will be how best to embody the patterns of the Kingdom and how to help people connect these Kingdom-patterns into the rest of their lives—not whether to use a worship band or an organ. Those "patterns" that we find in most traditional liturgies—gathering, praise, confession and forgiveness, baptism, hearing the Word, offering, passing the peace, Lord's Supper, prayer, blessing and sending—are what are important. But we may need to help people see why we do them, and we may need to give ourselves some freedom as to how we do them. You can practice those basic patterns in many ways, utilizing "traditional," "contemporary," or "emerging" styles.

This understanding of worship is different from the basic pictures of worship that naturally emerge out of Protestant liberalism, moral therapeutic deism, or certain versions of evangelicalism. However, it resonates deeply with the visions of worship of both the liturgical renewal movements of the twentieth century, as well as certain understandings of emergent, emerging or ancient-future worship movements. It is the vision of worship that underlies many of the explanations, structures and rubrics in the PC(USA) *Book of Common Worship*.

d. Implications for the Mission of the Church

The basic implication of this liturgical-missional vision for the church's mission is this: the mission of the church should flow out of our worship in a specific way. Namely, the presence of God in worship should not only "energize" our mission (corresponding to the work of the Holy Spirit), but also "shape" our mission (corresponding to the work of the Son).[20] You might say the basic DNA of all our activity as a church can or should be found in the core practices of our worship. Our worship should encode the basic patterns of what happens when the holy God encounters and shapes the sinful yet justified and sanctified people of God. Our confession of sin, assurance of pardon and passing of the peace is such a basic movement. Tornado-like, we should be caught up in that movement and spun out into the world to embody practices of reconciliation and peacemaking in our life together and then to extend them into the greater society. Similarly, the offering is a Kingdom pattern in a nutshell. It prompts us to lead lives of self-offering to God and each other, lives of financial responsibility and generosity in all that we do individually and corporately as Christians, and then to work to extend those gift-like economic patterns into the wider world. Likewise, our skillful presentation of music and art to God in worship should flow out into all kinds of engagement with music and art in the wider culture. This expansive vision of worship—that in it we encounter the Kingdom of God as it makes its pressure felt, forming human activity in a variety of ways, naturally lends itself it to an expansive vision of Christian cultural engagement as part of our mission as a church. Christians are or should be interested in evangelism, politics, economics, art—everything (Rev 21:26 "the glory and honor of the nations"). Such a vision has in fact been a hallmark of certain parts of the Reformed tradition.

In conclusion, I find this "liturgical-missional" vision of the Church to be extremely exciting and very important. Biblically, it provides a lens large enough to spot connections between the different genres and parts of the biblical witness in a satisfying way. Theologically, it rests on a Nicene vision of Christ, a Trinitarian view of God, and a sacramental understanding of God's action in the world. That combination of ideas is a golden key that unlocks the riches of the Christian theological tradition. Practically, as one

---

20. See Calvin, *Institutes*, I.13.18 for these distinctions between Father, Son, and Spirit. All of this is done according to the will of and for the glory of the Father.

is involved in the church's life, it provides an orienting yet flexible vision for thinking through and making decisions about the practical details of worship, mission, and ethics. Ecumenically, it opens up doors of conversation and a path towards greater unity in a tragically divided church. I highly recommend it.

Bibliography

Balentine, Samuel E. *The Torah's Vision of Worship*. Minneapolis: Fortress, 1999.
Bauckham, Richard. *Bible and Mission: Christian Witness in a Postmodern World*. Grand Rapids: Baker Academic, 2003.
Beale, G. K. *The Temple and the Church's Mission: A Biblical Theology of the Dwelling Place of God*. Downers Grove, IL: InterVarsity, 2004.
Brueggemann, Walter. *The Theology of the Old Testament: Testimony, Dispute, Advocacy*. Minneapolis: Fortress, 1997.
Calvin, John. *Institutes of the Christian Religion*. Edited by John T. McNeill. Translated by Ford Lewis Battles. 2 vols. The Library of Christian Classics. Philadelphia: Westminster, 1960.
Gorman, F. H., Jr. *The Ideology of Ritual: Space, Time, and Status in the Priestly Theology*. Sheffield: JSOT, 1990.
Guder, Darrell L., ed. *Missional Church: A Vision for the Sending of the Church in North America*. Grand Rapids: Eerdmans, 1998.
Johnson, Luke Timothy. *The Acts of the Apostles*. Collegeville, MN: Liturgical, 1992.
Kelsey, David. *Eccentric Existence*. Louisville: Westminster John Knox, 2009.
Küng, Hans. *The Church*. Garden City, NY: Image, 1967.
Leithart, Peter. *A House for My Name: A Survey of the Old Testament*. Moscow, ID: Canon, 2000.
MacIntyre, Alasdair. *After Virtue: A Study in Moral Theory*. 2nd ed. Notre Dame: University of Notre Dame Press, 1984.
Smith, Christian. *Soul Searching*. New York: Oxford University Press, 2005.
Stubbs, David. "Ending of Worship—Ethics." In *A More Profound Alleluia: Theology and Worship in Harmony*, edited by Leanne Van Dyk, 133–55. Grand Rapids: Eerdmans, 2005.
———. *Numbers*. Grand Rapids: Brazos, 2009.
Torrance, James. *Worship, Community, and the Triune God of Grace*. Downers Grove, IL: IVP Academic, 2008.
von Balthasar, Hans Urs. *Seeing the Form*. Vol. 1 of *The Glory of the Lord*. San Francisco: Ignatius, 2002.
Wellhausen, Julius. *Prolegomena to the History of Israel*. Gloucester, MA: Peter Smith, 1973.
Wolterstorff, Nicholas. "For Justice in Shalom." In *Hearing the Call: Liturgy, Justice, Church, and World*, edited by Mark R. Gornik and Greg Thompson, 109–13. Grand Rapids: Eerdmans, 2011.
Wright, Christopher. *The Mission of God: Unlocking the Bible's Grand Narrative*. Downers Grove, IL: IVP Academic, 2006.
Wright, N. T. *Jesus and the Victory of God*. Minneapolis: Fortress, 1996.

3

Worship as the Missional Church's Whence and Wither

Teresa Stricklen Eisenlohr

The mission of God in Christ gives shape and substance to the life and work of the Church. In Christ, the Church participates in God's mission for the transformation of creation and humanity by proclaiming to all people the good news of God's love, offering to all people the grace of God at font and table, and calling all people to discipleship in Christ. Human beings have no higher goal in life than to glorify and enjoy God now and forever, living in covenant fellowship with God and participating in God's mission.[1]

When I was in seminary, I had a dream one night. I was celebrating communion at the church where I was serving as youth minister. In reality, I wasn't ordained and couldn't celebrate communion, but in my dream there I was—celebrating at table. All was going well until someone with a gun burst into the sanctuary. In my dream the congregation disappeared so that the church was suddenly empty. The communion table in this church was very large, closed in front but open in the back with a long shelf in the middle of it for the storage of various worship items, so to protect myself from the gunman in the dream, I crawled inside the communion table. Lying there like a saint in one of the sleeping chambers of the Roman

---

1. *Book of Order*, F-1.01.

catacombs, I felt safe, sheltered beneath the wings of Mama Hen God, so safe that I began to fall asleep in my dream. The gunman went away, but then there was a growing uneasiness stirring within me even as I wanted to stay safe within the table, but I could not. I *had* to get out. I crawled out from beneath the table and was nudged to process down the aisle of the sanctuary and out the doors into the dazzling light of the world beyond the darkened sanctuary. This was a prophetic dream for me personally, but maybe the dream wasn't just for me. Perhaps it is a prophetic dream for the church at this time, too.

In the wake of the danger facing a disappearing church, the following is an attempt to construct a liturgical missional ecclesiology in order to help us move confidently into God's future through Christ as it was in the beginning, is now, and ever shall be. A liturgical-missional ecclesiology understands that we are in a time of institutional disestablishment that requires a re-examination of our tradition's treasures of biblical and theological resources. Doing this, we discover that these are not treasures from the past alone. They are eschatological in nature, calling us into the mission of God's beatific work in the world ("the Kingdom"). Indeed, as we learn in worship, this is why the church is called into existence and sent out in Christ's name.

Where We Are: A Crumbling Establishment in a Rich Tradition

The notion of church as an institution for a community's good that people will naturally want to be a part of is long gone in many places. Mega churches are not so mega anymore, admitting they may have compromised the gospel in their desire for others to embrace it.[2] Mainline Christian denominations in the United States are losing members in alarming numbers, and the evangelical church is troubled by the disappearance of its youth. In all the changes that we are seeing, what is unclear is what form the church will take in the wake of its disestablishment.

Whatever institutional form it takes, the church stands in continuity with centuries of Judeo-Christian tradition that cannot just be jettisoned for something new and improved. There is wisdom in the traditions our ancestors have bequeathed to us. But this is not tradition for tradition's sake. The wisdom bequeathed to us is not powerful because it links us to humans of the past, but because it helps us encounter the Holy here and now as we move into God's future. It behooves us, then, to revisit our tradition in order to be reminded of who we are in whatever culture or time we find ourselves.

2. Branaugh, "Willow Creek's."

Some Biblical Ecclesial Images

Biblically, we could say that the church is the body of Christ. Paul's use of this metaphor shows how our diversity is held within our unity in Christ. While still important, the image may be too static and individualistic in its actual use. It is often preached in such a way that it causes us to think about which part of the body we are and how we can use our gifts *for the body* without necessarily talking about what the body itself does and why it exists at all. If the body is of Christ is equivalent to the running of the church institution, then we have no distinction between the historical and spiritual nature of the church so that, in practical terms, to be a part of the body of Christ becomes merely suffering on the cross of a church committee. Such notions trivialize the power of the cross and can reduce Christianity to a social movement with God rhetoric—an abuse of power equivalent to the most oppressive regimes, as Marx argued.

Moreover, the body of Christ has functioned as an image that, at times, requires us to conform to a dogmatic institutional authority that has the power to whip us into shape or cut us off because we offend it. What is more, the body may not actually do anything other than exist on life support or run hither and yon through history without any clear purpose.

However, if the church body's face, like Jesus,' is "set on Jerusalem,"[3] the place of God's manifestation in the world, God's will may indeed be manifest through this body, and often is, in spite of our disabilities. But notice: this has the body moving toward a *telos*—the same end that Jesus served while on earth—namely, the Kingdom of God. The metaphor of the body may not be as apt an analogy of the church as being part of a musical group, a choir, or a theatrical company acting under the direction of the Holy Trinity as it seeks to fill the world with the story and music of the good news that, in Christ, God is at work to bless and redeem creation. This is the notion of the Kingdom that Jesus preached and called the church to continue, in whatever culture they encountered, as his earthly body filled with Holy Spirit. This way of understanding the body as an artistic group retains the essentials of Paul's use of the body as a diverse collection of parts working for a common goal—namely, God's work through the Spirit of Christ to reconcile the world. This is also in keeping with Paul's Christological and eschatological understanding of Christ as Lord of the new heaven and earth that is coming to pass. Moreover, this understanding of the body of Christ leaves individuals free to work out the details of their lives with Christ alone as Lord of their

---

3. Luke 9:51, alluding to Isa 50:7.

conscience while also being subject to the discipline of moving with a group of people on The Way toward the full manifestation of God's Reign.

The liberated, exodus people of God on the way to the Promised Land is another biblical vision of the church. Here is an image of oneness that pictures a people on the move toward a promised new day where God is Sovereign. There is no illusion in this image that this is anything but a sinful people in the process of being-formed by Torah as a good gift from God that teaches them how to live with the Lord and one another. Torah is more than a static set of regulations; it embraces the notion of law as way of life. This is why in its early days, Israel's judges discern how one should live in accord with Torah in the midst of concrete situations. Later, though, the Ten Commandments become more objectified as tablets in a box that Israel carried with them, and a sense of legalism reigned. Torah marked their unique identity, and, together with the tabernacle in which it resided, signified the presence of God.

Building upon this heritage, Christian parallels abound. Matthew depicts Jesus as the new Moses who delivers the Torah of the Sermon on the Mount (Matt 5–7). He is also our Passover Lamb and scapegoat who secures our freedom and forgiveness under the guidance of the *shekinah/* glory/divine presence that indwells him as he is brought up out of the water like Moses. The earliest Christians were known as followers of The Way. Christ's disciples are a people on The Way toward the Promised Land where God is sovereign. For Christians, though, the Promised Land is divorced from actual land, which Jesus also seemed to do by substituting talk of God's Reign for the restoration of the Davidic dynasty. God's Reign functions as a promised-land utopia in that it is "no place" (the literal definition of utopia) even as it is always "at hand" (Luke 17:21). Like the Kingdom of God that Jesus preached, it is as though this promised sovereignty exists in another dimension that is accessed when the veil between this world and God's world grows thin, so to speak, and we can perceive the divinity in which the world dwells like a baby exists separate from, yet dependent upon, its pregnant mother. The Holy Spirit, like the *shekinah* that encompassed and accompanied Israel, now dwells among us to guide, comfort, illumine, and lead the community. Though still being-formed out of all our sinfulness, Christians, too, are being taught by the Spirit of Christ to love God and neighbor, the essence of Torah.

While it has the advantage of being communal and on-the-move, the notion of the church being the people of God has led to supercessionism— i.e., Christians, not Jews, are the real people of God. Indeed, this is how the New Testament has been interpreted and enacted through time to the detriment of Jews. The Reformers also made a similar move in declaring themselves the true people of God over against Roman Church. Thus, as appealing as this image is, especially for a missional church, it is problematic at a time in history when our very survival on the planet may depend upon various religious people coming together in good will out of their desire to make peace. Lording it over others with our superior notion of what it means to be *the* people of God will not help such conversations occur. Moreover, lording it over people is not how we are to follow the Lord (Matt 20:24–26; Mark 10:41–43; Luke 22:24–26; 1 Pet 5:3).

Theological Options

Of course, we could take up classical discussions of the visible/invisible church or the institutional vs. spiritual nature of the church, which could be all the rage in our spiritual-but-not-religious culture. But, as Calvin knew, such distinctions are not ultimately ours to make[4] (though we make them all the time, perhaps to the detriment of our witness in the world). Calvin's struggle with the whole notion of what constitutes the church finally rests on where the word is preached and heard and sacraments rightly administered[5]—two of the major components of worship—to which communal accountability was added.[6] We could also revisit the marks of the church (one, holy, catholic, apostolic) according to our tradition.[7] The great ends of the church are also terrific: "The great ends of the Church are the proclamation of the gospel for the salvation of humankind; the shelter, nurture, and spiritual fellowship of the children of God; the maintenance of divine worship; the preservation of the truth; the promotion of social righteousness; and the exhibition of the Kingdom of Heaven to the world."[8] However, these are rather ecclesiocentric and although they do explicate the church's mission, they are also used as ways to establish a shining ecclesial institution as an end unto itself.

Though all of the above are worthy topics in and of themselves, for the purposes of this occasion, it behooves us to focus not on what has been done, but on what new thing God seems to be doing, as seen through the lens of ecclesial history. Following these classical theological affirmations, our new Form of Government in the *Book of Order* offers us the following:

4. Calvin, *Institutes*, IV.1.8.
5. Ibid., IV.1.9.
6. *Book of Confessions*, The Scots Confession, chapter 18. See also *Book of Order*, F-1.0303.
7. *Book of Order*, F-1.0302.
8. *Book of Order*, F-1.0304.

> *In Jesus Christ, who is Lord of all creation, the Church seeks a new openness to God's mission in the world. In Christ, the triune God tends the least among us, suffers the curse of human sinfulness, raises up a new humanity, and promises a new future for all creation. In Christ, Church members share with all humanity the realities of creatureliness, sinfulness, brokenness, and suffering, as well as the future toward which God is drawing them. The mission of God pertains not only to the Church but also to people everywhere and to all creation. As it participates in God's mission, the Presbyterian Church (U.S.A) seeks:*
>
> > *a new openness to the sovereign activity of God in the Church and in the world, to a more radical obedience to Christ, and to a more joyous celebration in worship and work;*
> >
> > *a new openness in its own membership, becoming in fact as well as in faith a community of women and men of all ages, races, ethnicities, and worldly conditions, made one in Christ by the power of the Spirit, as a visible sign of the new humanity;*
> >
> > *a new openness to see both the possibilities and perils of its institutional forms in order to ensure the faithfulness and usefulness of these forms to God's activity in the world; and*
> >
> > *a new openness to God's continuing reformation of the Church ecumenical, that it might be more effective in its mission.*[9]

What is striking about this statement is its forward-looking-ness. In this whole section titled "The Calling of the Church,"[10] the Presbyterian Church (USA)'s new Form of Government uses the past of tradition like a rear-view mirror to move us confidently into "the future toward which God is drawing" us. The emphasis is not on repristinating the past, but on embracing God's future. In short, the church exists to embody God's purposes, or God's mission of redeeming and blessing the world through the Spirit of Christ the Lord.

God's Future: A Missional Ecclesiology

This begs the question: what is God's future to which the church is called? God's future is the end or purpose God had for creating in the first place—to be in full communion with human beings in the shalom that characterized all of creation. As it was in the beginning, so it shall be in the end. God's purpose, or mission, is to move creation into its divine intention of

---

9. *Book of Order*, F-1.0404.
10. *Book of Order*, F-1.03.

harmonious relationship. This purpose is gathered up in the rich symbol of the Kingdom (*basileia*) of God. Since *basileia* denotes not a place, but the sovereign activity of God, *Kingdom* is a bad translation. *Reign* is a better translation, problematic homophone notwithstanding. God's sovereign activity is God's creative mission of redeeming and blessing a fallen world. Thus, God's mission is God's Reign, or Kingdom. Indeed, this is the gospel that Jesus preached: the Reign of God is at hand, working to restore creation's shalom. Repent and believe, i.e. turn around to live in accord with God's Rule (Mark 1:15). Jesus not only preached this, though; he lived it. He was crucified for it and, with the resurrection, vindicated and inaugurated to rule over it as Lord. It is thus "through Christ" that God is working to redeem creation. And it is in the same Holy Spirit that filled Christ that the church continues his work.

This does not mean that our deeds bring in the Kingdom, as nineteenth liberal theology thought. No, the church exists more like construction workers building a road that the Lord might travel, a la Isaiah 40:3. Our witness as a church prepares a space in time where people might encounter the living Lord and hear the divine invitation to come and follow him. The institutional church is not the reason why we exist as church. We are but servants of the Most High. The Reign of God is God's, not the church's. Nonetheless, God graciously invites us to participate as instruments of that work like flutes through which the divine music flows. As we offer ourselves unto the Lord, so God may use us to be instruments of blessing for others, but the salvific work of God is God's, not ours. We are but earthen vessels, like an ocarina, of the gospel's treasure. As followers of Christ, we preach and live the same gospel that he preached and lived with an additional affirmation that Jesus Christ is Lord.[11] This gospel of God's Reign thus functions as a touchstone for all our ministries as its end and source.

Here's the rub, though: God's Reign is amorphous. While it is always at hand, it is not within our grasp or our control.

The verbs that are connected with the kingdom of God in the New Testament are very different: "enter," "receive," "inherit," "wait for," and "proclaim" (or "preach"). The linking of these verbs to the kingdom of God makes clear that human beings have no role whatsoever in creating or sustaining it, much less in enlarging it or getting it noticed: it is whole and complete and comes as a gift or bequest, and that is the only way human beings can get it.[12]

---

11. See Dodd, *The Apostolic Preaching*.
12. Dally, *Choosing the Kingdom*, 50.

Nonetheless, there is a shape to God's Way that can be discerned by studying the Scriptures.[13] As George Hunsberger notes, we can trace the contours of God's reign by looking at the prophets' proclamations of God's coming reign in the Old Testament. Basically, these proclamations are characterized by shalom that

> envisions a world characterized by peace, justice, and celebration. Shalom, the overarching vision of the future, means "peace," but not merely peace as the cessation of hostilities. Instead, shalom envisions the full prosperity of a people of God living under the covenant of God's demanding care and compassionate rule. In the prophetic vision, peace such as this comes hand in hand with justice. Without justice, there can be no real peace, and without peace, no real justice. Indeed, only in a social world full of a peace grounded in justice can there come the full expression of joy and celebration.[14]

Shalom connotes not just peace, but harmonious well-being among all people. It is the abundant life that Jesus came to give to all (John 10:10), not just in the future by-and-by, but present in part here and now in our sinful world (cf. Luke 17:20; 2 Cor 5:17).[15] As Dally says it, God's reign "is present on earth whenever life accurately reflects the will and sovereignty of God. It is the way life and society would be if a compassionate God were in charge or imitated instead of" human powers that lord it over others.[16]

The Realm of God is what the church is called to proclaim and live as servant/citizens of. God's Reign, not the church institution, is what we're called to invite others to join. It is not a place to be equated with heaven or any culture or any church. It is a way of being in the world under the sovereignty of God. Inviting others to come join us on the pilgrim parade toward the Day when all of creation will be fully restored, the church exists as the Kingdom's advance guard of love, like the people waving palm branches shouting praises before Christ's triumphal parade. It does not exist to invite people to Jazzercise for Jesus or pancake breakfasts, as pleasant as these might be. God's Reign is so much bigger than simply joining the

---

13. For a helpful list of all of the scriptures that refer to the reign of God in the synoptic gospels, see ibid., 54–62.

14. Arthur Holmes, The Staley Lectures, Belhaven College, Jackson, Mississippi, 1980, referenced in George Hunsberger, "Called and Sent," 77–109.

15. The Greek of 2 Cor 5:17 literally reads, "If any in Christ new creation." This implies that those who are in Christ are of the New Creation begun through Christ's death and resurrection.

16. Dally, *Choosing the Kingdom*, 63.

church, and we are unfaithful to the gospel if all we welcome people to is church programs and not what the church itself exists to be—servants of God's the mission in the world.

Preaching the Realm of God is difficult, though, because there is no *there* to point people to, for God's Reign is not a place. It is God's mysterious activity among the stuff of everyday life that is as hidden as yeast in bread dough. Nonetheless, we are sent as Christ's ambassadors to proclaim this Reign in word and deed. This is what it means to be an apostolic church— to be sent with good news to the world that the way of oppressive human power has been judged and condemned in Christ's death and that, through the resurrection of Christ, God's Reign has begun. Like Lincoln's "Emancipation Proclamation," it will take awhile to fully institute, but, upon hearing its good news, we need to repent and believe that this is The Way things really are (despite evidence to the contrary) and live accordingly.

Worship as the Kingdom's Earthly Whence and Whither

The church, however, is a necessary agent of God's salvation as the premier place through which God's presence in the world is known. It is as necessary as a runway is to flying, although flying is the important thing. Similarly, the church exists to be about the work of God in the world (i.e. the Kingdom). According to Clark Cowden, the institution of a missional church functions like an airport terminal that helps people get to their destinations of serving the world in Christ's Spirit. No one wants to live, or even stay long, in an airport; we go there in order to get to our destination.[17] It is not the institution that serves as the terminus of the church's mission. Rather, it is the Reign of God, which is glimpsed most fully in worship. Worship is the center of the gathered church because it the place where we are patterned to see, celebrate, and rehearse the way of God in the world most clearly. Therefore, worship is not just one aspect of the church that can be placed alongside other ecclesial activities;[18] it is the primary place from which the church is sent to continue its worship in our work in the world, and worship is that for which the church gathers.[19] It is the whence and whither of the church's existence on earth as the antechamber of God's throne room of grace.

Worship is the space in time where the people of God assemble as citizens of God's Reign. In worship we begin to experience and understand the presence of God-with-us in Holy Spirit, hail the Sovereign, ask for mercy,

---

17. Cowden, unpublished sermon.
18. See Hirsch, *The Forgotten Ways*, 41.
19. See Schmit, *Sent and Gathered*.

listen to the divine Word of our Sovereign, respond with joyous loyalty, and sup at the royal banquet before being sent out with a divine emancipation proclamation. Worship is what shapes our perception of the activity of God for blessing and redemption in the world. In other words, worship is the place in time that best orients us toward life in God's Reign. It is a "thin place" where "we are caught up in God's future" that opens up in our Eucharistic remembrance of Christ in the present.[20] In worship we rehearse who it is we are before God—forgiven sinners who, by the grace of God in Christ Jesus, become children who inherit the Kingdom and are invited to sup with the Lord in the eschatological banquet. As we rehearse this remembrance, we learn more of God's Way so that we can recognize it as it becomes "presenced" in forms that are similar to past shapes witnessed by our ancestors in the faith who left their testimonies of God's Way for us in Scripture so that we, too, might come to know that Christ is Lord and follow (Luke 1:4; John 20:31). As Nicholas Wolterstorff says, "to participate in the liturgy is to enter the sphere of God's acting."[21] As we have seen, "sphere of God's acting" and "God's future" (from Moore-Keish above) are synonyms for the Reign of God. In worship we are lifted up into God's Reign. "We commune with and upon Christ," the Belgic Confession says, "not because he is brought down to us, but because we are lifted up to him"[22] who is "seated at the right hand of the Father," as Calvin explains the *sursum corda*.[23] In other words, worship is the premier place in time where we catch the clearest glimpse of God's Reign.

Worship Shapes Us for Kingdom Living

Worship is not just a celebration of God's Reign, however. It also shapes us for Kingdom living by tacitly teaching us the Way of God's Realm.[24] In fact, the structure of the fourfold order of worship serves as practice ground for Kingdom living, forming us to be church in the world as the body of Christ. Through its very structure, worship teaches us how we follow and embody God's Reign.

---

20. Moore-Keish, "Eucharist/Eschatology," 114.
21. Wolterstorff, "Reformed Liturgy," 290.
22. Belgic Confession, Article 35.
23. Calvin, *Institutes*, 4.17.38.
24. See Smith, *Desiring the Kingdom*.

Gathering

First, the church is constituted as those who follow Christ and consists of those gathered by the call of God. It is God and the divine call that prompts us to gather with others as church. We cannot be church by ourselves. Thus we gather with others upon God's initiative and invitation to worship and praise the Lord.

Even as we seek to glorify God, though, we understand that we fall short of God's good desires for us as we are called to confess our sin with the promise that we are forgiven, not condemned, in Christ. Thus, we confess our sin, which is as much a matter-of-fact admission of where we stand before God as it is a recitation of all the ways we fail. We gather as common sinners before the One who justifies and sanctifies us. Because this has been effected through Christ's life, death, resurrection, and Reign, the assurance of pardon evokes a sense of the deep, wondrous, mysterious love of God for us and all of creation. This prompts a desire to act as the new people in Christ whom we are, to live in accord with God's Way out of thanksgiving for all the Lord has done for us. Our gathering thus ends with praise and peace in Christ shared with one another. It is only in Christ and by Christ that we can be the Christian church.

Hearing the Word

It is not enough just to gather with the community of Christ's followers, though. Our order of worship teaches us that we are to hear and obey God's Word as it comes to us through the Holy Spirit at work in Scripture and the church's words that follow the same Kingdom trajectory. These words take many forms—sermons, drama, music, dance—but they are to be within the same beam of Scripture's flashlight that illumines the gospel of God's redemptive beatific activity in the world. This gospel, which Christ preached, embodied, died for, and was raised to reign, is what we are called to pass on by inviting others, as we have been invited, to live within God's future Reign that Christ's Spirit is at work in the world bringing to pass even now.

Responding to the Word with Thanksgiving

Upon hearing this invitation, we seek to respond to it with a more profound faith, often indicated by a reflective hymn of consecration. This faith is not just our own, though; it is the church's. Hence we stand with the communion of saints to profess the Apostles' or Nicene Creed or words from our Confessions or Scripture. This is the faith into which we are baptized and out of which we respond to the world as part of the church. Baptism/renewal of baptismal vows is the part of the service that gathers us into the church through a renunciation of our allegiance to the way of sin/death and an adherence unto Christ. Through water and the Spirit, our citizenship is transferred from this present age of death's decay to God's New Creation. Baptism's covenantal rite indicates that transformation into the image of Christ is a continual lifelong process of "being-savedness" in response to the Spirit's call and the Word's invitation. Our old, selfish life is continually being drowned as we walk in The Way with the pilgrim communion of saints, serving and praying for others.

Service and Thanksgiving

This way of life involves offering ourselves and our gifts to God to be used for the common good in accord with the Way of God's Reign. As we offer ourselves, so the Lord offers Godself to us. We serve one another and rehearse again the ancient story of God's mighty acts, and the Lord serves up nothing less than Godself in Christ through the Holy Spirit. So we commune with the Holy Trinity, participating in the proleptic feast of the Kingdom here and now in part, anticipating the Day when God's Reign is fully instituted. We do this by praising God, thanking God, serving one another, and continuing to pray for others as Christ prays for us and taught us to pray.

Sending

Then we are sent out from the Banquet table to continue our worship in service to the world as Christ's body, singing the eternal song of the church as we act justly for all of creation, seek all people's well-being, share so that all needs are met, bind up the brokenhearted and wounded, and help all have access to God's blessings. Departing to serve as charged, we are blessed with the power of God until we meet again. Thus blessed, we are sent out to be a blessing as the body of Christ on God's mission for the world.

This order of worship contains within it an implicit understanding of God's Reign and how, as Christ's body, we are to be church in the world, living as those who are called out (*ek-klesia*) by God to come commune with the Lord and then sent out to serve and invite others to come and see for themselves who Christ is by joining us along The Way. Thus, worship is the gathering and sending place of the church's ministries. To use an imperfect (and perhaps ludicrous) analogy, like a *Star Trek* transporter, worship is the platform in time that aligns us within the Light of God's Realm. It breaks us down and sends us forth reconstituted as part of the body of Christ until we are called and plucked up to return home.

Why Whence and Whither?

To review, we have argued that the church exists within the trajectory of a treasured tradition that need not be jettisoned, including some important biblical and theological understandings of the church. We have adopted a missional ecclesiology as a way that values our heritage as it embraces God's future, or the Reign of God. And we have asserted that the worship of the sent and gathered disciples of Christ occurs within God's Reign, helping us to see it and know its shape in the world so that we can offer our bodies for God's work.

Why? Why do these things matter? We are in the midst of a time that is witnessing a great tearing of the fabric of ecclesial life. Indeed, we are like growling dogs fighting over the cloth of orthodoxy, forgetting that orthodoxy means "right praise," not "right belief" or "right dogma." What is happening to the church is nothing less than a culture war over whose world view reads and interprets Scripture,[25] forgetting that we are all desiring to live faithfully within the sovereignty of God even though we have different understandings of what that looks like in actual concrete circumstances. If we can humbly (oh, so humbly!) gather together to worship the Lord and pay attention to what worship itself tells us about how to live in the world before God and one another; if we can talk about what our worship tradition seeks to do; if we can come together to sketch out the broad outline of what the Reign of God in the world is like even while admitting that none of us can control it or even completely understand it until we stand fully before the Holy One face-to-face; if we can get a clearer picture of what it is that all of the church is aiming toward, namely, embodying God's Reign; if we could shift our view from the past to God's future; and if we could focus our attention on right practice rather than on right believing, I wonder: will the gunman of our past dreams disappear as we find the Holy Spirit nudging us out from our safely established tables to be the church, the body of Christ, the people of God under the Spirit Rule of God's Way, in the world even now? Although this sounds pretty iffy, as part of the communion of saints, that's my hope. Dare I say it is our hope as well?

---

25. Ibid.

Bibliography

Belgic Confession, Article 35. Center for Reformed Theology and Apologetic. www.reformed.org/documents/BelgicConfession.html.

Branaugh, Matt. "Willow Creek's 'Huge Shift': Influential Megachurch Moves Away from Seeker-Sensitive Services." *Christianity Today*, May 15, 2008. http://www.christianitytoday.com/ct/2008/june/5.13.html.

The Constitution of the Presbyterian Church (U.S.A.), Part I, Book of Confessions. Louisville: Office of the General Assembly, 1999.

The Constitution of the Presbyterian Church (U.S.A.), Part II, Book of Order. Louisville: Office of the General Assembly, 2013.

Cowden, Clark. Unpublished sermon. Southwest Academy for Missional Preaching. Serra Retreat Center, Malibu, California, July 22, 2009.

Dally, John. *Choosing the Kingdom: Missional Preaching for the Household of God*. Herndon, VA: Alban, 2008.

Dodd, C. H. *The Apostolic Preaching and Its Developments*. New York: Harper & Row, 1964.

Hirsch, Alan. *The Forgotten Ways: Reactivating the Missional Church*. Grand Rapids: Brazos, 2006.

Hunsberger, George. "Missional Vocation: Called and Sent to Represent the Reign of God." In *Missional Church*, edited by Darrell L. Guder, 77–109. Grand Rapids: Eerdmans, 1998.

Moore-Keish, Martha. "Eucharist/Eschatology." In *A More Profound Alleluia*, edited by Leanne Van Dyk, 109–32. Grand Rapids: Eerdmans, 2005.

Schmit, Clayton. *Sent and Gathered: A Worship Manual for the Missional Church*. Grand Rapids: Baker Academic, 2009.

Smith, James K. A. *Desiring the Kingdom: Worship, Worldview, and Cultural Formation*. Grand Rapids: Baker Academic, 2009.

Wolterstorff, Nicholas. "The Reformed Liturgy." In *Major Themes in the Reformed Tradition*, edited by Donald McKim, 273–304. Grand Rapids: Eerdmans, 1992.

4

Opening the Doors of the Church

Identity and Mission at the Thresholds of Christian Worship

DAVID GAMBRELL

Pulpit, font, table—these fixtures of Christian architecture have, appropriately enough, received considerable attention as theological foci and liturgical symbols for the church's ministries of word and sacrament. They are centers of action in the liturgical assembly, charged with meaning, and as such offer rich resources for reflection on the identity and mission of the church. But there is another, more marginal and ambiguous symbol that merits our focused consideration, a neglected fixture (not necessarily so fixed): the doors of the church.

In this paper I will propose that, for the church of the twenty-first century, the sanctuary doors are a critical place for reflection on Christian identity and mission. By attending to these thresholds of Christian worship—in particular, to Christ's calling in gathering and sending the people of God, I will seek fresh insight on the nature and purpose of the church in the world. I will also suggest that the image of the door helps to open up our understanding of Christ's presence in word and sacrament—the matter at the heart of Christian worship.

The title of this paper alludes to a phrase heard during the altar call in some traditions: "The doors of the church are open." This invitation to discipleship can be a word of welcome to new believers; it can also be an opportunity for wandering souls to repent and return to Christ. The sense of a "double door" between the church and the world is important. At every occasion of Christian worship, when the church flings wide the doors to the world, two things are happening: (1) we are inviting those *outside* to come in and be baptized; and (2) we are asking those *inside* to go forth and claim their baptismal vocation. Simultaneously, through the doors of the church, Jesus welcomes new disciples with open arms *and* challenges his followers to go and embrace his calling.

Throughout this paper, I will rely on the "compact theology"[1] of hymn texts as a primary source for theological reflection on what the church does in worship, focusing on those that employ the metaphor of the door. I will also attend to images of doorways in the witness of Scripture. In each section, I will inquire about implications for the church's theology and liturgy, posing questions for reflection or discussion. And at the conclusion of the paper, I will offer a set of five practices intended to prompt further conversation around Christian identity and mission—all through the doors of the church.

1. Gathering: Baptismal Doors

1.1 *Assembling*

The very act of gathering for worship is a statement of faith and an expression of ecclesiology. We enter the doors of the church to stand together as the living body of Christ in a particular place and time, proclaiming Christ risen, here and now. This meeting of the people, called by God, constitutes the church—a baptized and beloved community. As Dutch Jesuit theologian Huub Oosterhuis frames the question:

> What is this place where we are meeting?
> Only a house, the earth its floor.
> Walls and a roof, sheltering people,
> windows for light, an open door.
> Yet it becomes a body that lives
> when we are gathered here,
> and know our God is near.[2]

---

1. This description of hymns is attributed to David Allan Hubbard, president of Fuller Theological Seminary from 1963 to 1993; see *Glory to God*, 926.

2. Oosterhuis, "What Is This Place?," 404.

Oosterhuis's verse helps illuminate the biblical metaphor of the church as house. The church is an ordinary place, grounded in earth—the dust from which we are made and to which we return (Gen 3:19). At the same time, it is a holy place, sanctified by the presence of Christ in the gathered community. The church is a bounded space, with "walls and a roof" that both provide safety or sanctuary and mark off a distinctive identity or location. At the same time, it is an open space, with a source of light that comes from beyond its walls and with unfettered access to and from the world. At this entrance, Oosterhuis introduces a second biblical metaphor: the church as body. Architecture becomes anatomy as we enter the church through baptism and are incorporated into the body of Christ. The people of God, "like living stones," are "built into a spiritual house" (1 Pet 2:5), "a temple of the Holy Spirit" (1 Cor 6:19).

As ecclesial communities explore new ways of "being church," many moving beyond the well-established brick-and-mortal models, we ought not to lose sight of these earthy, biblical images of house and body. What difference does it make to meet in a house of wood and stone, a body of flesh and blood? If the house has no walls, where is the door?

1.2 *Praising*

Christian worship begins (and ends) with the praise of the triune God. English poet and priest George Herbert gives voice to this praise in an "Antiphon" composed for his 1633 collection, *The Temple*:

> The church with psalms must shout:
> no door can keep them out. . . .
> Let all the world in every corner sing,
> my God and King![3]

The poetic ambiguity of Herbert's door is intriguing. Are the people of God streaming to worship, storming the sanctuary door with songs of praise? Or do the mighty psalms threaten to shatter the church's door and spill out into the world? Every door has two sides; yet Herbert seems to say that the praise of God has no respect for such distinctions (cf. Acts 10:34; Rom 2:10), resounding in "every corner" of the world.

Argentinian Methodist pastor and composer Pablo Sosa's setting of Ps 118 is somewhat more direct in its approach to worship:

> Open, now, open, the doorways of justice!
> Let us be glad as we pass through those gates.

---

3. Herbert, "Let All the World in Every Corner Sing," 636.

> This is the place where the righteous may enter,
> singing to God with thanksgiving and praise.[4]

This stanza of Sosa's hymn is a close paraphrase of Ps 118:19–20, one of a number of "entrance liturgies" in the Psalter (cf. Pss 15, 24). At first glance it might seem as though the faithful are able to unlock the temple gates by virtue of their own righteousness. In the larger context of the psalm, however, it is clear that a just and righteous God holds the key, and that God's saving grace alone will the door. This is why these verses are voiced in the jussive/subjunctive mode of prayer. And this is why, when the doors do open, the people gather with such gladness, singing thanks and praise to the one who has graciously welcomed them inside.

How is the praise of the triune God related to the church's mission and identity? Our purpose, above all else, is praise. The church is called to go "door to door," until every corner of the world has heard the glory of God and the call to baptismal discipleship (Matt 28:19–20). Furthermore, this praise of God flows from our understanding of who we are and what God has done for us in Jesus Christ: we are the people God has redeemed—the sinners God has saved; the lost, found; the outcast and dispersed, gathered up and drawn in.

1.3 Confessing

Thus our worship continues with confession. We don't arrive at this idea by our own initiative or desire; more often we run from it. Yet the God who has already called, chosen, and claimed us in baptism now calls us again: to confess, to repent. As an African American spiritual puts it,

> Somebody's knocking at your door;
> somebody's knocking at your door;
> O sinner, why don't you answer?
> Somebody's knocking at your door.[5]

In this song, Jesus stands at the door, offering salvation (Rev 3:20). In another hymn, Korean Presbyterian pastor Young taik Chun turns the metaphor inside out. Here the house belongs to Jesus and the door is left ajar; like a worried parent, Jesus keeps watch in the night:

> Jesus anxiously awaits you,
> with door kept open wide,

---

4. Sosa, "This Is the Day," 391.
5. African American spiritual, "Somebody's Knocking at Your Door," 728.

as one who waits throughout the night
for a lost child to come back home.⁶

These two songs reveal different facets of God's grace; there is wisdom on both sides of the door. With steadfast love, God pursues us. With faithfulness, God awaits our return.

Similarly, these hymns suggest two dimensions of the church's mission of reconciliation. We are called to go out and seek peace in the world, in Jesus' name, to be active in the pursuit of reconciliation within and among the nations of the earth. At the same time, we are called to keep the door open back at home, to "leave the light on" and wait patiently for those who "sit in darkness and the shadow of death" (Luke 1:79). How have we attended to each of these aspects of God's reconciling work? How have we neglected them?

2. The Word: Scriptural Doors

2.1 Hearing

The word of God is a gateway to truth and life. Like a door on its hinges, the book swings open and beckons us inside. A summary of Ps 119 by Mennonite hymnist Jean Janzen invites us to imagine the law of the Lord as a pathway to God's house:

> O God, I love your knowledge . . .
> It leads me to salvation's door
> where you have spread your table.
> O, lead me to your home.⁷

As this song suggests, Scripture is a doorway into God's realm. Paradoxically, the space we enter through these pages is larger and more real than the limited reality we have left behind. The gate may be narrow, but it leads to a broad place, an abundant pasture (John 10:9–10). When we take up the book of life and read, we discover that our stories are but a tiny part of God's great story; we find that our lives, our stories are held in God's hand.

Again, there are two sides to the metaphor. Scripture may also be understood as the door through which *God* enters our hearts and lives, as

---

6. Chun, "O Come unto the Lord," 416.
7. Janzen, "I Long for Your Commandments," 64.

demonstrated in a seventeenth-century German meditation on Ps 24 by Georg Weissel:

> Lift up your heads, ye mighty gates;
> behold, the King of glory waits . . .
> Fling wide the portals of your heart;
> make it a temple, set apart . . .
> Redeemer, come! I open wide
> my heart to thee; here, Lord, abide.[8]

As we approach the word of God in Scripture, we pray that, through these words, God will draw near to us, enter into us, and make a dwelling place within our hearts. Fittingly, then, a familiar prayer for illumination begins, "Lord, open our hearts and minds by the power of your Holy Spirit. . . ."[9]

Scripture shapes the church's identity and mission. So how *does* the church approach Scripture? As a doorway into the realm of God, or only a window? How might we frame a more compelling invitation to the word—both in public worship and in personal devotion—so that the people of God might enter in more fully and, by Christ's grace and the Spirit's power, be truly transformed?

2.2 *Proclaiming*

We might think of the preacher as a doorkeeper in the house of Lord (Ps 84:10). The one who opens the word of God to the people of God points to a doorway in heaven (Rev 4:1). John Mason Neale's English paraphrase of the medieval Latin carol *In dulci jubilo* supports this image:

> He has opened heaven's door,
> and we are blest forevermore. . . .
> Calls you one and calls you all
> to gain the everlasting hall.[10]

Of course, as this text reveals, Jesus Christ is the *true* doorkeeper. The hymn concludes, "Christ was born to save!" A contemporary song by Lutheran composer Marty Haugen elaborates on this point, employing similar imagery:

> Come as a baby, weak and poor
> to bring all hearts together,

---

8. Weissel, "Lift Up Your Heads, Ye Mighty Gates," 93.
9. "The Service for the Lord's Day," 5.
10. "Good Christian Friends, Rejoice," 132.

he opens wide the heavenly door
and lives now inside us forever.[11]

The preacher's task, then, is to point to Christ. Christ Jesus is the one who opens the door between heaven and earth—through his incarnation and life, his death and resurrection, his ascension and reign, and his promised return. In fact, he *is* that door, as he offers us a "new and living way" into the sanctuary of God through the curtain of his flesh (Heb 10:19–22). Again, as the latter song suggests, the door swings in both directions. The same portal that allows us this access to heaven is the one by which Jesus has chosen to enter into our lives. We are to abide in him as he abides in us (John 15:1–11).

In contemporary Presbyterian practice, when, where, and how is an invitation to Christian discipleship expressed? At what point in worship, or perhaps elsewhere in the life and ministry of the church, do we invite people to enter into deeper relationship with Christ, or to ask Christ to enter into them? How might a renewed and strengthened call to discipleship—in each service of worship—contribute to the renewal of the church's identity and mission?

2.3 Praying

The promise of the gospel inspires our prayer. Moved by the word of God in Scripture, we lift up our hearts to the Word of God enthroned in heaven, Jesus Christ, who intercedes for us, for the church, and for the whole world God so loves. A praise song by Karen Lafferty, with additional lyrics inspired by Matt 7:7, provides this entrance into prayer:

> Ask, and it shall be given unto you;
> seek, and you shall find;
> knock, and the door shall be opened unto you.
> Allelu, alleluia![12]

Lafferty's call to "seek first the kingdom" (based on Matt 6:33) echoes the form of prayer that Jesus taught: "Your kingdom come. Your will be done, on earth as it is in heaven" (Matt 6:10). In this stanza, Jesus invites us to "knock, and the door shall be opened." Prayer is a way of standing at the threshold between heaven and earth and boldly claiming the promises of God for the world.

---

11. Haugen, "Awake! Awake, and Greet the New Morn," 107.
12. Lafferty, "Seek Ye First," 175.

Do our prayers include genuine asking, seeking, and knocking? Too often we offer perfunctory prayers, hedging our bets or couching our petitions in courtly courtesy. Do we dare practice the kind of faithful and persistent prayer Jesus praises in the parable of the widow and the unjust judge (Luke 18:1–8)? Might we learn to pray more boldly from the language of the psalmists? And do we understand the ministry of prayer to be a vital and essential part of the nature and purpose of the church? This is, after all, our baptismal identity and vocation: to be "a spiritual house, to be a holy priesthood" (2 Pet 2:5), calling night and day on the mercy of God for the sake of the church and the world.

3. The Table: Eucharistic Doors

3.1 Taking

The church's eucharistic liturgy is shaped by Jesus' repeated action at table—taking, blessing, breaking, giving—whether in the feeding of the multitude (Matt 14:19), at the Passover meal (Mark 14:22), or on the road to Emmaus (Luke 24:30). Congregational pastor Robert Edwards points to the first of these actions, taking, in an offertory hymn:

> God, whose giving knows no ending,
> from your rich and endless store,
> nature's wonder, Jesus' wisdom,
> costly cross, grave's shattered door.[13]

The story of salvation is, in a sense, the story of God's extravagant giving. God's providence is poured out for us from the "rich and endless" treasury of nature, through the words of Jesus' lips, the blood of his cross, and even the door of his tomb. We take and use only what God has entrusted to us; indeed, we have nothing else, nothing but the grace of God. Therefore we lay our lives before the Lord at the eucharistic feast, an offering of gratitude for God's grace.

In some traditions, the bread and wine for the Lord's Supper are carried in procession from the doors of the church to the eucharistic table. In many congregations, ushers leave their posts at the church's doors to collect the monetary offerings. Some congregations have bags or barrels near the doors of the church where people deposit used clothing or canned goods. In John Calvin's Strasbourg, "a collection for the poor was probably taken

---

13. Edwards, "God, Whose Giving Knows No Ending," 716.

on the day the Lord's Supper was celebrated, most likely at the door as the congregation departed."[14] How might we draw stronger, closer connections between our self-offering in worship and God's self-giving for the world that waits beyond the church's doors?

3.2 Blessing

The second action of the eucharistic liturgy is blessing or giving thanks to God. The sixteenth-century German reformer Martin Luther (a theologian of doors, if ever there was one) offers this image of the Christ, the paschal lamb, in an Easter hymn:

> See, his blood now marks our door:
> faith points to it; death passes o'er,
> and Satan cannot harm us. Hallelujah![15]

At its heart, the eucharistic prayer is a shout of thanks and praise to God (Hallelujah!) for our liberation from captivity to sin and death through the body and blood of Christ Jesus. The life-blood of the lamb (see Exod 12:21–23) marks the dwelling-place that shelters us from sin, the passageway by which we journey from death into life. This is the glorious triumph of God we celebrate. This is why we keep the feast (1 Cor 5:7–8). John's gospel paints a complementary picture, using the same palette of images: Jesus as gate who saves and protects the sheep (John 10:7), as shepherd who lays down his life for them (John 10:11).

Do these eucharistic images resonate with our understanding of the church's identity and mission? Is the church a house made holy by Christ's blood? Is it a place where people pass from death to life? Is the church a gate of safety and salvation? Is it a place for laying down one's life for others, as Jesus' disciples are called to do (John 15:12–14)? If so, how might our eucharistic practice open or deepen such themes?

3.3 Breaking

The third action at Christ's table is the breaking of the bread and pouring or lifting of the cup. United Church of Canada minister Nigel Weaver alludes to the gospel accounts of Jesus breaking bread with his disciples on the day of his resurrection:

---

14. McKee, *John Calvin*, 134.
15. Luther, "Christ Jesus Lay in Death's Strong Bands," 237.

> The risen Christ, who walks on wounded feet
> from garden tomb through darkened city street,
> unlocks the door of grief, despair, and fear,
> and speaks a word of peace to all who hear.[16]

In Luke's Gospel, on the road to Emmaus the risen Lord first makes himself known in the breaking of the bread (Luke 24:35). Jesus comes again to a larger group of disciples in Jerusalem, the signs of his broken body still evident, to eat with them and share his peace (Luke 24:36–43). In John's account Jesus passes through locked doors, doors locked out of fear. But he commissions the disciples to go out, to go forth, "As the Father has sent me, so I send you" (John 20:21). Then he bestows the gift of the Spirit and the power of forgiveness of sin (John 20:22–23). Later, Thomas has the chance to touch Jesus' hand and side (John 20:26–29). Later still, Jesus breaks bread with his disciples beside the sea (John 21:13).

Perhaps being commissioned to ministry in Jesus' name means being willing to share our own brokenness, our own wounds. That is to say, in going about God's mission, we members of Christ's body should not attempt to conceal the church's hurt and shame: histories of participation in the systemic brokenness of racism, sexism, classism, for instance. We need to open locked doors—to move through and beyond our fear of confronting these issues—trusting the gifts of the Spirit and Christ's power to reconcile and forgive, looking forward to the day when all may feast together at one table.

3.4 Giving

The fourth action in the eucharistic liturgy is giving: the communion of the people. Baptist writer and dramatist Ragan Courtney draws a strong connection between the service of communion and the service of our neighbors:

> In remembrance of me, heal the sick.
> In remembrance of me, feed the poor.
> In remembrance of me, open the door
> and let your neighbors in, let them in.[17]

Courtney's song suggests that Jesus' call to "do this" has to do with more than a bite of bread and sip of wine. To be sure, communion with Christ begins with these elements, but it continues through the sharing of his life and ministry: healing, feeding, welcoming, teaching in Jesus' name. All of these things are an extension of the church's action at Christ's table. In

---

16. Weaver, "The Risen Christ," 257.
17. Courtney, "In Remembrance of Me," 521.

the words of a familiar eucharistic prayer: "As this bread is Christ's body for us, send us out to be the body of Christ in the world."[18]

In recent years, a number of mainline denominations have experienced debates over questions of baptismal integrity or eucharistic hospitality: whether persons who are not (yet) baptized should be invited to share the Lord's table. "Open the door and let your neighbors in," some cry; yet others wonder whether this might lead to the further breakdown of the body "re-membered" in baptism. I wonder whether this energy might be better directed toward *baptismal* hospitality: making a more compelling invitation to life and discipleship in Christ through baptism (see the questions under "Proclaiming," above). Focusing more on baptism might help us to connect the church's evangelical mission with its ecclesial identity.

4. Sending: Missional Doors

4.1 Loving

"Go in peace to love and serve the Lord" (see Deut 10:12–13). The final words of the Service for the Lord's Day, perhaps spoken by a deacon at the door of the church, send us forth to worship God through the service of daily living. Lutheran scholar Herman Stuempfle offers this striking depiction of Dorcas, a biblical paragon of diaconal ministry (see Acts 9:36–43):

> Lord, hear our praise of Dorcas,
> who served the sick and poor.
> Her hands were cups of water,
> her heart an open door.[19]

As Stuempfle envisions her, Dorcas is an embodiment of the humble service and love to which Christ calls us (see John 13:13–14, 34). Her heart, in particular, is a Christ-like door, open in love. This message of love for the world *is* Christ's mission.

With language echoing the poetry of the Song of Songs—"Arise, my love, my fair one, and come away" (Song 2:10)—United Church of Christ professor and poet Ruth Duck paraphrases Jesus' "mission statement" in Luke 4:16–21 (cf. Isa 61:1–2):

> Arise, your light is come!

---

18. *Book of Common Worship*, 72.
19. Stuempfle, "For All the Faithful Women," 324.

> Fling wide the prison door;
> proclaim the captives' liberty,
> good tidings to the poor.[20]

We are sent forth from worship with the blessing of the triune God on our heads and a hymn of love on our lips. We are called to love God and neighbor (Matt 22:34-40 and parallels; cf. Deut 6:4-5; Lev 19:18), and this love is meant to be a concrete action—borne out with heart, mind, soul, and strength, not only an abstract feeling. It is to be expressed through our engagement in the world: healing the sick, helping the poor, giving drink to the thirsty and food to the hungry, opening doors for strangers, visiting prisoners (cf. Matt 25:31-46), proclaiming good news.

The good news we proclaim is God's mission of love for the world through Christ (John 3:16-17). But *is* this the message we present or project to the world? Is this the quality by which Jesus' contemporary disciples are known to everyone (cf. John 13:34; 1 John 4:7)? The church in our time seems better known for its conflicts and controversies—hardly able to love one another, to say nothing of the wider world God so loves. How might we better reflect the humble love and service of Dorcas? How might we respond to the anointing of the Spirit and take up Christ's mantle: to bring good news to the poor and proclaim the time of God's favor?

4.2 *Serving*

When we exit the doors of the church, we enter into conflicted, contested spaces—geographies demarcated by social divisions, generation gaps, cultural chasms, economic barriers, political blocs. Of course, if we are honest, all of these lines run through the church as well, even though we claim that they are obliterated in baptism (Gal 3:23-29). Mennonite pastor and poet Adam Tice describes how Jesus leads us through such landscapes:

> Jesus crosses borders with the wandering poor,
> searching for a refuge, for an open door.
> Do our words and actions answer Jesus' plea:
> "Give the lowly welcome and you welcome me"?[21]

Walking with Jesus means breaching those boundaries, stepping into those spaces. It means choosing a life with the dispossessed, claiming a place with the disinherited, finding oneself among the undocumented. These are the lines we cross when we follow Jesus into the world.

---

20. Duck, "Arise, Your Light Is Come!," 744.
21. Tice, "Jesus Entered Egypt," 154.

Another of Tice's hymn texts addresses similar themes, but with an allusion to Jesus' humble service in the upper room (John 13:1–11):

> True faith will open up the door
> and step into the street.
> True service will seek out the poor
> and ask to wash their feet.[22]

Note that all four of the hymn texts cited in this section have rhymed "door" with "poor." This happy accident of English assonance points to something more profound: that the church's identity and mission are, in a fundamental way, bound up with the plight of the poor. Paul acknowledged this calling in his letter to the Galatians: "They asked only one thing, that we remember the poor" (Gal 2:10); this was a condition of his mission to the Gentiles, set by Peter, James, and John. Accordingly, one variation in the Service for the Lord's Day has the liturgy end with this commission: "Go in peace and in the name of Christ, remember the poor."[23]

In comparison with the rest of the order of worship, the "sending" portion of the Service for the Lord's Day is arrestingly terse, spare. A brief song, a few words—it often feels unfinished. Indeed, this is as it should be. The Sunday liturgy is incomplete, because the "work of the people" is meant to continue in the world. The service of God leads to the service of neighbors, as we "step into the street," following Christ. How might we make this step more explicit, underscoring the movement of the liturgy into the world?

5. Five Practices

In the spirit of the Presbyterian Church (USA)'s 2006 sacrament study, *Invitation to Christ: Font and Table*, I will conclude by offering five practices[24] for reconsidering the church's identity and mission at the thresholds of Christian worship. These practices are not intended to be strategies for renewal or solutions to a problem—renewing the church is God's work; our only help is in the name of the Lord (Ps 124:8). Rather, these practices are intended to provoke faithful questions, facilitate deeper conversation, and (perhaps, by God's grace) inspire transformation, as action leads to reflection and reflection prompts further action in Jesus' name.

---

22. Tice, "The Church of Christ Cannot Be Bound," 766.
23. "The Service for the Lord's Day," 13.
24. *Invitation to Christ*, 5–14.

5.1 Open the Doors between the Church and World on Every Lord's Day

In many congregations, the exterior doors of the sanctuary are no longer an active space or a living symbol. Members with "inside knowledge" access the church through an alternate entrance, often the one nearest the parking lot. Only hapless visitors stumble through the main doors, to be met (if they are lucky) by a startled usher. Sadly, in some settings, the original sanctuary doors are more or less permanently locked, even surrounded by gates, in order to prevent unauthorized entry to the facilities or to discourage homeless persons from sleeping on the steps. By opening the doors between the church and world on every Lord's Day, we might demonstrate that what happens in worship has something to do with how we live in the world. We might start to break down the assumption that faith is a private matter, disconnected from public life. With a little more fresh air and natural light in the sanctuary, we might be better able to sense the movement of the Spirit in the world.

5.2 Set the Font Nearer to the Doors of the Church and Fill It with Water

In the past decade, many Presbyterian congregations have rediscovered their baptismal fonts—in some cases, actually retrieving them from a closet where they were stored in case of baptism, and finding a place for them in the sanctuary. Some congregations have removed the heavy lids from their fonts, relics of the day when people believed the water of the font had intrinsic power, and tried to steal it for superstitious uses. Some pastors now pour water into the font at the opening of worship, or lift water at the declaration of forgiveness as a gesture of the grace of God proclaimed in baptism. Now that the font, once missing in action, has again found a place in worship, it is time to think about *where* it best expresses its relationship to the church's identity and mission. If baptism is how we enter the church, shouldn't the font be near the doors as a sign of Christian identity for all who enter? If baptism is related to our common vocation as disciples, shouldn't the font be near the doors as a symbol of Christ's call to mission in the world? Keeping water in the font will allow people to remember their baptism as they come in to worship and go forth to serve.

5.3 Lead Appropriate Parts of Worship from the Doors of the Church

As this paper seeks to suggest, the liturgical movements of "gathering" and "sending" have critical significance for the identity and mission of church in our age. If these movements are to have deeper meaning on Sunday morning and stronger ties to the lives of worshipers, they need to be reclaimed, reinterpreted, reinvigorated. An effective way to do this would be to lead certain portions of the service from the doors of the church. Wouldn't the invitation to "Worship the Lord with gladness; come into God's presence with singing!" (Ps 100:2) strike a different chord if it were uttered at the entrance to the sanctuary? Wouldn't the charge to "Go in peace to love and serve the Lord" be taken more seriously if it were spoken at the church's doors? The confession and pardon, too, might appropriately be led from the baptismal font at the door of the church; only by the grace of God, proclaimed in baptism, are we counted worthy to enter this assembly. Some will object that this will force them to turn, to stand, to move in order to participate in worship. Yes, exactly. God calls us to repent, to rise, to go in Jesus' name.

5.4 Let Book, Bread, Cup, and Cross Move to and from the Doors of the Church

We Presbyterians tend to view liturgical processions with some suspicion and disdain, as empty displays of pomp and pageantry. But there may be some wisdom in these rites of "passage." Stationary objects become idols, stumbling blocks, or simply fade into the background; they quickly lose their power to speak the living message of the gospel, to stir the spirit and engage the imagination. The pilgrim church of our time needs symbols that are portable. Let the Bible and cross (if applicable) be carried in procession from the doors to the chancel during the opening hymn and from the chancel to the doors at the closing song. Let the bread and cup be transported to the table during the hymn after the sermon or the offertory song. By giving these sacred symbols a more active role in worship we might start paying more attention to them, asking new questions about how they pertain to our faith and life. By allowing them to travel at these "threshold moments" or transitional times in the service, we might come to appreciate how the risen Christ, known through his word and action in the assembly of God's people, comes into our midst in worship and journeys with us in the world.

5.5 Increase the Number of Days on Which the Church's Doors Are Open

The fifth recommended practice is related to the first, but moves beyond the bounds of the Sunday morning assembly and, perhaps, the sanctuary itself. Many congregations already host support and recovery groups or smaller worshiping communities at other times during the day or week. But how might we expand on these offerings, elevating the church's profile in the community and expanding its outreach to neighbors? Start with services of daily prayer: encourage small groups in the congregation to gather at regular, appointed times to sing a psalm, read Scripture, and pray for the church and the world. Anyone can lead such services; in fact, it is best for elders and/or deacons to organize and preside at them. Beyond daily prayer, be creative; the church has often been a patron of artists. Make space available for musical recitals, art exhibitions, poetry readings, dramatic performances. Consider other possibilities: neighborhood meetings, service organizations, refugee ministries, interfaith groups. All of these can be opportunities for the church to deepen its engagement with the local community and enhance its witness in the world.

Bibliography

African American spiritual. "Somebody's Knocking at Your Door." *Glory to God: The Presbyterian Hymnal*. Louisville: Westminster John Knox, 2013.
Book of Common Worship. Louisville: Westminster John Knox, 1993.
Chun, Young tāik. "O Come unto the Lord. " Translated by Steve S. Shim. *Glory to God: The Presbyterian Hymnal*. Louisville: Westminster John Knox, 2013.
Courtney, Ragan. "In Remembrance of Me." *Glory to God: The Presbyterian Hymnal*. Louisville: Westminster John Knox, 2013.
Duck, Ruth. "Arise, Your Light Is Come!" *Glory to God: The Presbyterian Hymnal*. Louisville: Westminster John Knox, 2013.
Edwards, Robert L. "God, Whose Giving Knows No Ending." *Glory to God: The Presbyterian Hymnal*. Louisville: Westminster John Knox, 2013.
Glory to God: The Presbyterian Hymnal. Louisville: Westminster John Knox, 2013.
"Good Christian Friends, Rejoice." Translation and paraphrase by John Mason Neale. *Glory to God: The Presbyterian Hymnal*. Louisville: Westminster John Knox, 2013.
Haugen, Marty. "Awake! Awake, and Greet the New Morn." *Glory to God: The Presbyterian Hymnal*. Louisville: Westminster John Knox, 2013.
Herbert, George. "Let All the World in Every Corner Sing." *Glory to God: The Presbyterian Hymnal*. Louisville: Westminster John Knox, 2013.
Invitation to Christ: Font and Table. Louisville: Office of Theology and Worship, 2006.
Janzen, Jean. "I Long for Your Commandments." *Glory to God: The Presbyterian Hymnal*. Louisville: Westminster John Knox, 2013.

Lafferty, Karen. "Seek Ye First." *Glory to God: The Presbyterian Hymnal.* Louisville: Westminster John Knox, 2013.

Luther, Martin. "Christ Jesus Lay in Death's Strong Bands." Translation composite. *Glory to God: The Presbyterian Hymnal.* Louisville: Westminster John Knox, 2013.

McKee, Elsie Anne, ed. and trans. *John Calvin: Writings on Pastoral Piety.* New York: Paulist, 2001.

Oosterhuis, Huub. "What Is This Place?" Translated by David Smith. *Glory to God: The Presbyterian Hymnal.* Louisville: Westminster John Knox, 2013.

"The Service for the Lord's Day." *Glory to God: The Presbyterian Hymnal.* Louisville: Westminster John Knox, 2013.

Sosa, Pablo. "This Is the Day." Translated by Mary Louise Bringle. *Glory to God: The Presbyterian Hymnal.* Louisville: Westminster John Knox, 2013.

Stuempfle, Herman G. "For All the Faithful Women." *Glory to God: The Presbyterian Hymnal.* Louisville: Westminster John Knox, 2013.

Tice, Adam M. L. "The Church of Christ Cannot Be Bound." *Glory to God: The Presbyterian Hymnal.* Louisville: Westminster John Knox, 2013.

———. "Jesus Entered Egypt." *Glory to God: The Presbyterian Hymnal.* Louisville: Westminster John Knox, 2013.

Weaver, Nigel. "The Risen Christ." *Glory to God: The Presbyterian Hymnal.* Louisville: Westminster John Knox, 2013.

Weissel, Georg. "Lift Up Your Heads, Ye Mighty Gates." Translated by Catherine Winkworth. *Glory to God: The Presbyterian Hymnal.* Louisville: Westminster John Knox, 2013.

5

Ecclesiology Without Metaphor

JERRY ANDREWS

Why even try? The Scriptures rightly give us "aid," as Calvin would say, so that our faith can be supported, we being weak and constantly in need of assistance. The grand biblical metaphors for the church—bride and groom, vine and branches, shepherd and flock, head and body—give us aid. They each have explicatory and normative power in our thinking about the church. They are not to be neglected. And they are metaphors—similes some—referring by comparison to something not itself, not the church. No less true or necessary for being comparative, but the question comes to mind, is there a presentation of the church in the Scriptures without metaphor? If so, might this presentation be foundational for the metaphors that build up our ecclesiology, and might it even be prior in our thinking, perhaps even to be privileged, so that we can have a lens from the Scriptures by which we read the metaphors of Scripture?

Two literary forms in Scripture come to mind. First the narratives—perhaps the book of Acts. If Acts, a long book with few metaphors (can you think of one offhand?), were chosen as the appropriate object of study, I would argue that the narratives of the history of Israel are as important to the study. Founding the study of Acts with and on Genesis and Exodus would be most fruitful and remains, as far as I know, undone. It also would be a long work, too long for the first steps of the ecclesiology project at hand. For that reason I chose a second form in Scripture—those rare statements concerning the church that are declarative but not metaphorical. These have promise of being helpful in interpreting the metaphors for the church because these statements—usually propositional in form—do not presume we know much about the church yet and so do not attempt to embellish on a knowledge that may not be held with a comparative language that is fully useful only when the referents are better known. Rather the declarations announce what is not known making it known.

Four things need to be said here:

One, of course all language is metaphorical—the word analogical most often is used here. And yes, I've read David Tracy's *The Analogical Imagination* and I've read the feminists, like Sallie McFague's *Metaphorical Theology*, and with much profit. I've also read, indeed been taught by, Carl Henry (see his *God, Revelation, and Authority*) and others who argue that analogical speech is not a third way of speaking but a combination of the only two ways humans can speak—univocally or equivocally—again, with profit. (I've also read Wittgenstein's *Tractates* twice, and have no idea what he was talking about.)

Also, I would like to read a thorough account of what Calvin calls the "condescension" of God to our speech. Is divine speech limited to univocal, equivocal, and analogical, because our ears are? Or does the Word speak beyond, beneath, or behind these categories of human speech, and we hear it and are transformed by it precisely because it is more than human speech in its source and content, and in its category? I speculate here. The point is simple. Though all human speech is a metaphorical attempt to describe reality, divine speech need not be so limited. We'll return to this point in a moment. And, though all human speech is metaphorical it describes reality sometimes with intentional metaphor, and sometimes with the intentional absence of metaphor. Is there speech in Scripture—whether divine or human—which avoids metaphor in order to be more (what shall I say?) straightforward, probably more foundational, in the description of the church? Yes, I think so.

Two, the ecclesiologies that seem to motivate and which underlay the debates, deliberations, and decisions of the church are unexamined. They rely heavily on New Testament metaphors for the church and presume common understandings of those metaphors. "But, the church is the body of Christ . . ." one hears another say desperately to a dialogue partner, yet no common conclusion for thought or action comes from the plea. Good preachers—I've heard them—are able to explicate these metaphors one by one, but when we gather together for common conversation, the common conversation has less in common than what is necessary, and the meaning of the metaphors are not shared. Is there a more foundational (note: I am not saying more authoritative) expression of the church to the church in Scripture that, if explicated a bit, would help us get a fuller use of the dominating metaphors given for our aid in the New Testament? Yes, I think so.

Three, it is to be found in the Old Testament where we would expect the foundational to be. I don't think this should be problematic. Again Calvin's instinct, even theology, is at work here. If we remember that any good question about us must be in the context of the knowledge of God (Calvin is all over that statement), we want to know what God was doing prior to Pentecost, especially we want to know what God was and is doing in Christ, which has always required the Reformed to read as God's Word to us (and about us) what was said to and about Israel, or as Calvin would say "the Old Testament Church." Again, this is not about going to a more authoritative spot in the canon (nor a less authoritative spot), but it is a prior one and, I argue, a more foundational one, because it is the one on which the authors of the New Testament metaphors consciously built.

And four, after having made easy reference to Calvin several times above, this paper is not a Calvinistic project, it is a Zwinglian one. It does not seek the rich, even the full, expressions of the faith in matters of ecclesiology. It will not inspire. It does not have Calvin's aesthetic for language and theology. It is Zwinglian—simple, straightforward, severe, even intentionally austere. Stones at the foundation of a home are largely unadorned, for their beauty is not their essence. The foundational stones are clear cut, precise and, because trusted, permit the whole home to be built up in ways beautiful and which beautifully express the whole household. How's that for a metaphor? This paper begins at the beginning.

We are blessed by the Scriptures, for the Scriptures tell us not once but several times what is, I now argue, that foundational statement on which all ecclesiology, including the metaphors are built.

> I will take you to be my people,
> and I will be your God.

That's the Almighty telling Moses what to tell the people (Exod 6:7). Abraham had heard this Word earlier (Gen 17:7):

> And I will establish my covenant between me and you
> and your offspring after you throughout their generations
> for an everlasting covenant,
> to be God to you and to your offspring after you.

God will repeat this to Moses from Sinai, for him to tell the people again (Lev 26:12):

> And I will walk among you
> and will be your God,
> And you will be my people.

The prophets Jeremiah (30:22) and Ezekiel (36:28), among others, just to name two and one passage a piece, will declare it repeatedly in new circumstances, but with the same declarative, unadorned language:

> You shall be my people,
> And I will be your God.

And Hosea (1:9), when he wants to threaten Israel with the potential loss of all that is of value, says simply on behalf of God:

> You are not my people,
> And I am not your God.

And when Hosea announces the restoration of all that is good, says with equal simplicity:

> I will say, "You are my people."
> You will say, "You are my God."

This repeated phrase is, by the time of the exilic prophets, a *topos*—stylized, formulaic, familiar. But it never seems dull or dismissible. It is always on the lips of the Almighty, always declarative, always the critical moment into whatever conversation (or silence) it is spoken. It appears to be foundational. Though there is a beginning to this statement (I spoke this to your father Abraham), and though there is illustration of this statement (I brought you out of Egypt) there is no explanation for this statement. There seems to be nothing before it.

What can be known then by the priority, pervasiveness, and power of this statement—unadorned, straightforward, without metaphor—that can inform our ecclesiology? Again, four things.

First, God *speaks*.

Divine speech creates reality. The closest parallel to this statement may be "And God said, 'Let there be light, and there was light.'" The Almighty creates by the Word. The creation of the people of God is a work of God by means of the Word of God. The Almighty can and will eventually birth, adopt, and marry this people, but prior to all the relational metaphors and historical narratives there is the creation of the people as the people of God by the Word of God. The people of God are *creatura verbi*. Consider the opposite: the people of God are formed by human associations making application—speeches—to the deity for privileged status as the people of the deity. That's the pagan project—seeking, appeasing, even creating their own gods to be owned by them. The Old Testament people of God are sought out, formed, offered salvation, and owned by the Almighty in such a way as never to be let go. If there is a missing third line to the declaration "I will be your God, you will be my people" it sometimes seems to be "So get used to it." The Old Testament, it has been said, is the record of a people who did not want their God. This people never chose God; God chose, even created, them. This is the doctrine of election. The Almighty, taking only his own counsel, elects some for his own purposes. The people of God are created by the Word of God because elected by the inscrutable counsel of God, not and never by their own choosing.

Second, it is *God* who speaks.

Divine speech reveals reality. It reveals God. This is a declaration that not only creates the reality, it also reveals it—by revealing God. The declaration announces not only what they will be, but who God is and will be to them. The pagans would not be surprised to hear of a god who finally agrees to become a protector of a suppliant people, but they would be surprised to hear of a god who takes the initiative to reveal self to someone or some people, for the sake of both the deity and humanity. The lesser gods sought the favor of the great gods, always looking up, revealing their own lesser person and pitiable plight, and likewise expected humanity, lower still, in turn to seek them out, humanity revealing humanity because suppliant and subordinate. The initiator, the speaker, reveals self. This is the doctrine of revelation. The Almighty, again acting from his own counsel not from some external petition, initiates the conversation and reveals himself. In doing so, God presents and represents himself, defines, displays, and declares himself. Here, if there is a third line to the statement "I will be your God, you will be my people," it would seem to be "Because I say so." The Word that creates the people of God and reveals God to them is external to the people of God—*verbum externum*.

In both electing the people of God and in the self-revelation of God, the people of God are created and the Creator is revealed. The statement "I will be your God, you will be my people" is a statement of creation. The missing third line might be, "So there." Perhaps that is the third point. And perhaps I've already belabored it.

Fourth, God speaks to *us*.

Not much can be made of the Hebrew that is best and most often translated as a future in the statement "I will be . . . /You will be . . ." This is neither proleptic nor eschatological in any deep sense. But the past tenses of Hebrew are avoided in the many repetitions of this statement because, I think, they would sound pleading. This is not a request nor, though it should be a welcome statement, is it an invitation. The present tenses available in Hebrew are avoided for the same reason and perhaps also because they might connote command as in "I am the Lord your God. You shall have no other gods before me." God will, of course plead, invite, and command the people in due time and place, and this statement sometimes is found in contexts where those things are also present, but the statement announces an intention to establish what has not yet been or, at least, has not been known by the people. In this sense also it elects and reveals by announcing a creation, yet now, finally, here. I wish to call attention to what is established—a relationship, better said, a covenant within a relationship.

The statement is relational in that it names the two covenantal partners and brings them both into a stated relationship. One will be the God of the other; the other will be the people of the one. Again, this is news. The gods of the Ancient Near East, the Olympian gods of late antiquity and the all the minor, local, tribal gods before, during, and after the cultures in which the Scriptures were written, all stand alone, and certainly stand apart from humanity. They care little for humanity, are often at cross purposes to any affinity for humanity, indeed they are most often at cross purposes with each other.

If any god is for humanity it is Prometheus. He created human beings. A very ancient god—a Titan, to be specific—he decries the uniform absolute neglect of his creation by all the Olympians. Rebelling against them all, especially Zeus, he gives humanity fire which permits humanity to progress and build civilizations (which, it is presumed, will finally get the notice of the gods). They don't; he does. They gang up on him, defeat him, and punish him with an everlasting torment. No god will ever so identify with humanity again.

The gods of the pagans, whatever persuasion, stand alone, certainly apart, and do not create or value being in relationship with humanity. This God of the Scriptures clearly chooses to be in relationship. Indeed, a particular binding form of relationship—a covenant.

The statement of covenant is balanced grammatically; the relationship is to be mutual. "I will be . . . You will be." The election of the people of God is to a relationship that is mutual. They face each other. Though one is tempted to ask if there are any other kinds of relationships, again it is noted that reference to silent, absent deities unresponsive to desperate pagans fill the narratives and myths of the ancients, and the critiques of the biblical writers. Elijah on Mt. Carmel does not so much expose false gods but reminds the pagans of the falseness of the gods in relationship to humanity—they sleep, they are mute, frankly, they don't care. No one went home that day from atop Carmel thinking there were fewer gods, but Elijah had demonstrated there was only one responsive God. This God chooses to be in a relationship—a relationship that is mutual.

This is a statement of a relationship that, though mutual, is not equal; the covenant is not between equals nor does it name equal obligations.

Being God and being a people are not the same thing. In this sense there is a summons and response feel to the statement. I will do this; You will do that. The "this" and the "that" are parallel but not alike. This is not a division of shared, similar tasks between partners. The partners are unequal and the covenant names have unequal obligations. God is always God and to be imagined as ever having been, but a people can at one time have been no people and now become a people; which is Hosea's point, I think, in the threat of becoming—again—a "*non* people." There is *non*-you without me, says the Lord. What makes the people "the people" is that they are the people of God. There is no other reason for their existence offered. The "that" they are to do is to become a people in relationship to God. The Almighty has created the people and the covenant with the people at the same time, they are a covenanted people by definition.

The statement—"I will be your God; You will be my people"—was first spoken to Abraham in the context of and for the purpose of making covenant. It is interesting to note that the mutuality is missing here alone of all the passages cited above. "I will be your God" infers, in the mention of Abraham's offspring, the creation of a people, not the creation of God. But it is not until Sinai, and even after that, that the people are called to be a people. The context for the statement and frequent restatement is covenanting. These are all covenant-making, remaking, and renewing occasions. The language of covenant will often have additional terms and conditions, but at its core always stands the statement of relationship—"I will be your God; You will be my people."

From these four points found in the foundational ecclesial statement—election, revelation, creation, and covenant- making—we could go now in several directions. We could build out from each of them independently more implications toward a renewed doctrine of the church. But that is another set of papers for another day, which hopefully someday will help reestablish for the church a robust ecclesiology that is at once reformed, evangelical, and catholic. I prefer a different project to finish this paper—to keep the four together for a moment longer and draw out further from our foundational statement what may be obvious to all already but which, I argue, seems to be missing in many of the current ecclesiologies vying for attention.

The foundational statement is intensely personal. The one creates the other, chooses the other, reveals self to the other, and enters into a covenantal relationship with the other. God is thoroughly personal in all this. It is difficult to imagine how the Almighty could be more personal; no one has. The ancients, both limited to and thus perfecting personification, never imagined a deity like this.

Demeter, the goddess of harvest and a mistress of Zeus, lamenting the abduction of their daughter, Persephone, by Zeus' brother Hades, appeals to the Father of gods and men for their daughter's restoration from the place of the dead by threatening to stop all earthly harvests, thus, destroying all humanity. Zeus responds by saying he couldn't care less about his daughter's well-being or the destruction of humanity. Demeter appeals several times without success including a half-hearted appeal based on relationships. Finally she cleverly reminds him that the loss of humanity would mean not only the cessation of humanity but the cessation of humans sacrificing to him. "Oh, now I get it," he responds, and sets about rescuing Persephone by negotiating with his brother to let Persephone be above ground half the year and with him below ground the other half.

We have probably passed alongside the field of soteriology somewhere on our brief path through the four points, but let us note the grace viewed nearby which has constantly been within our reach. Who was not, now is; who was excluded, is now included; who knew not, now knows and is known to be known; and who was alone, now belongs. Is this not grace, starkly and beautifully stated?

The creating, electing, self-revealing, covenant-making God personally engages the people, declaring them to be his; and he to be theirs. They belong to each other. It will take centuries for the pagans to wrap their head around that one.

The rest of the Scriptures will narrate this, adding eternal qualities and historical particularities in the words of the prophets; flesh it out most perfectly and wonderfully in the life and ministry, person and work of Jesus of Nazareth; and finally explicate it all by helpful metaphors in the letters of the apostles. All that, I argue, is connected to the simple, stark, severe, austere, bold declaration of the Almighty early and often: "I will be your God; You will be my people."

Would someone dare to argue this is not love? It is as intimate and public as it can be. If we had only this, could we not foretell branches and vine, flock and shepherd, body and head, certainly bride and groom?

Convinced by the personal, I am as convinced that any ecclesiology that is not also intensely personal—intimate and public both—has diminished a, if not, the, central genius of the biblical record. And the personal is, I think, missing in some of our ecclesiology and much of our talk. We began at the beginning and found the intensely personal; let's go to the end to see if it survived.

Current eschatology has long since abandoned a dispensational framework, and Reformed ecclesiology, when true to itself, rejected it from the outset. The fundamental flaw of evangelical ecclesiology in the last century or so has been that, because of dispensationalism, it has been ecclesiology in the service of eschatology. No robust ecclesiology emerged from a movement that showed signs of strength in other areas of theology. But now, I worry, that among the Reformed the error has been repeated. I am not sure why. We think of the church more in terms of its end, than in light of its beginning. The church is being pulled, seldom pushed. Eschatology influences our ecclesiology more so than the reverse. I missed when that choice was made, but it seems dominant.

Closer to the point I wish to make, the end is now "realized" or "unrealized," "under-" or "over-" realized, and ubiquitously stated as "already not yet." The kingdom of God is here, near, coming. We live in it, work toward it, some would say help establish or build it, and we expect it. We experience, usher in, and await shalom. I confess, I hear all this as uninspiring. Where is God in all this? There is *us* to be sure, and probably enough of us together with each other, but too little of God for my taste. The kingdom of God is coming, but name the theologically respectable book or rigorous article that lately inspired you about the King who is coming. Shalom surely is on the way, we can see it from here maybe (and we seem to know with a high degree of certainty how that should inform our politics), but has anyone argued lately for the necessary arrival of the Prince of Peace? Heard or preached a sermon lately on the imminent return of Christ? Last week, the First Sunday in Advent, begs for it. I search my Presbyterian hymnal, both the one that has served me since ordination and one just now published, and remain at a loss to find much of anything that helps me to sing of the return of the Savior while I prayerfully await him.

Perhaps this is just my piety learned in childhood that lingers around my theology and haunts it. But can we not agree that, "I will be your God; You will be my people" is still awaiting its glorious consummation. That day, the last book of the Bible shows us, is very, very personal. God is present on the center stage of human history and seated central in the sanctuary of worship. God acts for us; we worship God. The feast enjoyed is a marriage feast for the Lamb (how's that for a mixed metaphor?). We are with God. Indeed in our individual eschatons, to be absent here is to be present with the Lord.

Alas. I don't suppose I really need to argue for all this, but wonder if I alone lament the absence of the personal God in our ecclesiology talk. And I wonder if our (impersonal) eschatology has, like it has for others, displaced our ecclesiology from its proper role and diminished its central genius—a personal God who makes us, chooses us, self-reveals to us, and makes covenant with us. God. Us.

I argue that our proper focus, indeed hope, is intensely personal, both in this life and the one to come. Kindgom, shalom, and the eschaton, are (I almost said "merely") the train that follows in the wake of the King, the Prince of Peace, the Spirit of eternity.

The statement "I will be your God; You will be my people" whether considering its individual companion doctrines—election, revelation, creation, covenant making—or all of them together assert, I argue, for the intensely personal nature of the church—God and us. Establish that and the metaphors of the New Testament find their true foundation. The statement announces that our ecclesiology is to be personal. The metaphors explain in what ways it is personal.

The metaphors can now be experienced with renewed life and used with more common understanding. Branches/vine, neither of which is human, can now be explicated more deeply, remembering the personal; flock/shepherd, one of which is human (and that referent assigned to the deity), is better positioned now to be recalled in our discussions; bride/groom, both of which are human, can now enrich us with its profound beauty; head/body, which is intrapersonal, can reveal more of its treasures now.

Personal. Then. Now. Forevermore.

It is not primarily for the event or the idea, or for the feast or even the wedding, but for the Groom that wise virgins still oil their lamps.

Part II

Hearing, Proclaiming, Sealing

6

The Church as Missional Community[1]

Darrell Guder

The term "missional" has, in a very short period of time, become a widely used cliché with little clarity about what it might mean. Its emergence can be traced back to the publication of a research project in 1998 entitled *Misional Church: A Vision for the Sending of the Church in North America*. That project was undertaken by "The Gospel and Our Culture Network," which continues the missiological discussion initiated by Lesslie Newbigin in Britain in the 1970s. On both sides of the Atlantic, the enterprise has been to continue exploring the missionary challenge of modern Western cultures as they rapidly secularize. Guided by Newbigin, we have come to recognize that the challenges we now face are basically ecclesiological and have to do with the very nature and purpose of the church. We are asking, "If our context has become a post-Christian mission field, how do the inherited churches within our context become 'missionary churches?'" The answer proposed by the 1998 study was to focus upon God's mission as it defines the nature, purpose and action of the church. It is that priority of mission for the theology and practice of the church that is expressed by adding "al" to "mission."

There is a long prehistory to the discussion of "the missional church." There has been a growing conviction over the entire twentieth century that mission and church belong inextricably together. Missional theology is an

---

1. Editor's note: Presented via Skype at the Moderator's 1st Colloquium on Ecclesiology at Austin Presbyterian Theological Seminary on April 23, 2013, this paper was adapted from Guder, "The Church as Missional Community," 114–28. In this essay, Guder updates conversations on missional theology since the 2005 essay. The editor thanks Mark Caton of Dictate Express for the *pro bono* transcription.

ecclesiological movement on both sides of the North Atlantic that, like the Ecumenical Movement, grows out of the Western missionary movement and the resulting global expansion of Christianity. The emerging discussion is documented in the consultations and conferences of the International Missionary Council from its inception in the late 1920s to its merger with the World Council in 1961. The emerging consensus claims that "the church equals mission." Put more bluntly, a church that was not defined by God's mission would not be an authentic church. The 1961 merger was to make it very clear that mission and church were inseparable.

For the missional church discussion in North America, especially in the Presbyterian and Reformed part of the family, there are particular individuals who are very important. Princeton Seminary is deeply involved in that history. John Mackay, from the time he arrived as president in the mid-1930s, was tilling the soil and forming the foundations of what would ultimately be called missional theology. Similar claims can be made for the dogmatic project of Karl Barth, to which we will return. Lesslie Newbigin laid out the cultural and theological challenges in his Warfield Lectures at Princeton in 1984.[2] He articulated the "missional" challenge to a group of North American missiologists a few years later, and the Gospel and Our Culture Network resulted from that initiative.

I have reviewed the process of this discussion we call "missionary theology" or "missional church." It has been lively, productive, insightful, and stimulating. It has resonated with many who are concerned about the ecclesiological crisis in which we find ourselves in Western Christianity. But it is clear that the discussion has been very hard to translate into the context of congregational life and practice. From the perspective of the seminary, student reactions to missional theological content are broadly supportive and even engaged. But it could not be claimed that this theological approach strongly influences the classical shape of seminary education. One of the major insights resulting from the missional discussion has been the absence of mission from Western theology's doctrinal engagement with the church. That separation of mission and church constitutes one of the major challenges with which we contend, but it is deeply embedded in the self-understanding of Western Christendom.

Western theology tends to do ecclesiology without mission. In our doctrines of the church, we focus largely on issues such as baptism and eucharist—the sacramental questions, and upon the ordering of ministry. There is little theological focus upon the missional vocation of the Church. Much of the seminary's work focuses on "practical theology," but a curricular

---

2. Newbigin, *Foolishness to the Greeks*.

connection between the doctrinal study of the church (ecclesiology) and the preparation of ministers in the practical theological disciplines is not clearly developed.

But that is changing. The conversation is informed by the growing recognition in the last decades that our context in North America and across the North Atlantic is rapidly changing. This has been well documented in Philip Jenkins' *The Next Christendom*, who has helped a broad readership to grasp the shift of the center of gravity of the Christian movement away from the West. In a remarkable irony, we are dealing today with the dynamic globalization of Christianity as well as the decline of what was once regarded as "the Christian West." Closely linked to this demographic and cultural transition are the historical traumas of the twentieth century in the West: the two world wars, the Great Depression, the Soviet empire, the Cold War, the Holocaust. Given that history, the claim that the West was Christian was difficult to make. Instead, the Western context has become one of the most difficult mission fields in the world! This is precisely the challenge that Newbigin articulates and that motivates the "missional church" discussion.

This very brief survey of the missional church discussion in its Western context leads us to comment briefly on the present state of the discussion, especially as it affects a mainline denomination like the Presbyterian Church (USA). Certainly, it is extremely important that ecclesiology has moved to the center of our theological discussions. One outcome of the turbulent twentieth century is that we no longer can be comfortable with the assumption that our inherited theological traditions adequately expound what the church is and what its purpose is. There's a lot of fundamental theology to be done. There's a growing awareness that this crisis of the Church in the West cannot be resolved by more strategies, more effective plans for outreach, more efficiency, more programs, or more attractive signs on our church campuses. We are dealing with a truly fundamental and biblical crisis.

This is directly related to the insight that the Western theological traditions have, for complex reasons, developed what I have called a "reductionistic understanding of the purpose and nature of the church."[3] The critique does not imply that the traditions are wrong but that their scope and vision of the nature and purpose of the church are too narrow and shallow. It is reductionistic to interpret the church's nature and purpose primarily in terms of the benefits that its members receive. Similarly, it is reductionistic to interpret the Gospel primarily in terms of the salvation of Christians. The effect of these reductionisms is to define the church as an end in itself,

---

3. Guder, *Continuing Conversion*, 97–144.

serving the savedness of its members. Of course the Gospel is about our salvation, but it is the salvation "of the nations," of humanity in all its cultural expressions, that is both its confidence and its hope. The church serves God's healing purposes for all of creation. When the church is defined inwardly, focusing upon itself, the savedness of its members, and the maintenance of its (necessary) institutions, then the Gospel it proclaims is too small. As long as Western cultures defined themselves as "Christian," describing their collective form as "Christendom," the reductionism was difficult to recognize. After Christendom, as we now see ourselves located in a difficult and complex mission field, the reductions of the Gospel and of our ecclesiologies are highly problematic. It is these inherited assumptions that are challenged by the missional discussion, not only on both sides of the North Atlantic, but in the global Christian movement. There is obviously much hard theological work to be done in order to illumine the complex history of the church's cultural captivities, to reframe our ecclesiologies and thus reshape our practices so that we can be faithful to our missional vocation.

The mainline churches, as direct heirs of Christendom, have a special responsibility to understand the history that shaped us in order to learn how to move into the next chapter of the Christian movement both obediently and confidently. We are helped in this endeavor by the pioneering theological work of Reformed theologians like John Mackay, David Bosch, Lesslie Newbigin, and Karl Barth—all of them embedded in the theological legacy of Western Christendom and at the same time insightful critics of it. Karl Barth, for example, constantly admonishes us to go back to the beginning, not in order to restore the ancient artifacts of Christendom, but rather to encounter the fundamental "strategy" (my word) of the Apostolic Church—remembering that "apostolic" is not merely a genealogical term but emphasizes rather the sentness, the missionary nature of the movement that began at Pentecost. The "apostolic strategy," as documented in the New Testament, was not merely to go out and save souls. The mandate was to form witnessing communities that were to be instruments for God's saving purposes for the whole world. This is linked theologically with a reclaiming, as Barth also teaches us, of vocation, as essential in understanding who we are and what we're for. Barth argues that the gospel of reconciliation is only fully grasped when we address justification and sanctification leading necessarily into vocation. In vocation we turn from the focus on ourselves and our saved-ness towards God's love for the world. In Barth's ecclesiology, the vocation of every Christian is to be a witness and thus to be part a witnessing community. The "missional community" is empowered, by the work of God's Spirit, to understand itself as God's people for God's mission, the so-called *missio Dei*.

The missional church discussion is seeking to identify and to concentrate upon the trajectories of theological work that need to be engaged in order for our congregations to be equipped for this witnessing vocation. That was the express purpose of the 1998 book. The work to be done is biblical, theological and historical. It has been very encouraging to see the growing numbers of biblical scholars who are responding to the challenge to engage in "missional hermeneutics." Their work is foundational for our pilgrimage "after Christendom." We need to learn together how do to engage Scripture as God's instrument for the formation of witnessing communities. We do so as we recognize that such formation was the apostolic strategy and thus informed the writing and the authority of the apostolic Scriptures.

The missional church discussion is developing its own momentum as theologians in many disciplines and traditions address the task of "equipping the saints for the work of service" in our post-Christendom context. I recently participated in a doctoral defense in which the candidate presented a project on missional homiletics, exploring how preaching informed by the apostolic strategy can contribute to the missional equipping of the church. The papers and presentations of this Moderator's Colloquium are an impressive demonstration of the expanding discussion. It is especially important to focus on the sacraments, asking how these practices serve the missional formation of the witnessing community. If the church is not an end in itself, then how shall we theologically interpret and practice the gathered worship of the community in order to emphasize the priority of public worship while linking it to the vocation of witness which defines the vocation of Christians both when they are gathered and when they are scattered as light, leaven, and salt in the world.

I conclude these remarks by referring to an example of "missional theology" serving "missional community." Benjamin Conner did his doctoral work at Princeton on the missional understanding of Christian practices. His work points to the important contributions of such scholars as Craig Dykstra, Dorothy Bass, Miroslav Volf, and many others around the question of Christian practices. But he respectfully and pointedly critiques the fact that their work is characterized by a complete absence of any reference to mission. Conner's book has opened up that conversation, stimulating the important exploration of ways in which all our practical theological disciplines can and need to be enlisted in the service of the formation of "missional communities."[4] It is my hope, as I soon retire as professor of missional

---

4. Conner, *Practicing Witness*.

and ecumenical theology at Princeton, that the broadening missional theological initiative will serve God's saving purposes by serving the formation of God's people.

Bibliography

Conner, Benjamin T. *Practicing Witness: A Missional Vision of Christian Practices*. Grand Rapids: Eerdmans, 2011.

Guder, Darrell L. "The Church as Missional Community." In *The Community of the Word: Toward an Evangelical Ecclesiology*, edited by Mark Husbands and Daniel J. Treier, 114–30. Downers Grove, IL: InterVarsity, 2005.

———. *The Continuing Conversion of the Church*. Grand Rapids: Eerdmans, 2000.

———, ed. *Missional Church: A Vision for the Sending of the Church in North America*. Grand Rapids: Eerdmans, 1998.

Jenkins, Philip. *The Next Christendom: The Coming of Global Christianity*. New York: Oxford University Press, 2002.

Newbigin, Lesslie. *Foolishness to the Greeks: The Gospel and Western Culture*. Grand Rapids: Eerdmans, 1986.

7

Preaching for Liturgical-Missional Congregations

Jennifer Lord

This essay focuses on preaching in relation to broader conversations about the relationship between Christian worship and mission. Preaching plays a part in any conversation about the connection between the church of Jesus Christ's liturgy and the church's mission: it is an integral act of worship which, in turn, is intrinsically a missional event. Though there are a variety of ways to talk about the nature and purpose of preaching I emphasize preaching as one of the central actions of the gathered Sunday assembly (the local congregation on the Lord's Day) and, here, propose particular ways that the preacher can conceive of and shape the sermon in order to serve preaching's missional purpose in the assembly. Preaching manifests and serves the assembly's self-understanding of its participation in the mission of God for the sake of the world.

Approach

Regarding vocabulary: in this essay the words liturgy and worship both, interchangeably, refer to

- the repeated actions Christians gather to do each Sunday;
- the triune God's presence and work through these actions (means of grace) and among us (who are the two or more gathered);

- this work that we do with God in the local worshiping assembly on the Lord's Day as a public instantiation of God's mission in the world and for the world.

For many Protestant Christians this last point can be a new idea: worship as a public instantiation of God's mission for the world. This claim means that the church, by God's grace and Christ's Spirit, has been invited into God's missional work and is *itself* a sign of God's mission in the world. And that each Sunday's worship is the primary enactment, in word and deed, of God's mission. To use liturgical theologian Aidan Kavanagh's shorthand: in the church's liturgy we are doing the world as the world ought to be done.[1] How do we *do* the world as it ought to be done? We again and again carry out certain things given by God, trusting in God's presence and use of them for us. The certain core, central things are scriptural, historical, and ecumenical and include the gathering of people, the reading and interpretation of Scripture, the prayers, the bath and table, and the sending forth. As we think about *things* it is important to remember that the gathered assembly is one of the central things. And that each central thing is surrounded by other (secondary) actions that amplify and nuance it: the secondary things assist in the ways that the central things are done in very different manners, for instance, always according to local culture.[2]

Preaching is one of these central things. It is a form of gospel proclamation, most commonly done—still—through one voice authorized by the assembly to speak, and in the liturgy it follows the reading of Scriptures and leads us to sing, acclaim, pray, greet in peace, offer, feast, and go forth. At times I refer to these actions as our common work. This is to emphasize that they are things done, things we do; they are actions that themselves are *loci* of God's work in our midst. In these definitions the use of *work* is in contradistinction to any sense of works-righteousness; these actions are God's work among us in Jesus Christ that we then repeatedly enact as sign and participation in God's mission to the world.

Three Approaches

When thinking about the relationship between liturgy and mission I am helped by Thomas H. Schattauer's work, *Inside Out: Worship in an Age of Mission*. "The assembly for worship is intrinsically connected to the mission

---

1. See Kavanagh, *On Liturgical Theology*.

2. See the Nairobi Statement prepared by the Department for Theology and Studies of the Lutheran World Federation for discussion of culture in relation to worship. For discussion of central and secondary things see Lathrop, *Holy Things*.

of God in Christ for the sake of the whole world (*missio Dei*), and consequently worship is integrally related to every form of the church's mission of witness and service."[3] Schattauer provides a threefold taxonomy of the relationship: *Inside and Out*; *Outside In*; *Inside Out*. He writes,

> In the first approach, liturgy is understood and practiced as the quintessential activity for those inside the church community. Mission is what takes place on the outside when the gospel is proclaimed to those who have not heard or received it or, to broaden the notion of mission, when the neighbor is served in acts of live and justice. The relationship between the inside activity of worship and the outside activity of mission is portrayed thus: worship nurtures the individual and sustains the community in its life before God and in its life together, and from where Christians go out to serve the church's mission as proclaimers and doers of the gospel. They return to worship, perhaps with a few more folk gathered by this witness, and the cycle begins again. In this model, worship spiritually empowers those inside the church who take up the church's mission in the outside world.[4]

According to this view worship does not do the same thing as mission though it sustains and propels us toward mission because of our repeated encounters with the means of grace in the Sunday gathering. According to this first approach, *Inside and Out*, the spheres remain separate; we are sent forth from corporate worship (inside) to do this missional work (outside). Missional work is always manifested outside of worship.

The second classification is *Outside In*. Here Schattaeur refers to two different ways that additional agendas become central in the Sunday assembly. "The sacred precinct of the liturgy becomes one of two things—either a stage from which to present the gospel and reach out to the unchurched and irreligious, or a platform from which to issue the call to serve the neighbor and rally commitment for social and political action."[5] According to this model the church's worship takes on a slightly different focus and purpose—the focus is turned to evangelism of those who have gathered or to transformation of the social/political commitments of those in the gathering.

The third category is *Inside Out*.

> This approach locates the liturgical assembly itself within the arena of the *missio Dei*. The focus is on God's mission toward

3. Schattauer, *Inside Out*, 3.
4. Ibid., 2.
5. Ibid., 3.

the world, to which the church witnesses and into which it is drawn, rather than on specific activities of the church undertaken in response to the divine saving initiative. The *missio Dei* is God's own movement outward in relation to the world—in creation and the covenant with Israel, and culminating in Jesus Christ and the community gathered in him. This community is created by the Spirit to witness to the ultimate purposes of God, to reconcile the world to God's own self (2 Cor 5:18–19). The gathering of a people to witness to and participate in this reconciling movement of God toward the world is an integral part of God's mission. The visible act of assembly (in Christ by the power of the Spirit) and the forms of this assembly—what we call liturgy—enact and signify this mission. From this perspective there is no separation between liturgy and mission. The liturgical assembly of God's people in the midst of the world enacts and signifies the outward movement of God for the life of the world. . . . The judgment and mercy of God enacted within the liturgical assembly signify God's ultimate judgment and mercy for the world. Like a reversible jacket, the liturgy can be turned and worn inside out, and by doing so we see the relationship between worship and mission—inside out.[6]

My discussion of preaching in the liturgical-missional church/liturgical-missional congregations is shaped by this third approach. This categorization is harder to pin down than the other two. The first two approaches are clear in an instrumental sense. In the first approach, worship enlivens us, empowers us, and directs us to go forth and share the good news: to speak and do unto others, neighbor and stranger, good news. In the second, worship is the place where we act out certain tasks of mission, evangelism and social change in the worship event itself (these may continue *outside* but, as compared to Schattauer's first and third categories, are particular works done within the worshiping assembly). In both categories worship itself is an instrument—either toward something that occurs later or toward something else that occurs in its context. But the third approach claims that we cannot separate mission from worship. To *do* worship, to *do* the actions of liturgy, is to participate in and be formed by the *missio Dei*.

Preaching According to These Approaches

A review of preaching's function within the first two categories sets the stage for thinking about preaching according to the third approach. Preaching

6. Ibid.

occurring in contexts defined by the first category, *Inside and Out*, is at its best when the preacher identifies textual-gospel ways that we are sent forth to preach the gospel ourselves—per St. Francis—with or without words. The preacher has identified a missional aspect of the text, or the gospel focus of the day's reading/s, and showed how we are to go forth and live out that mission in our times (e.g., feed the hungry, evangelize the nations, shelter the sojourner). Sermons that fit this category may very well end with the transitional phrase "and so let us go forth and . . ." They include some language directing listeners to move out in word and deed to spread the gospel. Preaching according to this category includes illustrations, stories, and other showings[7] of ways that the Faithful live their gospel lives in the world through service and witness. These showings, and the language of the sermon (i.e., choice of pronouns), may or may not emphasize a corporate response to the liturgy. Sermons could include emphases on both corporate and individual response to gospel in the world.

According to the second category, *Outside In*, preaching could be one of two things: for the purpose of instruction/conversion or for the purpose of information/change of heart. The sermon, in this construal of the relationship between worship and mission, either serves the broader purpose of evangelism in worship or serves the purpose of facilitating a social/political change of heart of those present in worship. Preaching according to this category could take many forms but generally aims to convert the hearers to faith, to bring about recommitment, or to strengthen particular social or political allegiances that are valued to carry out the gospel in the world. The preaching might very well have a more didactic, thematic, or topical quality than the preaching that occurs in the other categories. Most likely the sermon will be directed to the individual if its aim is conversion, though corporate language may be used as example or invitation. Sermons aiming for social/political instruction or change of heart may select language and showings for either the individual or corporate level.

The nature and purpose of preaching occurring in the first two categories seems straightforward though I do not intend to exhaust the possibilities through the descriptions I've offered. I am most interested in what preaching looks like in Schattauer's third construal of the liturgical-missional assembly, *Inside Out*. What is preaching in the midst of liturgy understood as that which "enacts and signifies the outward movement of God for the life

---

7. Homiletician Chuck Campbell uses the word "showings" to identify various ways that preachers use evocative language (story, metaphor, images, analogy, simile, other descriptive terms) in sermons. Personal conversation, August, 2011.

of the world"?[8] What is the purpose of preaching as it occurs in this understanding of the liturgical-missional relationship of the Sunday assembly?

By way of initial exploration here are three characteristics of preaching that are operative when the sermon functions according to this third way of construing the liturgical-missional relationship. While I don't think the homiletical characteristics are exclusive for any of these categories, this *Inside Out* approach to the nature and purpose of the liturgical assembly and its relationship to God's mission shapes a particular way of preaching in that context. The homiletical remarks that follow undulate between what is done and what ought to be done for this context.

Preaching in Liturgical-Missional Congregations: Preaching Today

Liturgical scholar Anton Baumstark drew scholarly attention to the concept of time in liturgies when he studied the use of the word *Hodie* in liturgical song. *Hodie* is the Latin word meaning *today* and its use in phrases of prayers and stanzas of hymns conflates time in a certain manner. For instance, at Christmas we sing, "Christ is born today." We know we do not literally mean the today of this year in the twenty-first century but, symbolically speaking (which is another form of truth-telling), we do mean this: Christ is born *today*. Our liturgies use the same sense of *today* at Christ's passion and resurrection: Christ dies *today*; Jesus Christ is risen *today*. Liturgists speak of this conflation of time in particular ways: the past and future become present by our ritual actions. This folding in of the past is *anamnesis* (Greek, remembrance) and is the way that our actions make a past event a present true claim on us. In the same fashion God's promised future is already breaking in upon us now; it is *prolepsis* (Greek, to take beforehand). It is the foretaste of all that is to be. While we live between the already and the not yet (the already of the full revelation of God through Jesus Christ and the not yet of the consummation of all things), the not yet breaks into our midst. God's *kairos* has taken up *chronos* and these things are possible: *today* these things are true in our midst.

There is a manner of reading texts according to this sense of *today*. There is a way of preaching that comes from this way of reading Scripture. Using short hand I would say it is preaching in the present tense. It is distinct from preaching that takes us back in time—to the historical time of various biblical texts and their settings. In these sorts of sermons the preacher tends to describe the scene of the past, which in turn has listeners engage

---

8. Schattauer, *Inside Out*, 3.

in time travel—backwards—to that scene. Often the sermonic claim is that God acted back in that time. Sometimes the preacher helps us see that God is still acting in the same ways now in our midst but often we are asked to believe, have faith, grow in the likeness and image of God because of what God has done in the past.

Preaching in the present tense, preaching *today*, neither locates God's actions solely in the past or in the future but announces these past actions and future promises in a manner that has a contemporary claim on us: now, in the present.

Homiletician Richard Lischer gets at this sense when he speaks about different ways of reading texts. What Lischer proposes relates to what I call present tense preaching or preaching *today*. Lischer calls preachers to theological exegesis and says "We read it (the text) as if it were addressed to our particular community and as if our lives depended on its conclusions, yet also with the conviction that its authority stretches well beyond our little congregation to the church of every time and place."[9] Lischer wants us to read in continuity with the church, one, holy, apostolic. Preachers read on behalf of the contemporary church and they read the church's book. This is to say that God's presence, faithfulness, and action are contemporaneous and that Scripture witnesses to this God. We do not have to look to the past or the future for God's actions, we proclaim the present tense truth and claim of God's deeds (past, present, future) on us *today*. This is Luke 4:21 preaching: "Today this scripture is fulfilled in your hearing."

One particular homiletic practice helps preachers preach *today*. Homiletician Paul Scott Wilson instructs all preachers to fashion a three-word statement for every sermon. The statement itself may or may not appear in the sermon but it is the sermon's orientation and focus. While many homileticians suggest such a focus statement, Wilson instructs preachers to prepare the three words as: *Subject* (The Trinity, God, Jesus Christ, Holy Spirit), an *Active Verb*, and the *Object* (Hearers, the World, the church local or beyond).[10] This construct requires us to put our focal proclamation in the present tense and in a form that proclaims an action done by God presently to us/in our midst. We are never the subject. And the verb is always active. A very good practice, I think, to help sustain preaching *today*.

---

9. Lischer, *End of Words*, 64.
10. See Wilson, *Four Pages of the Sermon*.

Preaching in Liturgical-Missional Congregations: Preaching to the Church

A second homiletical characteristic of this preaching is to preach to the church. Preaching to the church is different than preaching to an aggregate of individuals. When preachers do the work to prepare the sermon they keep the identity of church at the forefront of their preparations rather than focusing on individual persons or even the "bottom line" of shared humanity. This means to be mindful that our gathering as church is significant, even primary and constitutive, and preaching serves (among other things) to remind us whose we are and who we are and to calls us again to faith. This requires that preachers think with baptismal sensibilities: we preach to the local manifestation of the body of Christ and also, perhaps, to those not yet incorporated into the body through the sign and seal of baptism (all are invited to the waters). We preach to continue to form the faithful in baptismal identity and to invite those not yet incorporated to come to faith. Preachers have a Eucharistic sensibility too because the table forms and identifies us Sunday after Sunday: the Body of Christ for the sake of the world. Lischer again,

> Once we learn to read with the church, we will honor the church in our sermons. Linguistically, the sermon will create a symbolic world over time in which the reality of the people of God is central. It's odd, but we gather every Sunday as a group, pray for one another, receive the Eucharist shoulder to shoulder, and sing our hymns in unison. We read from a book that records the history of a people . . .
>
> The sermon is a word from one church to another mediated by the common use of Holy Scripture. It is a church word . . . The common denominator between Christians is not human nature but the church, which, as always, can be found gathered around lectern and pulpit, where it listens attentively for a word from the Lord, and scattered throughout the world, where it attempts to perform the word with integrity.[11]

It is one thing to conceive of preaching as that which is to give succor or direction to gathered individuals, though preaching surely does this. But it is another thing altogether to preach in order to shape the church, strengthen the church, to remind us—the church—of our life in the crucified-risen One. Our individual needs and sorrows are given their place in the larger narrative of the life of the church, which is to say in the paschal mystery,

---

11. Lischer, *End of Words*, 74–75.

the dying and rising of Jesus Christ. Our preaching tells the gathered local church who we are, already, in the grace and mercy of God through Jesus Christ. This shift from a sermon focus on the individual or aggregate of individuals to church becomes clear through sermonic language (pronouns), showings, and even sermon focus and theological claims.

Preaching in Liturgical-Missional Congregations: Primary and Secondary Mystagogy

A third homiletical characteristic of this preaching is to incorporate mystagogy into the sermon. By the fourth century great preachers were instructing the neophytes (newly baptized) in the mysteries (sacraments) of the church which they had received for the first time at their baptisms. Cyril of Jerusalem, Theodore of Mopsuestia, and Ambrose of Milan are three well-known mystagogical preachers. After the baptisms of the Great Paschal Vigil (the Easter Vigil) the newly baptized would hear special sermons instructing them after the fact in the mysteries of baptism and Eucharist. These were known as the mystagogical sermons: sermons that revealed, instructed, and enticed the new church members in the meanings of the sacramental actions that they had just experienced. Today we might preach such sermons for the newly baptized and their families.

But we also can preach in ways that not only open up the meanings of these primary things but also make connections to the secondary things that support these primary actions of the Sunday gathering (the confession of sin and assurance of pardon as part of the gathering rite; the passing the peace in between the prayers of the people and the Great Thanksgiving at the table; the prayer of illumination before the readings and preaching; the offering before coming to the table). Preachers can make connections between the scriptural texts and the meanings of the to the different things (primary and secondary) we do each Sunday. Our Sunday actions arise from the texts and preachers can help us see again that we are formed in being signs of God's work in and for the world through these repeated corporate actions. There are several connections to be made here—for why would a preacher refer in the sermon to something we have just done or are doing in that Sunday's worship? Because what we do is enactment of the promises of Scripture, because what we do repeatedly patterns our behavior, beliefs, and values for our daily lives, because what we do on a Sunday morning is the Christian life in ritual form. Preaching sets out the connections of Scripture-liturgical action-missional meaning. We need sermons that speak this truth—our congregating and doing the actions of church through our corporate worship is already a missional event.

Robert Hovda said this so well:

> What is most important about public worship is that we gather the sisters and brothers together for a festival, a special occasion, a celebration of the reign of God (not yet terribly evident in daily life nor in the institutions of society), that helps all of us feel so good about ourselves, so important, so dignified, so precious, so free, so much at one . . . not as escape, not merely in distinction to daily routine, but in judgment, in the Lord's judgment on those ways and institutions. A celebration of the reign of God that goes way beyond the tight, drab, rationalistic, verbose, pedagogical exercises we sometimes try to make of it—all those dreadful "themes" we love—into a large, broad fully human landscape, where Jesus is truly the firstborn of a new humanity, and where our other liturgical tools (festival excess and colors and tastes and textures and odors and forms and touches) penetrate the Babel of our words and points and arguments to heal the human spirit and to raise it up in the covenant community's vision of new possibilities. Good liturgical celebration, like a parable, takes us by the hairs of our head, lifts us momentarily out of the cesspool of injustice we call home, puts us in the promised and challenging reign of God, where we are treated like we have never been treated anywhere else . . .[12]

Hovda's words continue what Schattaeur has said about the third approach, *Inside Out*: what happens in the Sunday assembly is already the sign of and participation in the mission of God. It is our public enactment of the world as God intends for the world to be. We don't just rehearse it here, for it is already the real thing, a proleptic sign of what will be according to the judgment and mercy of God. Preachers, mindful of the day's texts and the season of the church's year, can name connections between the texts and our corporate actions alongside the current needs of the world, all to help us see how we, church, are already both sign of and participant in God's mission, God's reign. Much more can be said about preaching that serves this *Inside Out* approach to the relationship between the church's liturgy and the church's mission. But here is a start: it is spoken in the present tense. It is preaching *today*. It is focused on the life of the church. And it makes connections to all of the ritual ways that we enact, in the Lord's Day gathering, what is most true about neighbor, stranger, God, and us.

---

12 Hovda, "The Vesting of Liturgical Ministers," 220.

Bibliography

Hovda, Robert. "The Vesting of Liturgical Ministers" In *Robert Hovda: The Amen Corner*, edited by John Baldovin, 213–33. Collegeville, MN: Liturgical, 1994.

Kavanagh, Aidan. *On Liturgical Theology*. Collegeville, MN: Liturgical, 1984.

Lathrop, Gordon. *Holy Things: A Liturgical Theology*. Minneapolis: Augsburg Fortress, 1993.

Lischer, Richard. *The End of Words: The Language of Reconciliation in a Culture of Violence*. Grand Rapids: Eerdmans, 2005.

Nairobi Statement on Worship and Culture: Contemporary Challenges and Opportunities. Geneva: Department for Theology and Studies of the Lutheran World Federation, 1996.

Schattauer, Thomas H. *Inside Out: Worship in an Age of Mission*. Minneapolis: Augsburg Fortress, 1999.

Wilson, Paul Scott. *The Four Pages of the Sermon*. Nashville: Abingdon, 1999.

8

Baptism
The Already and the Not Yet

MARTHA MOORE-KEISH

We are gathered in Princeton to continue a conversation that began last spring, focusing attention on the liturgical-missional nature of the church. We have come together to think about the church universal—the one, holy, catholic, apostolic church—but we are also particularly committed to and concerned about the Presbyterian Church (USA). So together we are pondering the nature of *this* church, and how *this* church might renew its identity by focusing on what it means to be both gathered and sent.

Last spring, in Austin, several of the colloquium presentations focused on the Lord's Supper/Eucharist as a source for liturgical-missional identity. Here in the bleak nearly midwinter in Princeton, I am proposing that we pay attention to baptism as starting point for consideration of the same question. How might deeper reflection on baptism help the church renew its purpose?

So: how does baptism reveal to us the nature of the church as both (liturgically) gathered and (missionally) sent?

In order to answer this question, we need to back up and first ask: what do we mean by "baptism"? A few decades ago, New Testament scholar James D. G. Dunn described baptism as a "concertina word" expanding to refer to a whole process, or contracting to refer to the water rite alone.[1] (A concertina, by the way, is a small accordion, sometimes called a "squeezebox,"

---

1. Dunn, *Baptism in the Holy Spirit*, 5.

an instrument that makes music by expanding and contracting.) "Baptism" itself is a contested term, and theologians, liturgical scholars, and New Testament interpreters have argued vigorously about its proper meaning. On the one hand, it names a particular ritual event that involves water, word, and a specific individual head (or entire body). On the other hand, it names the identity of an entire community, lived out over time. What do we mean when we talk about "baptism"?

I propose that Dunn's concertina provides a helpful image here, because "baptism" does indeed have a double implication: it is both a defining event and an identity that unfolds over time. And in both cases, importantly, it pushes us out beyond ourselves. German Lutheran theologian Wolfhart Pannenberg said it this way: "Baptism is the basis of a new human identity outside the self—an identity that we have then to appropriate and work out in the whole process of our life history."[2] Baptism is first of all Christ's baptism, into which we are engrafted, giving us an identity outside of ourselves. This identity we then live out in a variety of ways, by the power of the Spirit, over lifetimes. Borrowing Oscar Cullmann's famous phrase, I will here call these two dimensions of baptism the "already and the not yet." Baptism is both an event that precedes us, anchoring our identity, and a process that sends us out from ourselves, and is not complete until the eschaton. Considered together, these two dimensions offer a way for us to see the baptized community as both centered in worship and sent into the world.

1. Baptism as an Event that Anchors Our Identity in Christ

From the beginning—or as early as we have any clear evidence about Christian communities—individuals entered the church by way of baptism. Baptism was understood to be the bath that washed away sin, and that marked one with the name of Christ. We see this, for instance, in Acts 2:38, when Peter says to the crowds in Jerusalem, "Repent and be baptized every one of you in the name of Jesus Christ so that your sins may be forgiven; and you will receive the gift of the Holy Spirit." We will return to the Holy Spirit later, but for now, notice the close connection between baptism, forgiveness, and the name of Christ. Those who had been baptized into the name of Jesus Christ were part of the messianic congregation that participated in God's saving work in the world. Their identities were now anchored outside of themselves, as they were literally placed "into" the wider and deeper name of Jesus the Messiah.

2. Pannenberg, *Systematic Theology*, 274.

Furthermore, the one baptized was not only part of a messianic congregation, but incorporated *into Christ*, and especially into his death and resurrection. As Rom 6 declares, "Do you not know that all of us who have been baptized into Christ Jesus have been baptized into his death?"[3] Baptism was not simply an act that confirmed or evoked a subjective experience of conversion; it was an objective event by which a person was joined to the crucified and risen Christ.

The basic baptismal service in the PC(USA)'s *Book of Common Worship* opens with words that affirm this "already" dimension of baptism. After selected sentences of Scripture (which may include Eph 4:3–6, Gal 3:27–28, 1 Pet 2:9, Rom 6:3, 4, and/or Acts 2:39) the minister continues: "In baptism God claims us, and seals us to show that we belong to God. God frees us from sin and death, uniting us with Jesus Christ in his death and resurrection."[4] The subject is clear: *God* claims us, seals us, frees us, and unites us to Jesus Christ. The first thing to say about baptism, then, is that it connects us deeply to something that is already true: Christ has died, and Christ is risen. From that point forward, we are named by that name, marked by that sign.

This is helpful to remember. For those of us North American Christians, at least, it is easy to act as though baptism is about us: our own commitments to Jesus, our own commitments to our children, the promises we make to be faithful and to nurture one another in paths of faithfulness. The temptation to focus on our own role in baptism only becomes stronger when we are anxious about our own life as a church: *we* need to baptize more people in order to survive! But the first thing we need to learn is that baptism is profoundly not about us—or at least, not about us in that way.

T. F. Torrance offers a refreshing, de-centering word on this point. In his reading of the New Testament, Torrance argued forcefully that in the New Testament, baptism refers first to the mystery of Christ crucified and risen, and only secondarily to the church's act by which we are engrafted into Christ.[5] At the beginning of his public ministry, Jesus was baptized by John in the Jordan, as an act of repentance which revealed his solidarity with sinners. Standing in the water, receiving the baptism by his cousin, he stood with all who were in need of forgiveness and new life. This same solidarity with "sinners" Jesus embodied in the way he ate, in the way he healed, in

---

3. See Bultmann, *Theology of the New Testament*, 133ff. for discussion of early Christian baptism "in/into the name of Christ" and 140ff. for discussion of baptism as participation in the death and resurrection of Christ. See also his discussion of Paul's more developed understanding of baptism as entrance into the church (311ff.).

4. From "The Sacrament of Baptism," *Book of Common Worship*, 404.

5. Torrance, *Theology in Reconciliation*, 90, 97f.

the way he spoke to those ignored by others. And this same solidarity with sinners led Jesus finally to the cross, where he stood in for all the tired, the poor, the huddled masses yearning to breathe free . . . for all of us, in other words. In that act, Jesus' baptism was complete.

"Baptism" then, first of all, names Jesus' baptism—in the Jordan, and on the cross. It is not an easy or sentimental thing. In Mark's gospel, when James and John ask to sit beside him in glory, Jesus asks them, "Are you able to drink the cup that I drink, or be baptized with the baptism that I am baptized with?" (Mark 10:38). Clearly his baptism entails suffering and death, and the disciples do not know what they are asking.

But Jesus' baptism, into which we are baptized, includes not only his death, but also his resurrection. According to John's gospel, the last words of Jesus on the cross were "it is finished." (John 19:30) We usually hear those words as a somber pronouncement of the end of his life on earth, and the end of his own bodily suffering. And so they are. Yet could we also hear them in another way—as the end of that struggle against sin and death that was finished at the death of Jesus? Could those words mark the end of his baptism, the completion of that work begun in the Jordan? Could they, in other words, be the pronouncement of a death sentence on death itself? If so, then we might see the sign of the cross on the head of the newly baptized not only as an identification with Jesus' suffering, but as a mark of the end of that struggle, as a sign that we do not need to struggle any longer. We need not fear death any longer, because that world no longer has a claim on us. We bear the mark of the end of that world on our foreheads.

Martin Luther famously reminded himself throughout his life, "I am baptized!" Especially in moments of struggle, this reminder called to mind this "already" dimension of baptism: as that event which joined him to God's saving work in Christ, in whom the battle was already won.

Baptism is first the baptism of Jesus—life, death, and resurrection. The New Testament (as Darrell Guder pointed out in his presentation) was not first of all interested in calling attention to the ritual act of worship, including the liturgy of baptism, but to that event that stands beyond/behind it, to Christ who is both content and agent of baptism.

Yet we cannot ignore the liturgical act of baptism, by which we are joined to the prior act of Christ. It is precisely in worship that we are most explicitly reminded of our identity in Christ. When we consider the baptismal ritual, one obvious feature is that we *receive* baptism. As Luther reminded us, we *are* baptized (rather than baptizing ourselves). Here we see the theological power of the passive voice: we do not add anything to this finished work. Baptism is a gift that comes to us from beyond ourselves, that we do not accomplish.

At its best, this is the dimension of baptism to which infant baptism particularly attests. In recent years, many Presbyterian and Reformed congregations have begun to use a baptismal declaration that powerfully articulates God's gracious work of salvation, accomplished apart from us, into which we are engrafted at baptism:

> For you, little one, the Spirit of God moved over the waters at creation, and the Lord God made covenants with his people. It was for you that the Word of God became flesh and lived among us, full of grace and truth. For you, [name], Jesus Christ suffered death crying out at the end, "It is finished!" For you Christ triumphed over death, rose in newness of life, and ascended to rule over all. All of this was done for you, little one, though you do not know any of this yet. But we will continue to tell you this good news until it becomes your own. And so the promise of the gospel is fulfilled: "We love because God first loved us."[6]

What does this mean for the church? We are baptized, claimed; we do not belong to ourselves but to Christ. At baptism, our identities are grounded outside of ourselves, in the life, death, and resurrection of the Baptized One, Jesus Christ.

2. Baptism as an Identity We Appropriate and Live Into Over a Lifetime—by the Spirit

So far we have focused on the "already" character of baptism, the way in which baptism anchors us in Christ. This is the most compressed form of the concertina of baptism (to return to Dunn's image). Now it is time for the expanded version.

Baptism is, as Pannenberg put it, "the basis of a new human identity outside the self—an identity that we have then to appropriate and work out in the whole process of our life history." I have already talked about the first part, the new human identity anchored in Christ. The second part is the "not yet" dimension of baptism, which is what sends the church out. While the "already" dimension points us, especially, to the accomplished work of Christ in his death and resurrection, the "not yet" dimension points us, especially, to life in the Spirit.

---

6. "Variations on the French Reformed Church Baptismal Liturgy," 2.

The Holy Spirit, of course, is present from the beginning, at Jesus' baptism itself. By the power of the Spirit Jesus is sent out, empowered for teaching and healing. We might say, by extension, that Jesus is led to the cross and raised from the grave by the Spirit (though the New Testament writers do not talk in this way). So Jesus' entire baptismal life is closely connected to his life in the Spirit. I do not want to suggest that we can separate baptism into Christ from baptism by the Spirit. There is only one baptism.

Even so, it is the Spirit-dimension of baptism that enables us to see more clearly how baptism is "not yet." When the wind and fire are poured out upon the gathered people at Pentecost, and they begin to speak in other languages, Peter interprets that occurrence as the eschatological gift of the Spirit, as spoken by the prophet Joel (Acts 2:1–21). That gift of the Spirit draws us into God's future, which has broken into the world in a new way in Christ. This is not just something that happens once; by the Spirit we live out our baptism over the course of a lifetime.

The Westminster Confession of Faith, not usually known for its strong views on baptism by the Holy Spirit, offers a helpful insight on this point. In the discussion of baptism, the Westminster divines affirmed that "the efficacy of baptism is not tied to that moment of time wherein it is administered; yet, notwithstanding, by the right use of this ordinance the grace promised is not only offered, but really exhibited and conferred by the Holy Ghost, to such (whether of age or infants) as that grace belongeth unto, according to the counsel of God's own will, in his appointed time."[7] What intrigues me here is the attention to both the certainty that baptismal grace is conferred and the recognition that such grace may not be evident in the baptized person's life until much later. Furthermore, it is *by the Spirit* that such grace is both "exhibited and conferred." This suggests that the authors of the Confession were seeking something like an "already and not yet" view of baptism: affirming that baptism is truly grounded in the already accomplished work of Christ, and that the grace of baptism manifests itself over time, according to God's will, by the power of the Spirit.

T. F. Torrance, despite his strong focus on the already accomplished baptism of Christ, does also hint at the dynamic, not-yet dimension of baptism in the Spirit: "On the ground of what Christ has done for us and in accordance with his promise, we are presented before God as subjects of his saving activity, and are initiated into a mutual relation between the act of the Spirit and the response of faith. . . . It is in the Spirit that God continues to act creatively upon us, uniting us to Christ so that his atoning reconciliation bears fruit in us, and lifting us up to share in the very life and love of God,

---

7. *Westminster Confession of Faith*, 6.159

in the communion of the Father, the Son, and the Holy Spirit."[8] This is the dynamic, the "not yet" dimension of baptism that can empower the mission of the church. In emphasizing this dimension of baptism, I am seeking to expand what Westminster meant by the "efficacy" of baptism, and what Torrance suggests in this passage about the Spirit lifting us up to share in the life of God over time.

As we glimpsed the "already" dimension of baptism in the baptismal liturgy of the *Book of Common Worship*, so too can we glimpse the "not yet" in that liturgical resource—and particularly in those portions of the service that name the Holy Spirit. For instance, one of the "Thanksgiving over the Water" prayers concludes, "Send your Spirit to move over this water that it may be a foundation of deliverance and rebirth. Wash away the sin of all who are cleansed by it. Raise them to new life, and graft them to the body of Christ. Pour out your Holy Spirit upon them, that they may have power to do your will and continue forever in the risen life of Christ." Here, the Spirit is invoked so that the baptismal water may convey deliverance, rebirth, forgiveness, new life, and union with Christ (which have particularly to do with the "already" of baptism), *and* ongoing power over the course of the lifetime of the baptized (the "not yet"). Even more clearly, the second prayer suggested at the laying on of hands makes an explicit eschatological connection: "Defend, O Lord, your servant N., with your heavenly grace, that she may continue yours forever, and daily increase in your Holy Spirit more and more, until she comes to your everlasting kingdom."[9]

The baptismal liturgy narrowly conceived rightly emphasizes God's saving work in Jesus Christ, which is accomplished apart from us, and which we receive by the power of the Spirit. It says relatively less about the "not yet" dimension of baptism, the lifelong process of appropriating that grace by the Spirit. If this were all the church ever said about baptism, it could lead to a lopsided view—that baptism is only about the recognition of what God has done for us, without attention to our response to that grace in our lives of baptism. In other words, if we only speak about the "already" of baptism, we could be lured into cheap grace.

Fortunately, our worship services and our lives together provide ample opportunities to recognize the dynamic, ongoing appropriation of baptism that sends us out. For instance, a worship leader might send the congregation at the end of the service from the font, reminding us of our baptism as the basis for our mission. Prayers of the people might also be offered

---

8. Torrance, *Theology*, 103. See also Calvin, *Institutes*, IV.15.6 for a similar understanding of the Spirit's role in baptism.

9. *Book of Common Worship*, 411, 413.

from the font, making the visual connection between our baptism and our intercessions for the world. Outside of worship, church groups gathering for social action or evangelism, healing ministries or visits to prisons might remind one another that they do this as the baptized community, empowered by the Spirit to share salt and light with the weary world.

3. An Already and Not Yet Church?

Anchored in Christ's baptism in the Jordan, secure in that identity, we appropriate that identity over the course of a lifetime—by the power of the Spirit. This twofold nature of baptism is above all an ecclesial, not simply an individual, reality. How does this help us think about the identity and mission of the church?

Conversations about baptism, both in local congregations and in ecumenical dialogues, often focus on the question, "what happens in baptism?" These conversations tend to explore the relationship of human action and divine action, the relationship of God to water, gesture, and words. These are important questions. But such conversations tend to fixate narrowly on a particular moment in time, and on an individual person. More important for our purposes is a different question: "who are we as a baptized and baptizing people?" If we focus on this question, then our answer has to do less with solitary individuals, and more with the church that receives baptism and invites others to the font.

Who are we as both baptized and baptizing people? If we attend to both dimensions of baptism, then the first thing we will say is that we are claimed, grounded, forgiven, washed, and freed in Christ. Our identity is anchored outside of ourselves. This can be a great relief for an anxious church, because it reminds us that we are not our own. We bear the mark of the cross on our foreheads, which testifies to Christ's solidarity with our suffering and his triumph over all that can hurt or destroy. We are baptized. Such a declaration can give us strength and hope. It is quite simply, a gift.

But if that is all we say, then we can grow complacent and inwardly focused. Baptism cannot remain compressed, the concertina forever stuck in the most inwardly directed position. As those who have been baptized, we are also sent out: seeking, inviting, witnessing, all by the power of the Spirit. We are not only those who have been baptized; we are sent to baptize others, to invite them into the new life that we have been promised. To do this, of course, means that we must actually have some sense of new life that we want to share. If we are only "not yet" and never "already," we will wear ourselves out with working for the kingdom, imagining that it is all up to us. But this is why we continue to return to the font, to reaffirm and receive anew those promises of new life and forgiveness, so that we go out not based on our own power, but in the power of the Spirit. Baptism, then, is always both *gift and call*.

By conclusion, I offer one implication of this way of thinking: if we understand ourselves as a baptized and baptizing church, then this might shape our response to unbaptized people who approach the table. The question of whether or not to invite unbaptized folks to the Lord's Supper has been before our church and many other Protestant churches in this country for several years. The PC(USA) report *Invitation to Christ*[10] addressed this very topic, and called the church to a season of sacramental renewal in response. I continue to be grateful for that report, and commend it to the church for study. Through these reflections on baptism as already and not yet, and on the church as both baptized and baptizing, I have come to a new angle on this old topic. If we as a church are both baptized and baptizing, then when people who are not baptized seek to participate in the Lord's Supper, we might see first not a "baptismal barrier," but an invitation to be who we are called to be. The "invitation to Christ" in this case goes both ways: the not-yet-baptized might be welcomed to Christ in the waters of baptism, and the already baptized might be invited to deepen our baptism through that act of welcome. In that case, the "already and not yet" refers to our baptismal identity as a whole (both grounded and unfolding) and to the people who are gathered for worship on any given day.

Already and not yet. United with Christ and sent by the Spirit. Baptized and baptizing. A church that moves and sings its way between these two poles may discover life it did not know it had: life behind us, in Christ, and life before us, called forth by the Spirit who renews the world.

Bibliography

Book of Common Worship. Louisville: Westminster John Knox, 1993.

Bultmann, Rudolf. *Theology of the New Testament*. Vol. 1. Translated by Kendrick Grobel. New York: Scribner's, 1951.

Calvin, John. *Institutes of the Christian Religion*. Edited by John T. McNeill. Translated by Ford Lewis Battles. Library of Christian Classics. Philadelphia: Westminster, 1960.

Dunn, James D. G. *Baptism in the Holy Spirit: A Re-examination of the New Testament Teaching on the Gift of the Spirit in Relation to Pentecostalism Today*. Naperville, IL: Allenson, 1970.

10. *Invitation to Christ*.

Invitation to Christ: Font and Table. Louisville: Office of Theology and Worship, 2006.

Pannenberg, Wolfhart. *Systematic Theology.* Vol. 3. Translated by Geoffrey W. Bromiley. Grand Rapids: Eerdmans, 1998.

Torrance, T. F. *Theology in Reconciliation.* London: Chapman, 1975.

"Variations on the French Reformed Church Baptismal Liturgy." Louisville: PC(USA) Office of Theology and Worship. http://www.pcusa.org/site_media/media/uploads/theologyandworship/pdfs/variations_on_the_french_reformed_church_baptismal_liturgy.pdf.

Westminster Confession of Faith. In *The Constitution of the Presbyterian Church (U.S.A.), Part I, Book of Confessions.* Louisville: Office of the General Assembly, 1999.

9

Is There Any Reason to Join a Church?
Baptism as Commissioning to Life Together

JOHN BURGESS

Let me begin with a story about the perils of church membership. A young woman joins a confirmation class in preparation for reception into active church membership. The confirmands meet every week over four months. Each confirmand seeks out a member of the congregation to pray for him or her and to stand by him or her at the time of the session examination. The confirmands' time together concludes with a weekend retreat at which they work on their personal statements of faith.

This young woman suffers from debilitating anxiety. She rarely speaks to others at church, even though she truly values the love and attention that they give her. She nevertheless participates actively in the class and gets up her courage to ask one of the church secretaries to be her mentor.

On the evening of the session examination, the young woman's anxiety is sky-high. The elders are kind, but when they ask her to read her statement of faith aloud, she panics and leaves the room in tears. Her mentor excuses herself, finds the young woman, prays with her, and persuades her to return to the meeting. The young woman agrees. Although she is unable to read her statement of faith aloud, she nods when the elders ask her to confirm her words.

Four years later, this young woman remembers that evening and how she was accepted into membership, despite everything that seemed to go wrong. She continues to come to church every week with her family. As before, she feels the congregation's love. Her confirmation mentor regularly greets her and hugs her. But no one gets up, so to speak, from the table anymore and seeks her out when she would rather hide. No one phones, no one tells her that they pray for her. What she has experienced in becoming an "active member" is that she is again alone with her faith, as she was before she became a confirmand. The only thing that has changed is that she gets a letter annually about pledging and another letter about attending the congregational meeting.

It is not surprising, then, that church membership makes little sense to many people today. If membership is primarily about money and governance, some would rather attend church without becoming members. Others treat membership lightly, ignoring their responsibility to support the congregation financially and participate in its decision making. Still others drop out of a congregation after a period of time and let their membership lapse. And most, like the young confirmand, sense that membership ought to mean something profound but are unable to say how their status is different from what it was before.

In this paper, I argue that attention to baptismal theology and practice can lead the church into a more faithful understanding of membership. For too long, baptism has been understood simply as a precondition to full, active membership in the church. Baptism, however, is a commissioning to ministry in the church and the world. It therefore represents full and active membership in a community of faith that exercises encouragement and accountability for each member's ministry.

In section 1, I briefly review how Presbyterian Books of Order over the past two hundred years have defined church membership and what has gone awry. In section 2, I examine a key New Testament text that can reorient our understanding of church membership in terms of a commissioning to ministry. In section 3, I suggest several changes to church baptismal practice that would strengthen this biblical understanding of church membership.

A Brief History of Church Membership

The current Form of Government has a section on "The Membership of a Congregation" (G-1.03). A subsection, "The Ministry of Members," enumerates 11 areas of involvement in Christ's mission and the ministry of his church.[1] Interestingly, most of these activities have to do with ministries

1. The full list reads, "proclaiming the good news in word and deed, taking part in the common life and worship of a congregation, lifting one another up in prayer, mutual concern, and active support, studying Scripture and the issues of Christian faith and life, supporting the ministry of the church through the giving of money, time, and talents, demonstrating a new quality of life within and through the church,

to which all baptized Christians are called, regardless of their membership status, such as proclaiming the gospel, participating in worship, lifting up others in prayer, studying Scripture, and working in the world for peace and justice.

In the nineteenth century, in contrast, the Form of Government of the Presbyterian Church in the U.S.A. (PCUSA) treated church membership sparsely. Church membership did not constitute a separate section of the Form of Government, and the Form of Government did not enumerate specific duties of membership. The 1823 Book of Discipline simply noted that "all baptized persons are members of the church, are under its care, and subject to its government and discipline: and when they have arrived at the years of discretion, they are bound to perform all the duties of church members."[2]

How then did we get from nearly no words about church membership two hundred years ago to long lists of responsibilities today, and what does the evolution of the church's *Book of Order* tell us about the idea of "church membership"? And even though "supporting the work of the church through the giving of money, time, and talents" and "participating in the governing responsibilities of the church" are only two of the responsibilities that the current Form of Government lists, how have they come to be perceived as primary?

The *Book of Order* of a predecessor denomination, the United Presbyterian Church in North America (UPNA), provides hints. Historically, the UPNA was shaped more strongly than the PCUSA by the Scottish Covenanter tradition. The nineteenth-century PCUSA Form of Government had required sessions to examine candidates' "knowledge and piety"; the UPNA added examination of candidates' "religious experience and purpose of life." The PCUSA did not call explicitly for a public profession of faith; the UPNA did. In contrast to the PCUSA's general language of "all the duties of church membership," the UPNA listed specific duties, including "separation from the world . . . household religion . . . [and] Christian giving and the evangelization of the world."

---

responding to God's activity in the world through service to others, living responsibly in the personal, family, vocational, political, cultural, and social relationships of life, working in the world for peace, justice, freedom, and human fulfillment, participating in the governing responsibilities of the church, and reviewing and evaluating regularly the integrity of one's membership, and considering ways in which one's participation in the worship and service of the church may be increased and made more meaningful." See the "The Ministry of Members" in *The Book of Order*, G-1.0304.

2. See "General Principles of Discipline" (chapter 1) in *The Constitution of the Presbyterian Church in the United States of America* (1823).

What brought one into communicant membership in the UPNA was not simply baptism and examination by session when one had reached the "years of discretion," but rather entering into a public covenant with the congregation. One professed one's faith before the congregation and promised to be diligent in using the means of grace and in performing "all duty as it may be made known to you." Sessions were to exercise accountability to the covenant by maintaining a roll of persons in "full communion" as well as a register of "all contributions of the congregation." Further, the *Book of Order* mandated that sessions remove members from the rolls who had been absent for one year or who had "practically withdrawn from the congregation," matters that the 19th PCUSA Form of Government did not address.[3]

By 1947, the PCUSA, while not requiring formal covenant-making, had edged closer to the UPNA. The Form of Government now asked candidates for membership to "make a public profession of their faith, in the presence of the congregation." The PCUSA also established different categories of church membership. The old PCUSA Form of Government had provided for two church rolls: one for baptized members and one for communicant members (including people suspended from the Table). The new Form of Government introduced further distinctions: communicant members, dismissed members, resident members, non-resident members, and even affiliated members. Members who had been given certificates of dismissal had no right to speak or vote in church meetings and were expected to join a new congregation within one year. Non-resident members could be suspended, as could resident members whose absence was "a serious injury to the cause of religion."[4]

When the PCUSA and UPNA united in 1958, the new church followed the UPNA at key points. The Form of Government had a separate section on "church members"; public profession of faith included promises "to make diligent use of the means of grace, to share faithfully in the worship and service of the Church, to give of [one's] substance as the Lord may prosper

---

3. For relevant sections of the UPNA *Book of Order*, see "Of the Admission of Members" (part II, chapter IV), "Of the Dismission of Members" (part II, chapter V), and "Of the Session" (part I, chapter XIV), in *The Confessional Statement of the United Presbyterian Church of North America*.

4. See "Of the Church Session" (Form of Government, chapter IX), "Of the Admission to Full Communion of Persons Baptized in Infancy" (Directory for Worship, chapter X), "Of Jurisdiction" (Book of Discipline, chapter II.2, "Dismissed Members"), and "Of Cases without Full Judicial Process" (Book of Discipline, chapter VII.3–4, "Suspension of Non-Resident Church Members" and "Suspension of Resident Church Members"), in *The Constitution of the Presbyterian Church in the United States of America* (1947) was even made to "erase" from the roll of communicants the names of members who felt that they could no longer come in good conscience to the Table.

[one], to render wholehearted service to Christ and his Kingdom throughout the world, and to continue in the peace and fellowship of the people of God"; and the session was charged to cultivate liberality in financial giving among church members. In addition, the church established yet another roll, this one for non-resident members.[5]

Other changes were in the offing. Historically, admission to the Lord's Supper required "full" membership. By mid-century, however, the idea of "communicant member" was eroding. In 1974, baptized children for the first time could come to the Table if their families deemed it appropriate and the session approved. While the Form of Government continued to emphasize members' responsibilities for worship and service, active membership was increasingly defined in terms of access to "the governing and decision-making life of the congregation." Baptized children could become active members when they were ready "to participate more deliberately in the total life of the church." What principally distinguished active members from inactive or affiliate members was exercise of power. Only active members had voice and/or vote in congregational meetings and could hold church office.[6]

By 1982, the distinct meaning of membership, apart from governance, was even smaller. The Form of Government had moved to speaking of the "privileges" available to nonmembers. If baptized, they were invited to the Table; if members of another church, not only could they receive the Lord's Supper, but they also had the "right" to have their children baptized. Again, what distinguished members from nonmembers was access to vote and office.[7]

This brief review suggests four major shifts of emphasis over the twentieth century. First, new Books of Order enumerated an ever wider range of duties incumbent on members. What had once been implicitly understood

---

5. See "Of Church Members" (Form of Government, chapter VI), "Of the Admission to Full Communion of Baptized Persons" (Directory for Worship, chapter IX), and "Of Cases without Full Judicial Process" (Book of Discipline, chapter VII.2–4, "Erasure of Name," "Provisions for Nonresident Church Members," and "Provisions for Resident Church Members"), in *The Constitution of the Presbyterian Church in the United States of America* (1958).

6. See "Of Church Members" (Form of Government, chapter VI), "Status of and Jurisdiction over Persons" (Book of Discipline, chapter II), and "The Sacrament of the Lord's Supper" (Directory for Worship, chapter VI), in *The Constitution of the Presbyterian Church in the United States of America* (1974).

7. See "Of Church Members and Their Ministry" (Form of Government, chapter VI), in *The Constitution of the Presbyterian Church in the United States of America* (1974).

had to be made explicit. Second, the responsibility of members to make financial contributions became more prominent. Third, the church developed different categories of membership in response to growing social mobility and changing attitudes about church attendance. Fourth, church membership was no longer primarily about admission to the Lord's Supper, but rather about voice, vote, and office.

Today, sessions are reluctant to remove people from the rolls who continue to make a financial contribution, even if they are otherwise uninvolved. The *Book of Order* assures inactive members, affiliate members, and nonmembers alike that they can participate fully in church life except for voting and holding office.

It is no wonder that people can't see the point of membership, if it just means being hounded to give money, to attend congregational meetings, or to "take one's turn" on session. The church desperately needs a clearer theological basis for church membership. Attention to baptism as commissioning to ministry can help.

Baptism as Commissioning

The church has typically turned to passages in Acts and the Epistles for its understanding of baptism. Key images for baptism have included repentance and cleansing from sin, dying to sin and rising to new life in Christ, incorporation into the church as the body of Christ, and receiving the Holy Spirit.[8] Karl Barth famously suggested beginning instead with Christ's own baptism. For Barth, to be baptized is publicly to declare, as did Christ in the Jordan, allegiance to God's cause in the world. Barth therefore dismissed the practice of baptizing infants.[9]

I wish to start at yet a different place: Jesus' calling of the twelve disciples (Matt 10:1–15; Mark 6:7–13; and Luke 9:1–6). While these texts are not explicitly baptismal, they can help us understand the call to new life in Christ, to which baptism gives expression, as a commissioning to ministry.

The Gospels make a special point of naming the twelve, just as the church gives those who are baptized a "Christian name." Jesus calls the twelve to give up everything to follow him, just as the church calls those being baptized to break with the past and begin a new life. The calling of the disciples confirms Barth's point that baptism marks a realignment of loyalties: One is joined to God's cause in the world, the kingdom of God. The calling stories, however, make clear that this alignment is not so much our

---

8. See *The Book of Order*, W-2.3000.
9. See Barth, *The Teaching of the Church*, and Barth, *Gespräche*, 339–45.

decision in response to God's grace as God's gracious decision for us. When Jesus later says that his disciples must be like children, we can conclude that children, like adults, can become disciples (Matt 18:2; also see Matt 11:25).

In three respects, the calling stories challenge understandings of baptism that focus primarily on the individual's salvation. First, they help us understand that life in Christ, as set forth in baptism, is not a precondition for full membership in the Christian community. Rather, baptism itself constitutes full membership. Those who are baptized, whether as infants or adults, have been called by name to follow Christ. Second, the calling stories teach us that those who have been claimed by Christ through baptism are sent into the world to declare by word and deed God's salvation of the world. Third, the calling stories help us see baptism as entry into a community that encourages us in, and holds us accountable to, this calling.

Baptism Itself Constitutes Full Membership in the Church

In calling his disciples, Jesus does not appoint junior or senior members. The separation of baptism from the Lord's Supper has led to such strange aberrations as the Puritan halfway covenant, in which baptized Christians were denied the Lord's Supper because they had not made a profession of a personal experience of conversion. Barth sought to reintegrate baptism and full, active membership by reserving baptism for professing adults. The calling stories suggest, however, a different possibility. If the church knows what it is doing when it baptizes, it will continually remind the baptized, whatever their stage of life, that they are members of the church, the body of Christ.

Parents walk to the front of the church with their child. They let go of it, placing it in the hands of the pastor. Like Hannah bringing Samuel to the temple, they are implicitly acknowledging that this child is no longer just theirs, that indeed it has never been just theirs. Holding the child, the pastor speaks God's word of promise, applies water to the child, and calls the child by name—in my case, "John Paul, I baptize you in the name of the Father, and of the Son, and of the Holy Spirit"—as if the child in that moment has a new family name: John Paul, son of the triune God. Whether we affirm that new identity or not, whether we wander away from it or embrace it, we have been marked once and for all as God's own. The baptized therefore deserve the church's love and prayers.[10]

---

10. See Burgess, *After Baptism*, 1–7.

To Be Baptized Is to Be Sent to Declare God's Salvation of the World

Too often church tradition has focused on baptism as personal salvation. The calling stories are different. They do not speak of the salvation of the one who has been called, but rather of the salvation that God is offering the whole world. Those who belong to Christ are called to all ends of the earth to declare that the "the kingdom of God is at hand" (Mark 1:15 RSV).

Baptism therefore marks one as a minister. If the church knows what it is doing when it baptizes, it will constantly remind the baptized that they have been called to live not for themselves, but rather for others. They are to be salt and light. They are to grow in holiness so that others can see God's image in them. They are to cast out the false identities that hold them or others captive to powers and principalities that would define "the good life" in terms of particular national, economic, or political interests, rather than in terms of God's kingdom of righteousness and peace.

A pastor baptizes a child and places it again in the hands of its parents. The church and parents now bear a responsibility to guide the child into ministry. Active membership does not begin after a personal profession of faith or with attending a congregation's annual meeting. Baptism itself is the moment of our commissioning to active membership.

Baptism Is Entry into a Community of Mutual Encouragement and Accountability

A number of years ago, theologian and liturgical scholar Ronald Byars wrote that the problem with baptizing infants is not that they are unable to understand what is going on, but rather that the church too often fails in its promise to nurture them in Christian faith.[11] Similarly, my comments about baptism as full membership will only make sense if baptism, whether of adults or infants, is understood as entry into a community that offers people encouragement for, and accountability to, the ministry of witness to which baptism commissions them.

The calling of the twelve is not only about identity and sending, but also about such a community. Matthew names the twelve in pairs (Matt 10:2–3); Luke makes the same point about a community of discipleship when speaking of the seventy whom Christ sends ahead of him in pairs (Luke 10:1). The emphasis on community is again apparent when these gospels report that commissioned disciples are to seek out those who will provide them

---

11. Byars, "Indiscriminate Baptism," 36–40.

hospitality. Disciples need each other's help and encouragement in a world that will resist their witness.

The disciples also exercise accountability. Should they fail to find hospitality at a house, they should withdraw their peace from it.[12] The *Didache*, a second-century church manual, adds that travelling apostles must not stay more than one or, at most, two days with their hosts, lest they become freeloaders. Disciples call each other to remain true to the ministry that God has given them.

Congregations cannot force faith from those whom they baptize, but congregations can commit themselves to practices of mutual encouragement and accountability that lay claim on all in its midst who are baptized. Those who are baptized need encouragement and accountability, and the Christian community needs the encouragement and accountability that the baptized offer each other.

In sum, church membership is best grounded in an understanding of baptism as marking one with a new identity, commissioning one to witness, and joining one to a community of mutual encouragement and accountability. Questions of financial giving and church governance should not be dominating criteria, nor should record-keeping become an obsession.

Implications for Baptismal Practice

On the basis of the baptismal theology that I have sketched out, I would like to make several practical proposals:

1. Eliminate Language of "Active" Membership from the Book of Order

If our baptismal theology is correct, we will regard all who are baptized as full, active members of the church. Membership is a matter not of one's intentions to "assume greater responsibility in the life of the church and God's mission in the world,"[13] but rather of God's intention for one's life. In baptism, God has commissioned an individual to ministry and joined an individual to a community of faith. That community has responsibility for identifying, cultivating, and directing the individual's gifts for witness. While the way in which the individual makes this witness—and the ways in which the community offers encouragement and accountability—will vary

---

12. The reference to "house" is probably a reference to a house church.
13. *Book of Common Worship*, 447.

(e.g., depending on the individual's age and gifts), the church must resist distinguishing baptismal membership from full, active membership.

Equally problematic is the idea that those who were baptized as infants must later make public profession of faith. While those who were baptized as infants have not always made a "public profession" according to the procedures of the *Book of Order*,[14] they have already made public profession of faith regularly and perhaps frequently, e.g., when they have received the Lord's Supper or joined the congregation in reaffirming the baptismal covenant. For pastoral reasons, congregations may ask young people to profess their faith publicly before the session and congregation, but this act would no longer represent a transition to "active" membership. Rather, these young people would be reaffirming the status they already have as full, active members.[15]

Eliminating language of "active" membership and removing public profession of faith as a requirement for active membership (except perhaps for older children or adults seeking baptism) has implications for how congregations think about confirmation / communicants classes. Christian education is a continual process from infanthood to adulthood. Membership therefore should not be dependent on "graduation" from a confirmation/communicants class—a graduation that in practice is too often graduation from the church altogether. Rather, membership entails a dynamic, lifelong process of growing in theological understanding, in a capacity for witness, and in a commitment to the church community.

Congregations may still wish to establish criteria for voting and holding church office, but these criteria would no longer define membership. An appropriate analogy may be national citizenship. All who are born in the United States are citizens, but one can vote or hold office only after additional qualifications are met. Nevertheless, categories of "active" or "inactive" citizenship do not exist.

2. Interpret Baptism as Entry into a Community of Mutual Encouragement and Accountability

The church has the responsibility to help those who seek baptism (for themselves or their children) understand what baptism means as church membership. On the one hand, baptism does not guarantee personal salvation;

---

14. See *The Book of Order*, G-1.0303.

15. Richard Osmer argues for preserving the practice of confirmation, but as a reaffirmation of the baptismal covenant within the context of a lifelong process of participating in congregational life. See his *Confirmation*, 168–218.

on the other, it is more than a social rite of passage or a congregational welcoming ceremony. Rather, baptism identifies one as belonging to Jesus Christ and to the community that he has commissioned to witness to him. Those who would be baptized must know that after their baptism, they will not be left alone, whether by default or by their own choice. God has claimed them for active witness.

In this matter, the burden of responsibility falls on the congregation, not on the individual. The individual does not have to prove how active he or she is in order to retain membership; rather, the congregation has the responsibility to encourage the baptized in their commission to witness and to hold them accountable to it.

Mutual encouragement and accountability take time and practice. Sometimes church communities can become harsh and judgmental in disciplining members, but at other times congregations can become so consumed by institutional survival that they fail to cultivate what German theologian Dietrich Bonhoeffer called "life together." As Bonhoeffer noted, idealism about these matters can only lead to disappointment and even disaster.[16] We can, however, make progress, even if limited, in living out our responsibilities to each other.

More than thirty years ago, Joseph Small, former PCUSA pastor and head of the denomination's Office of Theology and Worship, described one session's efforts to frame baptism in terms of mutual encouragement and accountability. Every month the church newsletter published anniversary dates of people baptized by the congregation, along with a reminder of the congregation's responsibility "to tell [them] the good news of the gospel, to help them know all that Christ commands, and, by our fellowship, to strengthen their family ties with the household of God." At its monthly meeting, the session would pray for these members and then send each (or their parents) a letter expressing the church's "continuing care and . . . hope for growth in common discipleship."[17]

Other sessions have explored appointing older members to serve as mentors to new members. Or a congregation may invite new members into small groups that study Scripture, pray for each other, and enjoy fellowship. Mutual encouragement and accountability can also occur when sessions annually review the rolls. Rather than simply eliminating the names of inactive members, sessions can become aware again of who has not been present, make inquiries about them, and determine how the church can best minister to them.

---

16. Bonhoeffer, *Life Together*, 23–47.
17. Small, "Salt and Light," 178–87.

I have proposed eliminating language of "active" membership. One may nevertheless protest that some church members really do become inactive. When people have become inactive because they have moved to another congregation, a session can responsibly remove them from its rolls. More difficult are those cases in which people simply drop out of church life and efforts to keep them connected with the congregation bear no apparent fruit. Here a session has a couple of options. It could disqualify such persons from voting, without removing them from membership. It could, however, also determine whether these people have implicitly or explicitly renounced their baptismal vows (though, of course, we do not believe that they can renounce their baptism). Short of such a renunciation, a congregation could continue to reach out to them, if nothing else by regularly naming them in prayer.

3. Introduce into the Baptismal Service Symbols and Words of Commissioning to Witness

Baptism sets forth God's claim on us. It commissions us to witness, by word and deed, to what God has done and is doing in Christ. If a congregation understands that baptism means active membership, it will continually help its baptized members identify, develop, and express the particular gifts for ministry that God has given them.

Congregations are often better at representing baptism as incorporation into the community of faith than as a commission to witness. While the now common practice of walking the newly baptized infant or adult through the congregation dramatically expresses that he or she belongs to the family of God, it fails to mark him or her as a disciple whom God sends into ministry both in and beyond the congregation. To make that point, the pastor would have to walk the person down the aisle and out the front door!

To be sure, the words for the baptismal service in the Presbyterian *Book of Common Worship* do not neglect the theme of baptism as commissioning to witness. In the thanksgiving over the water, the pastor praises God for "filling us with a variety of gifts that we might proclaim the gospel to all nations."[18] An emphasis on commissioning is even stronger in the prayer for those reaffirming the baptismal covenant: "Send them forth by the power of your Spirit to love and serve you with joy, and to strive for justice and peace in all the earth."[19]

---

18. *Book of Common Worship*, 440.
19. Ibid., 443.

Words alone, however, are not enough to commission us. Visible, tangible symbols help strengthen the sacramental significance of the waters through which we pass. Joseph Small's essay of thirty years ago is again suggestive. He reports that after more than a year of study and reflection, the session made several changes to the congregation's baptismal practice. Of particular interest was its decision to present two gifts to the newly baptized: salt and light.

> Next to the baptismal bowl on the communion table we place a small pottery salt dish filled with salt and a pottery candle holder with a small candle. . . . The elder lights the small candle from the paschal candle (which is present during Eastertide and then whenever there is a baptism or a funeral), holds the candle and the salt out to the baptized person, and says, "(Name), you are the salt of the earth; you are the light of the world . . ." (Matt 5:31ff. RSV). Thus we proclaim discipleship in the life of the baptized person.[20]

It may be hard for us to imagine how a newly baptized infant can have a commission to ministry. We nevertheless trust that its gifts for witness will become clearer over time. And even now the infant is salt and light. A congregation that knows what baptism is all about will see the very existence of the infant as a witness to Immanuel, "God with us." The child's witness calls forth our own, and together we are called to grow into a community of ministry, to encourage each other's gifts for witness at each stage of life, and to hold each other accountable to our baptismal commission.

∼

So, is there any good reason to join a church? It all depends on what we mean by membership. I have been encouraging us to focus on baptism as membership, rather than on membership as something that happens separately from baptism and perhaps many years later. Those who come into our congregations as baptized Christians are already members of the church universal. It is not quite right to ask them to complete a "new members class" before joining our congregation. We would more appropriately ask them what needs to happen so that they can reaffirm their baptism as a call into this particular community of mutual encouragement and accountability, for the sake of our common witness to Christ in the world.

That reaffirmation of the baptismal covenant might or might not happen as a separate liturgical act in which the church publicly poses questions

---

20. Small, "Salt and Light," 182.

to one who has entered into the congregation's life. More important is whether the congregation makes clear that if you attend worship here, receive the Lord's Supper, and participate in acts of reaffirmation of the baptismal covenant, such as confession and assurance of pardon, this community of faith will take responsibility for encouraging, and holding you accountable to, your growth in the Christian life and the ministry to which God has called you. Moreover, the community will call on you to encourage those around you and hold them accountable to their baptismal commission.

I do not know what my approach to these questions would mean for membership numbers in the Presbyterian Church (USA), but membership numbers have never told us much about faithfulness to Jesus Christ anyway. Our challenge today is less about beefing up the rolls and more about how to shape congregations that are disciplined by care of one person for another and by common witness to the world.

> You are salt . . . but if salt has lost its taste . . . it is no longer good for anything except to be thrown out and trodden under foot . . . . You are the light of the world. A city set on a hill cannot be hid. . . . Let your light so shine . . . that [others] see your good works and give glory to your Father who is in heaven. (Matt 5:13–16 RSV)

> And [thus] the Lord sent them on ahead of him, two by two, into every town and place where he himself was about to come. (Luke 10:1 RSV)

Bibliography

Barth, Karl. *Gespräche: 1959–1962*. Edited by Eberhard Busch. Zurich: Theologischer Verlag, 1995.
———. *The Teaching of the Church Regarding Baptism*. London: SCM, 1948.
Bonhoeffer, Dietrich. *Life Together*. Edited by Geffrey B. Kelley. Minneapolis: Fortress, 1996.
Book of Common Worship. Louisville: Westminster John Knox, 1993.
Burgess, John P. *After Baptism: Shaping the Christian Life*. Louisville: Westminster John Knox, 2005.
Byars, Ronald. "Indiscriminate Baptism and Baptismal Integrity." *Reformed Liturgy and Music* 31 (1997) 36–40.
The Confessional Statement of the United Presbyterian Church of North America. Pittsburgh: United Presbyterian Board of Publication, 1926.
The Constitution of the Presbyterian Church (U.S.A.), Part II, Book of Order. Louisville: The Office of the General Assembly, 2013.
The Constitution of the Presbyterian Church in the United States of America. Newark: Benjamin Olds, 1823.

The Constitution of the Presbyterian Church in the United States of America. Philadelphia: Office of the General Assembly, 1947.

The Constitution of the Presbyterian Church in the United States of America. Philadelphia: Office of the General Assembly, 1958.

The Constitution of the Presbyterian Church in the United States of America (Part II: Book of Order). Philadelphia: Office of the General Assembly, 1974.

Osmer, Richard. *Confirmation: Presbyterian Practices in Ecumenical Perspective*. Louisville: Geneva, 1996.

Small, Joseph D. "Salt and Light." *Reformed Liturgy and Music* 15 (1981), 178–87.

10

The Centrality of the Eucharist

Thomas E. Smith

I have come to the conclusions of my paper as a result of a liturgical journey best captured in the historic phrase: *"lex orandi, lex credendi, lex vivendi,"* which translated loosely means *"so we pray, so we believe, so we live."* Because of the living context within which I have been doing ministry for the past twenty-eight years at the Presbyterian Chapel of the Lakes (PCL), I have arrived at my convictions about the centrality of Eucharist. From within the liturgical life of this congregation I have forged my three pastoral convictions about Eucharist, namely that Eucharist is central to Christian identity, central to Christian evangelism and central to Christian mission.

I believe Eucharist is central to Christian identity because it commemorates our union with Christ, and thus it unities us with one another in Christ's Body, the Church. And I believe that Eucharist is central to Christian evangelism because it proclaims the saving work of Christ on behalf of the whole world, and thus the whole world is invited to our Lord's Table. And I believe that Eucharist is central to Christian mission because the sacramental significance of Eucharist lies in it effecting what it signifies. And to effect what Eucharist signifies there must be a missional transformation of the participants or the elements themselves remain empty and barren.

I argue these intrinsic connections by noting that the New Testament's emphasis upon our salvation as a *"union with Christ"* includes an inseparable ontological and ethical dimension. And I note that this same dual emphasis can be found in Calvin's understanding of our spiritual union with Christ as *"the special fruit"* of the Lord's Supper and is also broadly consistent with the patristic tradition's historic teaching on deification. Thus, it is my belief that our Eucharistic worship not only fuels the Church's mission in the world, but it also spurs the Church to greater ecumenical oneness.

Lex Orandi, Lex Credendi, Lex Vivendi

The Presbyterian Chapel of the Lakes is a congregation in which most of the members and visitors are non-Presbyterians who have retired to a resort area and have come to the Chapel mostly because it was nearby and also because it has a breezy "*come as you are*" worship style. The congregation on any given Sunday is composed of Quakers and Catholics, Methodists and Lutherans, along with a few Presbyterians sprinkled in here and there.

So when communion is celebrated those who are not Presbyterian have often wondered aloud if they are permitted to participate. I assure them that Presbyterianism is long past the days of "*fencing the table*" by requiring celebrants to first get a communion token from the elders before being allowed to participate in our Eucharistic worship.[1] But I take their concerns seriously and began to adopt a practice of offering a more expansive and ecumenical introduction to the Lord's Table by saying more or less the following just prior to offering the Eucharistic prayer of thanksgiving:

> Friends, this is the Lord's Table. This is not a Presbyterian table. If it were a Presbyterian table you could all go home now because this would be meaningless. But this is the Lord's Table, which means that Jesus Christ presides as Host at this table. And He invites all to come to His table, and so all are welcome at His Table. Sinners are especially welcome at the Lord's Table!
> Come to this table just as you are, for it is here that we learn again and again that God has first come to us, shared our common lot, and invites us now to share in His love.

I often receive positive comments following Eucharist from visitors at the Chapel who remark on how hospitable the invitation is, but also at how startled they are by it. It forces them to realize that the Lord's Table is truly meant to transcend the denominational boundaries that we have created within the Church at large, boundaries which obscure if not trivialize the

---

1. Communion tokens were commonly used in eighteenth and nineteenth-century Scottish Presbyterian Church to fence the table from those deemed unworthy to celebrate as a mechanism of church discipline. Prior to Eucharist those who wished to commune had to receive the approval of the elders in the form of a small token, usually lead and embossed with a biblical phrase or emblem such as the burning bush. The goal here was to close communion to only those deemed worthy and thus protect the Table from being profaned, though, as I will argue below, an emphasis upon such external and legalistic criteria of worthiness itself risks profaning the Table.

meaning of our Christian unity. Those whose backgrounds are from more restrictive, closed communions are usually the most grateful for the inclusiveness of the Lord's Table invitation.

Eucharist Is Central to Christian Identity

And while my practice of ecumenical invitation may be heard as merely a prudent pastoral accommodation, I believe it is more than this. I believe that such Eucharist hospitality is essential and necessary in order to honor the true meaning of our Lord's Table.

> When we bless "the cup of blessing," is it not a means of sharing in the blood of Christ? When we break the bread, is it not a means of sharing in the body of Christ? Because there is one loaf, we many as we are, are one body; for it is one loaf of which we all partake.[2]

In 1 Cor 11:17f. Paul upbraids the Corinthian congregation for injecting their worldly socioeconomic boundaries into their Eucharist celebrations. Paul found this kind of behavior reprehensible and regarded it as a spiritual problem of *"not discerning the Lord's body."*[3]

Because they failed to discern the meaning of the Lord's body, namely they failed to understand the inclusive unity of the Church and the essential oneness of Christ's body they brought down judgment on themselves. By their exclusionary practices they desecrated the Lord's body.

The New Testament is emphatic on this score. In Gal 3:28 Paul famously argues that: "There is no more Jew and Greek, slave and freeman, male and female; for you are all one person in Christ Jesus."

And when he repeats this formula in Col 3:11 he sharpens his point by insisting that even the "Scythian" is included in the oneness of this new humanity in which *"Christ is all and in all."* The thrust of Paul's sharp rebuke to Peter in Galatians 2 was because of his refusal to eat with Gentile believers, which Paul saw this as a threat to the gospel itself. And in John 17 Jesus was clearly praying for more than just His immediate disciples when he says, "May they all be one: as thou, Father, art in me and I in thee, so also may they be in us, that the world may believe that thou didst send me." Therefore our unity and oneness in Christ and with one another is meant to serve as

---

2. 1 Cor 10:16–17.

3. 1 Cor 11:29. Apparently the rich were shaming the poor by beginning without them and not waiting for them to arrive. Presumably the poor were slaves whose duties delayed them from arriving to join the assembled in a timely manner.

a powerful witness of gospel love to the world. And my pastoral experience testifies to the truth of this prayer. Eucharist has been for us a powerful expression of our Christian unity, as it was always meant to be.

Thus, the scandal of Christian worship to this day is the Corinthian divisiveness we display in our Eucharist celebrations. It is scandalous that we insist upon majoring on minors at a time and place when we ought to be majoring on majors. The Eastern Orthodox refuse to commune with the West, both Roman Catholic and Protestant; the Roman Catholic refuses to commune with Protestants; Missouri Synod Lutherans refuse to commune with other Lutherans let alone other Protestants. Taken to its logical and most neurotic extreme, Roger Williams eventually decided that he could only commune with his own wife, and then started having doubts about her too!

Yes, there is a time and place to be a Presbyterian, but the Lord's Table is not the time or place. And so I would regard it as an essential expression of the catholicity of our Christian faith that our invitation to the Lord's Table welcomes all Christians to come and participate with us.[4] We should not fence visitors from other denominations of the Christian faith away from our celebration of Eucharist. We should extend to them the benefit of whatever doubts we may otherwise have.

Eucharist Is Central to Christian Evangelism

That being said, how far are we willing to go down this road of Eucharist hospitality? Well, I argue that our Eucharist hospitality should be modeled upon our Lord's hospitality. And it is the consensus of even the most radical of New Testament critics that our Lord ate and drank with sinners, with those who were deemed unworthy to participate in Israel's liturgical life and were treated as ritual outcasts.[5]

---

4. Calvin, *Institutes*, IV:1:9 states, "Individual men who, by their profession of religion, are reckoned within such churches, even though they may actually be strangers to the church, still in a sense belong to it until they have been rejected by public judgment . . . For it may happen that we ought to treat like brothers and count as believers those whom we think unworthy of the fellowship of the godly, because of the common agreement of the church by which they are borne and tolerated in the body of Christ. We do not by our vote approve such persons as members of the church, but we leave to them such place as they occupy among the people of God until it is lawfully taken from them."

5. God's love is to be lavished indiscriminately upon the just and the unjust alike, just like the rain. Only in this way can we enter into the perfection of God's goodness, a goodness that knows no bounds. Cf. Matt 5:43–48.

So, I believe that the *Didache* got it exactly wrong when it said, "[And] let no one eat or drink from your Eucharist except those baptized in the name of [the] Lord, for the Lord has likewise said concerning this: 'Do not give what is holy to the dogs.'"[6] And I believe that the PC(USA) sacramental study paper, *Invitation to Christ*, got it exactly right when they argued for "strong, expressive, participatory, lavish, loving and grace-filled sacramental practices," including the unconventional practice of open and evangelistic communion that temporarily disrupts the conventional order of first font and then table.[7]

It is clearly presumptuous to assume that every person receiving communion is a devout believer or faithful disciple of Jesus Christ. Many may be only nominal at best, and some may no doubt be ambivalent about various aspects of the Christian faith. They have doubts on many levels. Yet they attend worship in spite of their doubts, no doubt seeking answers to their doubts.

That being the case, no one can presume to have some kind of special insight into the faith of their hearers. The apostles were taught to make their appeal to all knowing that the faith of some is shallow and does not have enough of a root system to withstand the heat of the day while the faith of others is compromised and will be choked out by the cares of this life.[8] They make their appeal to all, taking at face value their professions of faith and knowing full well that not all who say "Lord, Lord, shall enter into the kingdom of heaven."[9] They give their hearers, in other words, the benefit of the doubt.

All the people who attend Sunday services experience the whole of Christian worship. They experience the gathering music, the hymns of praise, the public confession of sin, the prayers of the people, the recitation of the Lord's Prayer, the doxology, the *Gloria Patri*, the public reading of Scripture, the public preaching of the gospel, and the public invitation to the assembled who have gathered to come to the Lord's Table and in holy remembrance to celebrate His death until He comes again in glory.

Now at this point in the service, if they wish to come to the Lord's Table, why would I not welcome them? Why would I not give them the

---

6. See Milavec, *The Didache*, 23. The context in which Jesus made this statement is one in which He in fact is teaching us by His example to extend his healing grace to an "unbaptized" outsider such as the woman from the region of Tyre and Sidon.

7. *Invitation to Christ*.

8. Cf. Luke 8:4f.

9. Matt 7:21.

benefit of the doubt? Who am I to bar anyone from coming to Jesus at this point? That would make no gospel sense to me at all.

Yes, there are boundaries of exclusion to be observed in the kingdom of God. But when Jesus was once asked "Are only a few to be saved?" He clearly warned against presuming one had a reserved seat at His kingdom feast. In this respect, Jesus' stern "Out of my sight, all you, you and your wicked ways," is very much of the same spirit as John the Baptist's warning: "Do not presume to say to yourselves, 'We have Abraham for our father.' I tell you that God can make children for Abraham out of these stones here!"[10]

And yet in both cases these warnings against presumption are directed at the religious elite in stark contrast to the generous welcome and gracious hospitality directed to those who had been deemed ritually unworthy by the religious elite. The common people flocked to John the Baptist "from Jerusalem, from all Judaea, and the whole Jordan valley."[11] And Jesus follows up his warning to the religious elite that they may find themselves thrown out of the kingdom feast by noting that people "from east and west, north and south" will nonetheless be welcomed into at His kingdom feast, a kingdom in which "some who are now last will be first and some who are now first will be last."[12]

Again, in a context in which Jesus affirms His principle of exclusion by upbraiding those towns in which most of miracles had been performed for their unbelief, we nonetheless hear Jesus give God thanks for "hiding these things from the learned and wise, and revealing them to the simple," along with His invitation: "Come to me, all whose work is hard, whose load is heavy; and I will give you relief. Bend your necks to my yoke and learn from me, for I am gentle and humble-hearted; and your souls will find relief. For my yoke is good to bear, my load is light."[13]

The disciples clearly had to be taught to imitate Jesus' generous welcome and gracious hospitality. Once when mothers brought their infant in arms to Jesus to be blessed, the disciples thought it best to rebuke them and restrain them from coming to Jesus. But they quickly learned that was a mistake. Jesus shapely rebuked them and noted, "The kingdom of God belongs to such as these."[14]

When Jesus was once asked to make a discriminating judgment about who was or wasn't His follower, He said, "Whoever is not against us is for

10. Matt 3:9 and Luke 13:27.
11. Matt 3:6.
12. Luke 13:29–30.
13. Matt 11:25, 28–30.
14. Luke 18:15–17.

us."[15] I take this to mean that we are to give people the benefit of the doubt and not to overly narrow the gate and contradict the gospel we preach when we invite people to the Lord's Table. Our invitation to celebrate Eucharist is to be in the spirit of the consistently generous welcome and gracious hospitality extended by our Lord to all prodigals, including "tax collectors and sinners."[16]

In pastoral life there are discriminating judgments to be made to be sure, but such discrimination is to be the product of a love that has grown "ever richer and richer in knowledge and insight of every kind."[17] Granted, this meal is intended to be a means of grace by which the faithful are fed and nourished, but the crumbs from this Table are intended to feed any and all.

Again, if our table worship is modeled after our Lord's Table hospitality then we should extend to the world the benefit of whatever doubts we may otherwise have. As St. Augustine once observed with respect to the inherent ambiguity involved in all such judgments: "For, in that unspeakable foreknowledge of God, many who seem to be without are in reality within, and many who seem to be within yet really are without."[18]

Added to this ambiguity is the inherent mystery of Christ's presence in Eucharist which can only be experienced by the secret power of God's Spirit at work in the participant by faith. Hence, where faith is absent, so too the Spirit's power is absent. Calvin says that in such cases the bread and wine, become "empty and trifling" and of no more value than "the splendor of the sun shining upon blind eyes, or a voice sounding in deaf ears."[19]

So, only by the Spirit's secret power working in us by faith can our Eucharist celebration be said to be a feeding upon the divinized flesh and blood of our resurrected Lord. Only by faith can it effect what it signifies, for as Calvin notes: "it is one thing to be offered, another to be received."[20]

And so we risk much if our Eucharist hospitality is too exclusive. And we risk little if it is judged by some to be too inclusive. And in such a damned if you do, damned if you don't sort of situation, I believe we should be damned on the side of a too inclusive invitation. Our invitation to the Lord's Table ought to be as inclusive as the grace and gospel to which it testifies and itself evangelistically proclaims.

---

15. Mark 9:40.
16. Luke 15:1–32.
17. Phil 1:9.
18. Augustine, *Of Baptism*, V.27.38.
19. Calvin, *Institutes*, IV:XIV:9.
20. Ibid., IV:XVII:33.

Eucharist Is Central to Christian Mission

My third thesis, namely that the sacramental significance of Eucharistic worship resides more in a moral transformation in the lives of the participants than it does in any metaphysical transformation of the elements themselves, is both controversial and uncontroversial. It is controversial in as much as sacramental theology is normally entangled by tortuous explanations about how Christ is objectively present in the elements, such as the Lutheran notion of the ubiquity of Christ's divinized human flesh or the Roman Catholic notion of the transubstantiation of the Eucharistic elements, explanations that rarely satisfy and usually only end up generating more questions than answers.

But my third thesis is uncontroversial in as much as it is really just an extension of a very common argument found throughout the New Testament, namely the argument that we must become what we are, that the resurrection life in which we participate must necessarily give life to our mortal flesh.[21] It cannot lie dormant in us. A faith that is not energized by love, a faith that does not issue in a changed life, a salvation by grace through faith that does not walk in those good works to which it is foreordained to walk is no faith at all.[22]

Essentially, all I am arguing for here is the inseparability of Christian faith and life. I am extending this to include Christian worship and witness. Calvin argued early on in his *Institutes* that God cannot be known apart from piety, "that reverence joined with love of God which the knowledge of his benefits induces."[23] Calvin goes on to brand as "idle speculations" a merely intellectual interest in God:

> What good is it . . . what help is it, in short, to know a God with whom we have nothing to do? Rather, our knowledge should serve first to teach us fear and reverence; secondly, with it as our guide and teacher, we should learn to seek every good from him, and, having received it, to credit it to his account . . . Besides, this mind restrains itself from sinning, not out of dread of punishment alone; but, because it loves and reveres God as Father, it worships and adores him as Lord. Even if there were no hell, it would still shudder at offending him alone . . . all men have a vague general veneration of God, but very few really reverence

---

21. Rom 6:1ff.
22. Cf. Gal 5:6; Jas 2:14; and Eph 2:10f.
23. Calvin, *Institutes*, I:II:1.

him; and wherever there is great ostentation in ceremonies, sincerity of heart is rare indeed.[24]

So, in my pastoral ministry I do not stress "ostentation in ceremonies" but instead stress to my congregation that a sacramental transformation must take place within us if this sacrament is to become "real" in our world in any meaningful sense. I tell them that only as the love of Christ that we hallow in this meal becomes "real" in us can it become "real" in our world. In words attributed to St. Aquinas: "See what you are. Be what you see."

Otherwise Christ's continued presence with us and our union with Him is reduced to some kind of metaphysical magic. Christ's continued presence with the Church encompasses more than just a sacramental transaction that occurs from time to time in Eucharistic worship. It includes the continued incarnation of His love that is empowered by that very worship and offered to the world by His priestly people. The central identity of the people of God is as a thankful people, a people whose central mission is to proclaim good news and to embody in deeds of love what we otherwise celebrate in Eucharist.

The sacrificial love we hallow and remember in Eucharist celebration is the very same sacrificial love we preach to the world and that we are called upon to incarnate in the world. And so by gospel necessity, the Christian faith we celebrate and preach must issue in Christian mission or it is reduced to a faith without works and thus proves to be of no value whatsoever.[25]

A Union That Defies Understanding: Union with Christ

These otherwise uncontroversial gospel observations can be linked up with Calvin's teaching on our mystical union with Christ, as well as with the Eastern Orthodox's teaching on deification. Calvin was emphatic that our union with Christ is a spiritual union, but by "*spiritual union*" Calvin has in mind not only the mystery of our mystical union with Christ but also our communion in love, a union of our will with God's will.

> The Lord's Supper, as Calvin presents it, is thus the occasion of a twofold self-offering: in it Christ gives his crucified body to his people, and they in turn present their bodies as a living sacrifice to God, which is their spiritual worship. But, of course, neither self-giving—Christ's or his people's—takes place only in the Sacrament . . . The spiritual gift of the holy banquet moves

---

24. Ibid., I:II:2.
25. Jas 2:17.

the communicants, on their side, both to gratitude and to love: indeed, obedience to the commandment of love is thanksgiving, which for Calvin is not only a liturgical but also an ethical concept. Hence in 1539 he actually added to his first thoughts on the sacrifice of praise the assertion that it includes all the duties of love—duties by which, in embracing our brothers and sisters, we honor the Lord himself in his members.[26]

The gist of Calvin's teaching on Eucharist is that it effects "a wonderful exchange" and a spiritual union with Christ that has both an ontological as well as a moral dimension, both a forensic and an ethical application. For Calvin, Eucharistic gratitude is the pinnacle and realization of all human life. And speaking specifically of our union with Christ as the special fruit of the Lord's Supper, Calvin states,

> This is the wonderful exchange which, out of his measureless benevolence, he has made with us; that, becoming Son of man with us, he has made us sons of God with him; that, by descent to earth, he has prepared an ascent to heaven for us; that, by taking on our mortality, he has conferred his immortality upon us; that, accepting our weakness, he has strengthened us by his power; that, receiving our poverty unto himself, he has transferred his wealth to us; that, taking the weight of our iniquity upon himself (which oppressed us), he has clothed us with his righteousness.[27]

And in his language of "a wonderful exchange" Calvin is clearly echoing the language of Irenaeus, which means that he is joining up his discussion of "the special fruit" of the Lord's Supper with what has been said historically about deification in the Eastern tradition, i.e., "God became what we are so that we might become what God is."[28]

The terms of this analogy—spiritual union versus deification—are not exact equivalents, of course, but they are in the same zip code.[29] In my

---

26. See Gerrish, *Grace and Gratitude*, 126–27. See also Calvin's *Institutes*, IV:XVIII:16.

27. Calvin, *Institutes*, IV:XVII:2.

28. For similar arguments on behalf of the missional meaning of Eucharist see Purves, "The Mission of the Church," 57–70. See also Scandrett, "Reclaiming Eucharistic Piety," 155–69.

29. The Eastern Orthodox tradition speaks of our deification by means of our sharing in God's nature, i.e., God's uncreated energies/attributes. But beginning with Augustine and his version of divine simplicity, i.e., "God is what God has," this distinction is lost in the West. So, there are indeed critical differences to be noted between Orthodox and Roman Catholic/Protestant views of sanctification/glorification/deification.

opinion, both are trying to express something of crucial importance about the transformative power of Christ's presence in our life. And both involve a mystical union with Christ celebrated in sacramental worship, a mystical union that is intended to transform our whole character.

As to just how exactly such a mystical union adheres to the elements of wheat bread and grape wine I am content with Calvin to simply say "I have no idea!"

> Now, if anyone should ask me how this takes place, I shall not be ashamed to confess that it is a secret too lofty for either my mind to comprehend or my words to declare. And, to speak more plainly, I rather experience than understand it. Therefore I here embrace without controversy the truth of God in which I may safely rest. He declares his flesh the food of my soul, his blood its drink [John 6:53ff.]. I offer my soul to him to be fed with such food. In his Sacred Supper he bids me take, eat, and drink his body and blood under the symbols of bread and wine. I do not doubt that he himself truly presents them, and that I receive them.[30]

So there is a theological humility and an apophatic silence to be observed here. We need not worry about having a handy explanation for "how" the phrases "This is my body . . . this is my blood" make metaphysical sense when applied to the sacramental elements. It is enough to speak in the generalities of "a wondrous exchange," "deification," and/or "a mystical union." I argue that we should sit loose on the specifics of what is meant by these phrases just as the Christian Church did for centuries.

But we cannot sit loose on the moral and spiritual application of this truth to our life. The New Testament is emphatic that "the will of God is that you should be holy" and "Everyone who takes the Lord's name upon his lips must forsake wickedness."[31] There is an intrinsic relationship between our union with God and our union with God's selfless love in Jesus Christ. And so those who would walk in the light of God's truth must live in love. "Here is the test by which we can make sure that we are in Him: whoever claims to be dwelling in Him, binds himself to live as Christ Himself lived."[32]

In keeping with the New Testament's emphasis on this intrinsic connection all branches of the historic Church, Orthodox, Roman Catholic, and the Protestant Reformers, et al. universally agree that the gospel that

---

30. Calvin, *Institutes*, IV:XVII:32.
31. 1 Thess 4:3 and 2 Tim 2:19.
32. 1 John 2:6.

offers us eternal life must begin its eternal work of transformation and restoration in this life.

So, call it what you will and describe it theologically as you please, in Eucharist we are both celebrating and receiving again and again the grace of God in all its fullness. And we must not receive this grace in vain.[33] For if Eucharist does not engender in its celebrants a whole new way of life, then it truly has become an empty and barren sign.[34]

Only when Christians go forth in love to fulfill their calling as Christians, only then does their love become a "real" expression of and a "true" witness to what they have celebrated in Eucharistic worship, namely, "God is love. Jesus Christ is Lord." Hence, the reality of Eucharistic worship depends upon the moral transformation of the recipients as much if not more than the metaphysical transformation of the elements.

And the fact that Christian love is drawn from Eucharistic worship is precisely what makes Christian love Christian.

> What makes it Christian is not its "matter" but the "form" which is given it by love understood as a response to God's love, which came first (1 Cor 13). The liturgy is the place where this priority of the love of God freely bestowed is attested (see the gesture of Eucharistic communion). In the measure in which the ethical life of service to others is lived as a response to this primary gift, and therefore takes its source in the sacraments, in that same measure it finds its Christian identity.[35]

So, our spiritual *"union with Christ"* by faith that allows us to participate in Christ's body and blood mystically, a union in, Calvin's words, that is

---

33. 1 Cor 15:1–2; Gal 4:8–11.

34. My argument seeks to restore a faithful Eucharistic piety that ensures that the sacramental worship of the Church is fruitful and not barren. To that degree my emphasis falls on the "well being" of the Eucharist more than the "being" of the Eucharist, more on the horizontal than on the vertical. But I am also arguing that these are inseparable. What I am after is a restoration of balance in our Eucharistic piety. For instance, Louis-Marie Chauvet adds his lament that St. Thomas Aquinas' sacramental discourse was imbalanced and too one-sided: "Thomas was not ignorant of this twofold circuit. He had even sketched the place the sacraments could have in the 'moral' part of his Summa, and more precisely in the framework of his analysis of the 'virtue of religion.' In this latter case, the sacraments . . . would have been considered the summit of the Christians' ethical life, the revelatory expression of their daily life inasmuch as it is lived in the theological virtues of faith and charity. Unfortunately, Thomas did not develop this perspective for itself. This is regrettable because it would have helped to balance his sacramental discourse, too strongly centered on the objective efficacy of the sacraments as 'source' of salvation" (Chauvet, *The Sacraments*, xvii).

35. Chauvet, *The Sacraments*, 41–42.

"a secret too lofty for either my mind to comprehend or my words to declare" is only fulfilled morally when we perform, in Calvin's words, "all the duties of love" to which it testifies. And only in this way can we then grow as God's children in conformity to God's nature, to which we presumably have been united. Thus, only a sacramental worship that includes *both* will experience "the special fruit" of the Lord's Supper, namely that "wonderful exchange" in which the love which is God's by nature becomes ours by grace.

Our mystical union with Christ, a union that defies understanding, nonetheless clearly and inescapably involves an ethical dimension, a moral and missional application to the whole of our life and to the whole of our world. And it goes without saying at this point that in my opinion the efficaciousness of the Eucharist primarily swings, not on the metaphysical transformation of the elements but on the ethical transformation of the participants.

The breadth and scope of the relevance of this truth is staggering.[36] To a world debased by the metaphysical reductionism of scientific materialism, where "matter is all that matters," where reality is merely "matter in motion," and where human beings are reduced to "moist robots," the Eucharist proclaims that we do not live by bread alone, that life is more than biology, more than the food we eat and the clothes we wear, that human life is a sacred gift of God for which the only appropriate response is "Eucharist."

To a world demystified by the epistemological reductionism of modern rationalism the Eucharist proclaims that at the heart of life is a celebration of mystery, the mystery of God's continued presence in sacrificial love for the world, a mystery that defies rational explanation because its meaning resides in selfless love and not rational calculation.

To a world demoralized by the ethnic tribalism and political polarizations of modern nationalism the Eucharist proclaims the world's true oneness in a feast that celebrates Christ's kingdom, a feast to which all the peoples of the world, north, south, east and west are to be invited and welcomed.

And to a world deluded by its own hubris and self-inflated sense of power and manifest destiny the Eucharist sets forth the Church of Jesus Christ as the true community of the end times, a community made up primarily by the weak and not the strong of this world, the foolish and not the wise of this world, the nothings and not the supposed "somethings" of this world. A community that is to serve as a real, albeit it the proleptic and

---

36. I'm drawing out these observations from something Peter J. Leithart has written on his blog.

provisional, demonstration of the coming kingdom of God, central to that calling and identity stands the Eucharist.

Bibliography

Augustine. *Of Baptism*. Translated by J. R. King and revised by Chester D. Hartranft. Nicene and Post-Nicene Fathers, First Series 4. Edited by Philip Schaff. Buffalo: Christian Literature, 1887.

Calvin, John. *Institutes of the Christian Religion*. Edited by John T. McNeill. Translated by Ford Lewis Battles. 2 vols. Philadelphia: Westminster, 1960.

Chauvet, Louis-Marie. *The Sacraments: The Word of God at the Mercy of the Body*. Collegeville, MN: Liturgical, 2001.

Gerrish, Brian. *Grace and Gratitude: The Eucharistic Theology of John Calvin*. Minneapolis: Fortress, 1993.

Invitation to Christ: Font and Table. Louisville: Office of Theology and Worship, 2006.

Milavec, Aaron. *The Didache: Text, Translation, Analysis, and Commentary*. Collegeville, MN: Liturgical, 2003.

Purves, Andrew. "The Mission of the Church through the Celebration of the Sacraments." In *A Passion for the Gospel: Confessing Jesus Christ for the 21st Century*, edited by Mark Achtemeier and Andrew Purves, 57–70. Louisville: Geneva, 2000.

Scandrett, Joel. "Reclaiming Eucharistic Piety: A Postmodern Possibility for American Evangelicals?" In *Ancient and Postmodern Christianity: Paleo-Orthodoxy in the 21st Century; Essays in Honor of Thomas C. Oden*, edited by Kenneth Tanner and Christopher A. Hall, 155–69. Downers Grove, IL: InterVarsity, 2008.

11

Missional Eucharist

MARNEY WASSERMAN

When we enter the sanctuary and see a loaf of bread on the Lord's table, it's a reminder that we've been invited to a meal, a meal with Jesus and his friends. And it should invite us to wonder: who's *hungry* here? and for what? what am I hungry for? and who else needs to be fed? We all *do* get hungry for the *gift* of this meal we call the Lord's Supper, for the *grace* we receive in it, for the spiritual nourishment it provides. In a demanding, fast-paced, superficial, soul-draining world, we need that time with our risen Friend, when *we* are fed, when *we* can get centered and draw close to Christ. That's partly a legacy from the sixteenth-century Reformers, of course: communion is a gift of grace, they insisted, not a good work to perform, not a sacrifice we are required to offer. And we have learned that lesson well.

In fact, maybe we've learned it too well, since sometimes we miss the *call to discipleship* that is also integral to this feast. We come to the table so needy, so hungry, so focused on the gifts Christ has to give us, that we can lose sight of the life of the world into which the Lord's Supper *sends* us. We can neglect the kingdom work *for* which it nourishes us. We can ignore the servant lifestyle in which it aims to *form* us. We can forget what the church, including Calvin, has always known: that the Lord's Supper, like baptism and the Word of God proclaimed, contains *both a gift, and a call*. From the Lord's table, we are always being sent to feed others—spiritually, physically, communally—as we ourselves are fed. It would be hard to get much more missional, more turned towards the world, than that! So how is it that in our eucharistic practice, it's the missional link we most often miss?

Twenty years ago when our youngest was an infant, I took three years off from pastoral ministry and joined the ranks of the worshipers at a nearby Presbyterian church. It was a wonderfully alive, active congregation, with a gifted pastor. But this pastor had one sacramental practice that I came to see as emblematic of our overly self-absorbed approach to the Lord's table. On every communion Sunday, he repeated the words of institution not just once, or even twice, but three times—first in the Invitation to the Table, second as he broke the bread, and finally again at the serving of the elements. *On the night before he died, the Lord Jesus took bread . . . This is my body given for you . . . Do this, remembering me.* Three times over. That communion service never failed to give me the feeling of being so totally trapped in the past, that the present was entirely out of reach, barely even perceivable. The present moment, the present company of worshipers, the meal we were eating right then and there, the present presence of God in our lives, all got ignored in favor of that past moment on the eve of his death when Jesus sat at table in the upper room with his disciples. The Lord's Supper in that church often felt like nothing more than a memorial of the last supper.

Now that last statement, as you might guess, has proved to be a provocative one in congregations I have served. *What's wrong with that?* I've often been asked. *Isn't that what the Lord's Supper is supposed to be? The words of institution help us remember Christ's suffering and sacrifice. We can't have communion without recalling the last supper, can we?* Of course not. But remembering is not the only thing we are invited to do at the Lord's table. In fact, remembering is not even the primary thing we are invited to do here. We are invited first and foremost to eat and drink together, to love and serve one another, to "do this"—this meal, this life and love—as Jesus commanded. The Lord's Supper is *a meal*. It happens in the present tense, with real bread to eat and sweet wine to drink. The fare is simpler and the conversation more formal than at some other meals we eat, but the sacrament is still a meal, with good food and each other's company to enjoy, along with the joyful companionship of the risen Christ. Shall we remember the last supper at the Lord's table? By all means. We couldn't celebrate the sacrament without remembering. But we can't stop there, or we get stuck in the past and do not make the vital connections to the present and future that the meal itself invites us to make.

The Lord's Supper and the last supper are related, of course, but they are not the same meal. The last supper took place before Christ's death; the Lord's Supper happens only and always after his resurrection. The last supper was held just once; it is the Lord's Supper the church has been celebrating ever since. The last supper is remembered at the Lord's Supper, but so are dozens of other biblical meals—like the post-resurrection meals in

Jerusalem and Emmaus and by the Sea of Galilee, like the ancient manna provided for Israel in the wilderness, like the sumptuous wedding feast with the Lamb at the end of time, to name just a few.

In fact, some of these other stories help us remember that the Lord's Supper is a glad occasion as well as a sobering one, a moment for holy joy, because we feast together, in *our* time and place, with our risen Lord. The Lord's Supper is, as the liturgy keeps trying to tell us, "the joyful feast of the people of God!" When, in our well-intentioned piety, we are too quick to explain away the elemental satisfactions of hearty bread and good wine, of keeping company with one another and with our risen Friend, as if these were *only* signposts pointing back in time to the broken body and spilled blood of the Savior—then we trade in the rich fullness of the Lord's Supper for a mere reenactment of the last supper. We confuse the once-crucified body of Jesus of Nazareth with the body of Christ risen to life in his church. We miss the food God is giving us *now*, good solid spiritual food, and the things that God is doing *here* with bread and wine, among *us*. And in all likelihood, with our eyes on the crucified Savior, we miss the risen Lord. Then, when the meal is over and we get up from the table to go, we are just as likely to miss the hungry world that is waiting beyond the church doors, overburdened with present need for help here and love now.

This is where the sacrament becomes missional, turned towards the world, bent on sending us to do God's work in that world, forming us lovingly in the practices we will need to do it. It's like the old custom of family suppertime around the kitchen table, where we received the day's nourishment. In part, it was the nourishment of food, but also the nourishment of companionship, of belonging, along with lifelong lessons in table manners, values, family traditions. The supper table is where most of us learn as children, not only how to eat, but how to behave: how to share, how to serve, how to express gratitude, how to make room for others, how to clean up after ourselves. Even when the family's meals together are infrequent, they're still the best place there is to learn the stories and practices that define what it means to belong to the family. Just so at the Lord's table, we are fed on bread and wine, on one another's company, and on the shared practices of receiving, giving, thanking, sharing, and serving. These are table practices meant to equip us not just for participating in the sacrament, but for living in the world: receiving, giving, thanking, sharing, serving.

In fact, the Lord's table is intimately related not only to a wide array of biblical meals but also to all the other meal tables we sit around in *our* lives. There are the family tables, where we've enjoyed ordinary meals and holiday feasts, hosted friends and fed occasional strangers, and there are wider gatherings with others around picnic tables, potluck tables, banquet tables, soup kitchen tables, the tables of the poor. After all, Jesus didn't get a reputation for being "a glutton and a drunk" for nothing—he was always sitting down to eat with people. In fact, that's how they knew he really was risen, wasn't it? He ate with them; they recognized him. . . breaking the bread. The table manners we practice at the Lord's table—receiving, giving, thanking, sharing, serving—shape how we relate to all those who eat with us around other tables, and even more broadly, all those who share this life with us.

If we have a hard time getting the Lord's Supper out of the past and into the present, we have an even harder time imagining ourselves into the future tense. But that's part of it too, a foretaste of the messianic banquet, at the end of time. If the last supper invites us to remember the past, if the Lord's Supper invites us to eat and drink together in the present, to learn the practices of servanthood and joyful living—then the kingdom meal pushes us towards the future. Here the missional connections become inescapable as we taste the bread and drink the wine of yet another banquet where all wrongs will be made right, all tears wiped away, all comers fed. We can hardly take our place at this table, without seeing that what we are offered in bread and wine is not only a gracious *gift*, but a bold, outrageous and persistent *call* to join the company of God's people who are doing God's work in the world towards this great tomorrow—the work of evangelism and justice, saving and setting free, prayer and reconciliation and mercy. Anticipating this great banquet helps us learn the core gospel stance of hope: learn to speak the language of hope, rather than words of defeat, put-down or sarcasm; learn to do hope in the ways we live, rather than succumb to fear or apathy, or too easy accommodation.

A re-membrance, a meal, and God's mañana: these are the three tenses of the Lord's Supper. And we need all three of them, because the Lord's Supper is both a gift we are given and a call we may answer with our lives. If we stay stuck in the past, focused only on the last supper, we miss the call to discipleship and missional living that the Lord's Supper, the church's glad meal with its risen Savior, so compellingly extends.

We Presbyterians claim our identity as a church of Word and Sacrament. What's probably closer to the truth is that we are a church of Word and sometimes Sacrament. We forget that we need water in the font, not just to baptize, but to remind us week by week of our baptismal identity and calling. We forget that we need regularly to eat and drink the Word of God, as well as to hear it—Sunday by Sunday to take it into our bodies and our lives, to do the Word with our hands and our actions and interactions. These sacramental signs are equal, we profess, to the sacred Book that we always read, to the Word of God that we hear from its pages and from the mouths of preachers. But too often on a Sunday, the table is bare, or cluttered with things that are not bread. Too often the font is covered, and there is no water in sight.

We tell ourselves that weekly communion is too much: that the Lord's Supper will become dull and ordinary, lose its "specialness" with too frequent repetition. But I suspect it is a different reason altogether that keeps us from coming to the Table more often. I suspect it's because the Lord's Supper pushes us too clearly out into a hungry and thirsty world to live our discipleship, to wear our faith on our shirtsleeves, to reorder our entire lives around the claims of the gospel. We're not so sure we really *want* to be sent out filled every week, to feed others with all that we have and are. We don't want to consider how we may need to be broken for the sake of a broken world. We resist coming empty-handed before God every Sunday asking for bread, and learning all over again to trust the sufficiency of the gifts we're given. We're not eager to practice serving one another, because we know full well that's on-the-job training for a servant life.

Is that possible, that we don't *want* to come to the Lord's table week in and week out, precisely because the sacrament's missional call to be about God's work in the world is so strong and clear we wouldn't be able to avoid it?! If it is, then that's precisely the reason we *need* to come to the Lord's table, way more often than we do. Movement towards weekly eucharist is the most important step we can take towards celebrating the Lord's Supper as a missional meal that makes a difference in the present tense. Rediscovering the joy of this feast with our risen Savior is another key.

One additional practice is commended by Dr. David Gambrell of the Presbyterian Church (USA) Office of Theology, Worship and Education. We can separate the *action* of breaking the bread from the *speaking* of the Words of Institution—so that instead of appearing to mimic Jesus at the last supper, the presider breaks open the loaf with alternate words that locate the meaning of the meal we are sharing in the here and now. *Jesus Christ, the bread of life for the life of the world. Jesus Christ, the vine in whom we abide as branches. Jesus said: Come to me and never be hungry, trust in me and thirst no more.* This pattern, I believe, could help us "see" more clearly the gift of the present moment, present context, present company, risen and present Lord, just at the point when we are ready to eat and drink together. At the same time, this leaves Jesus' Words of Institution to be spoken earlier, and most appropriately, as part of the remembrances included in the prayer at the Lord's Table. The Great Thanksgiving faithfully recalls all God's mighty acts from creation to redemption, culminating in Christ's sacrifice on the cross and resurrection to new life, and for these gifts offers grateful praise. What better place than here, as the crowning remembrance of this sacred story, to speak the words of Jesus instituting the feast that invites us into his resurrection from death? In a eucharistic practice often overly focused on the past, maybe even this small change can provide a bridge to the sacramental present in which we eat and drink and live together.

A remembrance, a meal and God's manna. The Lord's Supper pulls both past act and future hope into the present moment, and invites us there to meet our risen Lord over bread and wine, and to be changed again and again by his powerful life and love. The meal he gave us to celebrate is missional to its core: it nourishes us in the depths of our being. . . *so that* it can send us out with bread for the hungry, with hope for the broken, with love for the world, with the good news of the risen Christ for all.

12

The Space Between Acts 2 and Acts 10
An Ecclesiology of Text, Time, and the Holy Spirit

FRANK YAMADA

> JAKE: Oh yeah? Well me and the Lord. We got an understanding.
> ELWOOD: We're on a mission from God.
> —*The Blues Brothers*

Of Conversions and Interruptions

The quote above comes from an iconic Chicago-based movie, *The Blues Brothers*, starring Dan Ackroyd and John Belushi. Jake and Elwood are bearing witness to a calling that they received after their journey through the penitentiary system lands them at Triple Rock Baptist Church, the Reverend Cleophus James presiding (played by James Brown). The brothers face a crisis. The orphanage where they grew up will close if they can't come up with $5000. So they seek to get "churched up" and cleaned up. During the gospel frenzy that ensues, a literal light from heaven emerges from the clouds. They receive the revelation that will guide them on their calling—a calling that is summed up in two words: "THE BAND." They must get the band back together. God interrupts. Their calling and mission becomes clear. Their lives and the clubs of Chicago are never quite the same.

As a Presbyterian, I understand that this type of scene would never have happened at First Presbyterian Church of the Midwest. The hand clapping, dancing, shouting, and improvisation, which characterizes Triple Rock Baptist would be inconsistent with what most would deem good Reformed worship. There was also obviously no committee planning for this service, not even a bulletin. While we try to make room for the sometimes disruptive movement of the Holy Spirit in our worship, my guess is that most PC(USA) churches would have deemed this expression of worship to be not decently executed and not in good order. Our tradition, for better or worse errs toward planned process rather than disruption, well-wrought scripts rather than improvisation. Our theology suffers from the same tendencies.

My biblical reflections on ecclesiology focus on interruptions, more precisely on the interplay between continuity and discontinuity in the narrative and life of the church—on the recovering of tradition, which is held together at the same time with disruptions from the Holy Spirit. I will argue that in our current crisis, we have privileged continuity in our current understandings of the church and have failed to embrace the confrontational and often disruptive moments that may actually open us up to the *missio Dei*. Such confrontations are not mere digressions or differences of opinion regarding tradition. I would argue that these holy interruptions both challenge us to think radically different thoughts about the nature and makeup of the church, i.e., who is in and who is out, and enliven mission in the process.

Before I unpack the biblical texts under discussion, some background will prove useful. I am no theologian, nor a theologian's son. I, like many Gen-Xers, did not grow up in a Christian church. I did not have a pedigree that would lead me naturally to be Presbyterian in general to say nothing about becoming a PC(USA) teaching elder, biblical scholar, and seminary president.

As a *Sansei*, a third-generation Japanese American, growing up in Southern California in the 1970s and 1980s, I was an even less likely candidate to be part of mainline Protestantism. I was barely religious. The only "church" I attended was the Buddhist church.[1] I would describe my family as "twice-a-year" Buddhists, which meant that we went to temple when someone died or when someone was getting married. The Buddhist church, in ways very similar to Christian churches in Asian American communities,

---

1. The phrase "Buddhist church" represents an Americanization of the practice of Buddhism among East-Asian groups. In the Japanese American community, this change of name came about shortly after World War II and the internment of over 120,000 Japanese and Japanese Americans, mostly on the West Coast. The effects of war galvanized this process of Americanization among Japanese American Buddhists.

functioned as a way to gather Japanese American families in order to rehearse and maintain idealized cultural values from the homeland. However, for my particular family, religion played a minimal role.

Religious awakening, when it happens—and it happened for millions of people living in Southern California during the last third of the twentieth century—usually embraces a narrative of abrupt divine intervention into one's lifestyle, a holy discontinuity, a conversion. It is not necessarily good Reformed theology to use this terminology. However, I converted or was converted to Christianity when I was nineteen. My first heightened religious experience was certainly disruptive. Ask my family, and they will tell you as much. I won't go into detail, but my conversion included a tract with the question, "Are you going to heaven?" on it, two young, whacked-out-for-Jesus Christian men, and my eventual refusal months later of a "ritual of spiritual circumcision." I'm not kidding.

My journey within Christian communities includes:

- Being recruited into high school ministry at a charismatic megachurch of about 10,000 members in Southern California only three months after my conversion
- Being on the leadership team of a church plant just up the street from the aforementioned megachurch, which emphasized teaching and discipleship
- Getting my undergraduate degree in religion and Bible from an Assemblies of God liberal arts college, where I studied with both a reader-response critic and a fundamentalist Old Testament professor, who still believed in Mosaic authorship
- Going to a prestigious PC(USA) seminary in order to be better prepared for full-time ministry
- Joining a Presbyterian congregation while attending Princeton, where I first joined a PC(USA) congregation; and
- Serving as a high school, English-ministries pastor at a Korean immigrant church with about twenty-five first-generation members and a youth group of about half that size.

For the past fourteen years of my ministry, I have had the privilege of working in theological education as a professor in Hebrew Bible/Old Testament, a director for an Asian American ministries center, and now a senior administrator of a PCUSA seminary, which was founded in 1829.

I am starting my paper on this contextual, even personal note, for at least two reasons First, I believe that all of theology and biblical interpretation, and, therefore, by consequence all ecclesiologies, are necessarily situational and culturally contextual. My thoughts on an ecclesiology, grounded in Scripture and open to the movement of the Holy Spirit, emerge from my various experiences as an Asian American, as a West Coast Asian American, as a former evangelical charismatic and current mainline progressive Christian, who is facing into the changes and challenges that confront the church and theological education in the twenty-first century. This practice of identifying my own social location is part of our educational model at a cross-cultural, urban, and ecumenical seminary like McCormick.[2] Part of the problem in both the church and academy is that we tend to universalize our own experiences, social location, and theology, while imposing these perspectives on other peoples. Foregrounding our own social and theological situated-ness helps us remember that we see from a particular place in society, time, and history, from a particular cultural location. As well, if we read the Acts 2 passage carefully, we can see the Holy Spirit's disruption has everything to do with truth expressed in radical cultural particularity (cf. Acts 2:8–11).

My second reason for this contextualizing exercise lies in the very different expressions of congregation represented in my faith journey, which call into question for me oppositions that exist in our current public discourse about Christianity, the PC(USA), and religion in general. The differences between conservative/liberal, mainline/evangelical, Christian/Buddhist, Christian/non-Christian become more difficult to navigate cleanly when one thinks of the many intersecting complexities of twenty-first-century North American religious experience. I would guess that my experience is not unique. We all come from a variety of complex and even contradictory traditions; and yet we continue to speak of the church's future as if it is singular, that our denomination's destiny is one with the future of God's mission.

Thus, I am arguing that an ecclesiology of disruption and particularity may be instructive for this century characterized by both unprecedented change and diversity.[3] One might guess that I am not a fan of polarizing binaries. In one of my first essays articulating a later-generational Asian American approach to biblical interpretation, I argued that cultural binaries, which characterize much of Christian theology and biblical interpretation,

---

2. The practice of identifying one's own social location in interpretation was a requirement for contributors in the cross-cultural study Bible edited by DeYoung et al., *The Peoples' Bible*. For a description of the context, theology, and pedagogy of McCormick Seminary, see Esterline and Kalu, *Shaping Beloved Community*.

3. I address more specifically the implication of twenty-first-century diversity on theological education and the church in my inaugural address, "The View from 2040."

including immigrant Asian American theology, represent meaningful categories of experience for these groups, and have found particular traction among early generation Asian American theologians and communities. Therefore, notions such as marginality and liminality, which require the maintenance of binaries such as center/margin, dominant culture/minority culture, have been prominent in early-generation Asian and Asian American theologies.[4] These themes have helped to give voice to the theological witness of communities that have been marginalized from dominant American culture. These themes were also a dominant way of thinking in modernity.

I argue, however, that such categories assume a certain amount of stability in the assumed cultural categories—East vs. West, Asian vs. American—that when pressed often do not hold up to scrutiny. For later generations of Asian Americans, notions such as hybridity or heterogeneity provide a better way of understanding both the identities of Asians living in the North American context and the theologies that emerge from these communities. In fact, the high degree of interracial intermarriage among later generation Asian Americans suggests that hybridity is represented in the very bodies of fourth, fifth, and sixth generation Asian Americans. The notion of hybridity, made prominent by theorists such as Homi Bhabha, refuses oversimplified dichotomies of God/human, colonizer/colonized, black/white, male/female, or Asian/American, preferring to speak of the complicated and often conflicted space "in-between," what Bhabha has called the Third Space, where identity and meaning are constructed and negotiated in often messy ways. The Chinese concept of yin-yang provides a useful metaphor for understanding the non-binary nature of hybridity. Contrary forces, for example light and dark, are viewed not simply as oppositional or polarized. They are interdependent, each containing a part of the other, and the whole relying on the interaction and mutuality of the constituent parts.

For our current topic, I would argue that our present ecclesiologies, at least as they are expressed on the ground, rely too heavily on a narrative of the church that seeks unity over diversity, continuity over discontinuity, purity over hybridity. While this impulse is understandable, it also makes us inattentive to the ways that God interrupts our particular narrative or tradition, a symptom that causes us to retreat into overly romanticized projections of the "church as we see it," whether those projections are from an idealized past or a hoped-for future. I would argue that taking seriously

---

4. For examples of Asian American theology that use the categories of marginality or liminality, see Lee, *Marginality*, and S. H. Lee, *From a Liminal Place*. For an exploration of hybridity and Christology, see Joh, *The Heart of the Cross*.

the conflicted and yet interdependent nature of church and its constituent parts requires us to pay just as much attention to the disruptions in the church's story as much as the dominant plot lines that have shaped Christian identity through the centuries. Hybridizing contradictions are nothing new for Christian theology. These themes help us to make sense of a Christology that thinks of life emerging from death and a community of saints, who are also always sinners. The way of Christ would not have these separated. For ecclesiology, hybridity would recommend that notions and dynamics that punctuate our current discussion in the PC(USA) regarding the future of the church—church/world, life/death, conservative/liberal, contemporary/traditional, past/future, hope/fear—are inseparable and intimately connected to our common destiny. The fullness of our humanity will only reach its completion and full maturity in Christ and, therefore, we should refuse the temptation to read our own narrative as the metanarrative for the whole church.

This framework of hybridity and heterogeneity, which emerges from my social location as a later-generation Asian American Christian, punctuates my interpretation of the biblical texts, including my reading of the book of Acts and the role of the Holy Spirit. It is to this interpretation that I now turn.

Continuity and Discontinuity in the Book of Acts

The book of Acts, which most scholars read as a narrative unity with the Gospel of Luke, recounts the continuation of the work of the risen Jesus as it is carried out through the apostles.[5] This unity, however, is punctuated with two contradicting theses. First, the author seeks to answer the question, "Did God keep God's promises to Israel given the people of God's rejection of Jesus?" To this question, the author responds affirmatively. Thus, the book of Acts seeks to build a continuous tradition from Israel to the first Christians, from the prophets to the apostles and disciples. Like the prophets of Israel, the Spirit of the Lord falls upon the followers of Jesus, enabling ecstatic speech acts that proclaim the divine intention to the people. In a similar way, the apostles, like Jesus before them, perform mighty works of God—healings, the casting out of demons, and raising the dead—in the same way that the prophets did. Thus, the early Christians, as depicted in the book of Acts, show the efficacy of God's word in both speech and sign, word and deed. The author of the book of Acts makes a compelling case that the early church is a continuation of God's promises made to Israel,

---

5. See Johnson, "Luke-Acts," 403–19, and Tannehill, *The Narrative Unity*.

and in this way, demonstrates God's *hesed*, covenantal faithfulness, to a new generation.[6]

The second thesis, however, represents a departure from tradition, at least as it was received in most segments of early Judaism, including among the first Christians. Following the theology of certain traditions like those found in Deut 7, interactions with the nations (*ethnoi*) or Gentiles was forbidden and represented a threat of impurity to the people of God:

> When the Lord your God brings you into the land that you are about to enter and occupy, and he clears away many nations before you—the Hittites, the Girgashites, the Amorites, the Canaanites, the Perizzites, the Hivites, and the Jebusites, seven nations mightier and more numerous than you—and when the Lord your God gives them over to you and you defeat them, then you must utterly destroy them. Make no covenant with them and show them no mercy. Do not intermarry with them, giving your daughters to their sons or taking their daughters for your sons, for that would turn away your children from following me, to serve other gods. Then the anger of the Lord would be kindled against you, and he would destroy you quickly. But this is how you must deal with them: break down their altars, smash their pillars, hew down their sacred poles, and burn their idols with fire. For you are a people holy to the Lord your God; the Lord your God has chosen you out of all the peoples on earth to be his people, his treasured possession. (Deut 7:1–6)[7]

The book of Acts, however, makes the incongruous case that the mission of God extends to the Gentiles, to the nations. While one could certainly argue that this theme is present within Israel's scriptures (e.g., Abram's being a blessing to the nations in Gen 12:3 or the Lord's Abrahamic-like promises to Hagar in Gen 16:10), the author of Acts clearly characterizes Peter's vision sequence in chapter 10 as being discontinuous with tradition. Peter's vision conflates the inclusion of the Gentiles, which occurs later in the chapter, with prohibitions in Jewish dietary law, an issue of no small consequence as the later council of Jerusalem makes clear (Acts 15).

In short, the author of Acts holds together two seemingly incongruent theses: 1) the Holy Spirit falling on the apostles/disciples at Pentecost connects the early Christians to the legacy of Israel's prophets, showing God to be faithful to God's promises to Israel through the church's witness to

---

6. For a good treatment of *hesed*, which she translates as covenantal loyalty, see Sakenfeld, *The Meaning of* Hesed.

7. All biblical quotations are from the New Revised Standard Version.

the risen Christ; and 2) the Holy Spirit falling on the Gentiles opens up the faithful community to those who are, by definition, outside of Israel. Thus, the narrative underlying this author's ecclesiology is simultaneously congruent and incongruent with Israel's salvation history. The Holy Spirit both animates the continuity of God's mission from the prophets through the apostles at Pentecost while disrupting the same received tradition by falling on the Gentiles, those believed to be "unclean" or "profane."

There is another theme, which scholars identify in the book of Acts, namely, that the word of the Lord will accomplish its purpose. Isaiah 55:11 reads, ". . . so shall my word be that goes out from my mouth; it shall not return to me empty, but it shall accomplish that which I purpose, and succeed in the thing for which I sent it." Put another way, the gospel cannot be stopped. Neither resistance, persecution, conflict from within or from without can prevent the apostles from witnessing to the risen Jesus. In fact, as I will argue below, not even the church itself or its lead apostle can get in the way. In order to more fully unpack the spaces in-between Acts 2 and Acts 10, I will briefly explore the function of the Holy Spirit and its effects on the mission of God within these two narratives that hold together the author's incongruous continuity.

Acts 2 and Continuity

Acts 2 recounts the Holy Spirit falling on the disciples in Jerusalem. The author utilizes tropes that are familiar to the Israelite ear, drawing from the Deuteronomistic prophetic traditions. This history recounted from Joshua to 2 Kings uses a prophecy/fulfillment formula. In this way, the faithfulness of the Lord is enacted in history as the word of the Lord comes to pass just as the prophets had spoken. Jesus instructs his disciples in Acts 1: "But you will receive power when the Holy Spirit has come upon you; and you will be my witnesses in Jerusalem, in all Judea and Samaria, and to the ends of the earth" (1:8). The Deuteronomistic traditions also privilege the prophetic speech act. These speeches provide the critical moments of decision that carry the plot forward in God's salvation history. Jesus like the prophets of old instructs his disciples about how God will carry forward the prophetic tradition through them. They will be God's witnesses first in Jerusalem and then will move outward into greater areas of influence to the surrounding regions to the ends of the earth. The author of Acts uses this prophetic speech formula to demonstrate the continuity of the early church to the legacy of the prophets of Israel. In fact, the deliberation of the disciples that results in the selecting of Mathias as the twelfth apostle makes the more general connection of continuity to Israel itself, each apostle representing the twelve tribes.

Jesus' prophetic speech reaches fulfillment in Acts 2, when the *ruach 'elohim* blows through house, filling the disciples with the Holy Spirit. Note that the author evokes language reminiscent of Gen 11, the Tower of Babel story, by describing that the followers of Jesus were "all together in one place" before they disperse to speak in different languages. Acts 2 does not represent a reversal of Babel, but the former evokes the latter in order to provide continuity from the creation of languages and cultures in Genesis to the understanding of many languages among those gathered from the nations in Acts.[8] If anything is redeemed in this passage, it is the resulting lack of understanding among the nations in Gen 11. In Acts 2, the disciples are bearing witness to God's deeds of power in the languages of the gathered crowd so that all understand the words being spoken even if the people struggle to interpret what this display of tongues means.

Ted Hiebert, an Old Testament/Hebrew Bible scholar from McCormick Seminary, at the PC(USA)'s National Multicultural Church Conference in 2010, drew a more significant point of connection between Gen 11 and Acts 2, arguing that in both texts, God prefers diversity to unity, many cultures to "one language and the same words" (Gen 11:1).[9] This preference for diversity is echoed in Jesus' words from Acts 1, declaring that the disciples will be his witnesses not just in Jerusalem but indeed to the ends of the earth. Peter's speech in Acts 2, which interprets the events of Pentecost through the prophet Joel, echoes this same theme:

> In the last days it will be, God declares, that I will pour out my Spirit upon *all flesh*, and your sons and your daughters shall prophesy, and your young men shall see visions, and your old men shall dream dreams. Even upon my slaves, both men and women, in those days I will pour out my Spirit; and they shall prophesy . . . Then *everyone* who calls on the name of the Lord shall be saved. (Acts 2:17–21)

Similarly, in Acts 10, the same Spirit falls on the Gentiles, which creates the possibility that God has opened up the boundaries that construct the faithful community through the democratizing work of the Spirit.

---

8. Ted Hiebert makes the case that Gen 11:1–9 is not a story of judgment and punishment but is an etiology about the creation of the world's cultures. See Hiebert, "The Tower of Babel," 29–58.

9. As presented by Hiebert at "H2o: Deepening our Faith, Widening our Culture," the National Multicultural Church Conference of the PC(USA), May 27–30, 2010, Chicago, Illinois.

In all of this, the author of Acts is making a strong case for the continuity between the early church and Israel, between the work of the apostles and the prophets of old. Note, however, that this argument for continuity contains within it a discontinuous idea, namely that the work of the Holy Spirit, the same creative and empowering wind of God that enables the prophetic speech, also has the ability to disrupt social categories and boundaries, even those that are reinforced within the traditions of Israel. Thus, though the Holy Spirit is a sign of God's ongoing work in salvation history for the people of God, and is the empowering agent that propels that history forward. It also has the ability to disrupt the very nature of the faithful community, who is in and who is out (cf. Num 11:16–30). This idea is developed more fully in the tenth chapter of Acts.

Acts 10 and a Discontinuous Continuity

Acts 10 recounts two visions, one given to Cornelius the centurion and the other given to Peter. Ironically, Cornelius' vision hearkens back to Peter's quotation of the prophet Joel in Acts 2:17, "In the last days it will be, God declares, that I will pour out my Spirit upon *all flesh*." Of course the passage in Joel understands "all flesh" to mean "all Israel"—sons, daughters, young and old, slaves and free, etc. The disruptive moment in Acts 10 is that this vision, a line of sight usually reserved, though not exclusively, to the prophets, is first given to Cornelius, a Gentile, and then to Peter, the apostle. The text makes clear that the word of the Lord came to Cornelius saying, "Thus says the Lord . . ."

Peter's vision is instructive of the disruptive work of the Holy Spirit in this passage. Peter is hungry and goes into a trance. He sees a vision of a sheet with all kinds of unclean animals. The word of the Lord is clear, "Get up, Peter; kill and eat" (v. 13). As a faithful Jew, Peter refuses on grounds consistent with the laws of kashrut. He will not eat anything unclean. God's correction is equally clear: "What God has made clean, you must not call profane" (v. 15). In this way, the word of the Lord directly challenges the received tradition, not just in terms of what food is proper to eat but with whom you may properly eat such food. This implication is made clear as the chapter proceeds to describe the eventual encounter between Cornelius and Peter.

Peter's initial refusal echoes a theme within the Hebrew Bible in which the prophets initially resist the word of the Lord. Of course, this happens in many call narratives (e.g., Moses and Jeremiah). A particularly compelling echo for Acts 10, however, exists in the book of Jonah, in which the prophet literally runs from the word of the Lord. There are also deeper echoes to the current chapter in Acts in the repentance of the wicked Ninevites, an event that is very disturbing to Jonah. In fact, as the reader later understands, Jonah's resistance is motivated by the prophet's displeasure of God's anticipated compassion for the inhabitants (and cattle) of Nineveh.

As Peter is speaking, the Holy Spirit falls on the Gentiles, and they begin to speak in tongues and extol God, echoing the Pentecost event in Acts 2. The response from the circumcised believers is one of great surprise. Eventually Peter and those gathered respond to this disruption by baptizing the new Gentile converts. In Acts 10, like the story of Jonah, the world has turned upside down; the unfaithful have now repented and are among the faithful. The prophet is the one who requires conversion.

The genius of the book of Acts is, therefore, not simply in the way that the author draws a congruent narrative of salvation from Israel and the prophets to the early church and the apostles, but is also found in the reorientation, I would argue a hybridization, of this *Heilsgeschichte* through the recovery of the discontinuous theme of God's work among the nations—a theme, that disrupts the stream of tradition, especially as it relates to the composition and identity of the people of God. This theme weaves irony into the fabric of the story of Israel and the church. The faithful in this disruption are "those people" who are typically identified as outside of the covenant circle. The covenanting God shows signs of God's *hesed* through the falling of the Holy Spirit on those who are labeled as unclean and profane. Again, ironically, it is Peter, the holy apostle, who is converted in the process.

This theme of discontinuity also creates a wrinkle in the idea that the word of God will not return void. In Acts 10, however, it is not Saul, the persecutor of the Way, or Rome, or the religious leaders, who pose a threat to the forward movement of the message. It is now the apostles, first Peter and then those in Jerusalem, who struggle to understand this new development in the history of salvation. Eventually, the church gets it right, but only after much discernment. In other words, even the church cannot get in the way of the word of the Lord and its fulfillment. In some cases, the gospel must even overcome the church.

Implications and Conclusions

So what does this reading of Acts mean for us in the twenty-first century, who are facing enormous challenges in the church, threats from within and without? How does a hybridous ecclesiology of a discontinuous continuity or a theology of disruption speak to the church today? Let me posit a few provisional conclusions.

First, while we tend to emphasize Acts 2 in our liturgical year as the birth of the church, we need to also recognize the disruptive work of the Holy Spirit as found in texts like Acts 10, as way to reclaim the ongoing repentance of the church from idolatry, especially when it takes shape as an overly rigid understanding of who is inside and outside among the faithful. We must stress instead the various ways in which the church is converted anew to the surprising mission of God. This disruption can often challenge the very nature of how we understand the church and who are members of the beloved community.

Second, being open to the disruptive potential of the Holy Spirit's work is one of the only ways that true innovation can happen in the lived realities of the church on the ground. God knows that our churches and, therefore our ecclesiology are in need of a healthy dose of disruptive innovation.[10] In an age where innovation is the buzz word in business, social organization, and in our denomination, it would be wise to recover both in Scripture and in our understanding of the history of the church those moments where the movement of the Spirit overturned the apple cart of our ecclesiological status quo in ways that, ironically, gave life and vitality to those very traditions. Disruption and innovation go hand in hand. This is not only good business, I believe it is also good ecclesiology.

Finally, holding together both the continuity with our past with the sometimes disruptive work of the Spirit will allow for us, when we encounter something that seems on the surface to be absurd, even unclean or profane, to discern and hold in mystery the powerful deeds of the Lord. The Spirit's disruptive work is hardly finished. The Spirit hovers over chaos before the Lord's utterance brings forth light and order to creation (Gen 1:2). I pray that we the church might be converted afresh and anew as we accept the continuous discontinuity of God's life within us in the Spirit. Embracing such an uncertain hope opens us up to the possibility that Moses envisioned when the Spirit exceeded the boundaries of Israel's camp in the book of Numbers, saying: "Would that all the Lord's people were prophets, and that the Lord would put his spirit on them!" (Num 11:29).

---

10. Clayton Christensen differentiates between sustaining and disruptive innovation. The former describes ways to substantially improve core business, the latter challenges the status quo of a business by beginning as a small component within the business, but which later moves up market leading eventually to a dominant position within it (e.g., online bookstores like Amazon vs. traditional bookstores like Borders). See Christensen, *The Innovator's Solution*.

Bibliography

Christensen, Clayton M. *The Innovator's Solution: Creating and Sustaining Successful Growth.* Boston: Harvard Business School Press, 2003.

DeYoung, Curtiss Paul, et al., eds. *The Peoples' Bible.* Minneapolis: Fortress, 2008.

Esterline, David V., and Ogbu U. Kalu, eds. *Shaping Beloved Community: Multicultural Theological Education.* Louisville: Westminster John Knox, 2006.

Hiebert, Theodore. "The Tower of Babel and the Origin of the World's Cultures." *The Journal of Biblical Literature* 126 (2007) 29–58.

Joh, Wonhee Anne. *The Heart of the Cross: A Postcolonial Christology.* Louisville: Westminster John Knox, 2006.

Johnson, Luke Timothy. "Luke-Acts, Book of." In *The Anchor Bible Dictionary*, edited by David Noel Freedman, 4:403–20. New York: Doubleday, 1992.

Lee, Jung Young. *Marginality: The Key to Multicultural Theology.* Minneapolis: Fortress, 1995.

Lee, Sang Hyun. *From a Liminal Place: An Asian American Theology.* Minneapolis: Fortress, 2012.

Sakenfeld, Katharine D. *The Meaning of* Hesed *in the Hebrew Bible: A New Inquiry.* Eugene, OR: Wipf & Stock, 2002.

Tannehill, Robert C. *The Narrative Unity of Luke–Acts: A Literary Interpretation.* Vol. 2, *The Acts of the Apostles.* Minneapolis: Augsburg Fortress, 1992.

Yamada, Frank M. "The View from 2040: the Futures of Theological Education." http://mccormickpresident.wordpress.com/2012/02/15/the-inaugural-address-the-view-from-2040-the-futures-of-theological-education/.

Part III
Sending and Serving

13

Worship and Justice

The Church's Identity and Calling[1]

MARK LABBERTON

These are a set of musings and reflections on the life of the church. I think one of the great gifts of the day that we live in is the gift of the so-called "Nones." This group of people who have basically, in one way or another, washed their hands of the church, and have done so out of a sense of conviction that there's really nothing there for them. I think that that is actually quite an important gift, especially given the percentage of the so-called "Nones" who have in their background been very active in the life of the church, but who have come to a point now of saying that this is no longer the case, that they look at the life of the church and consider it to be something which they are more than ready to disregard. And I think the value of that is that it holds up to us, I think, a set of lenses, an opportunity to see again how it is that we are actually perceived despite whatever it is that we think we're doing, despite whatever it is that we are trying to do, despite whatever it is that we're trying to affirm.

The affirmation back to the church is it has nothing to do with me, it has nothing to do with the world that I'm a part of, it has nothing to do with something that I would consider to be weighty, substantial, or worth being a part of. I think that's a very disturbing finding, but it's very illuminating

---

1. Editor's note: This is an edited transcription of Mark Labberton's address to the plenary gathering of the Moderator's Third Colloquium on Ecclesiology held at Fuller Theological Seminary in Pasadena, California, on March 17, 2014. The editor thanks Mark Caton of Dictate Express for the *pro bono* transcription service.

in a number of different ways and it's the primary biblical text that I want to reflect on for a few minutes this morning, which is the prophet Isaiah, chapter 58.

One of the things that strikes me the most about the connection between worship, mission, and the life of the church, or the people of God, is this sense that often there is this brokenness that exists in the way that those three things relate to one another and then the way that they actually fail to converge and fail to mutually confirm the identity and practice of what it means to be God's people in the world. If Israel was confident of anything, it was confident of its worship—confident that its worship reflected the one true and living God, that it reflected the God that made and kept promises, the God who had chosen Israel, the God who provided the law, the God who had delivered them throughout the history of their life together, that had given them ultimately in succession the temple and all of its practices. It was confident that it had its worship right and yet, it's obviously as we know Israel's worship, that is actually one of the most dramatically critiqued parts of the major/minor prophets in Isaiah, and is among those voices and texts that stand out.

> Shout out, do not hold back! Lift up your voice like a trumpet! Announce to my people their rebellion, to the house of Jacob their sins. Yet day after day they seek me and delight to know my ways, as if they were a nation that practiced righteousness and did not forsake the ordinance of their God; they ask of me righteous judgments, they delight to draw near to God. "Why do we fast, but you do not see? Why humble ourselves, but you do not notice?" Look, you serve your own interest on your fast day, and oppress all your workers. Look, you fast only to quarrel and to fight and to strike with a wicked fist. Such fasting as you do today will not make your voice heard on high. Is such the fast that I choose, a day to humble oneself? Is it to bow down the head like a bulrush, and to lie in sackcloth and ashes? Will you call this a fast, a day acceptable to the Lord? Is not this the fast that I choose: to lose the bonds of injustice, to undo the thongs of the yoke, to let the oppressed go free, and to break every yoke? Is it not to share your bread with the hungry, and bring the homeless poor into your house; when you see the naked, to cover them, and not to hide yourself from your own kin? Then your light shall break forth like the dawn, and your healing shall spring up quickly; your vindicator shall go before you, the glory of the

Lord shall be your rear guard. Then you shall call, and the Lord will answer; you shall cry for help, and he will say, here I am.[2]

This text is provocative for many different reasons, but let me just walk through some of the things that stand out the most to me. First, of course, it is a piece of what our themes come throughout the writing of the book of Isaiah, the themes of God's indictment of Israel's worship. In the context of this particular text it's described as rebellion, it's described as the rejection of God because of their sins. "Yet day after day they seek me and delight to know my ways." I think these are words which could virtually be put in quotes, they "seek me," they "delight" to be near to God. Why? Because it's "as if they were a nation that practiced righteousness and did not forsake the ordinance of God; they ask of me righteous judgments, they delight to draw near to God." I think the entrance to this text is that there's this incredible sense that what Israel is practicing is what could be called, on this English translation, "as if worship"—worship that appears to be one thing when in fact it's something really quite different. It's worship that appears to be about God, but in actual fact, as the prophet goes on to say, it's actually worship that ultimately is more about them, not primarily about God. And the rift between those two things is enormous, "as if they were a nation that practiced righteousness." The assumption is if you seek a God who is righteous then our life is meant to be conformed to that character of God. The evidence of whether our worship is faithful is whether it brings our life into the conformity of the God that we worship; we become like the one that we worship, that's the assumption of the Bible. The great deliverance in following in God's righteous way is that we become like the God that we worship, we become like God in character, we become like God in the connection what we affirm and what we do, what we say and what we actually enact in the world.

In this context, the indictment is they are a nation that seeks to know God's ways, delight to know his ways, as if they were actually going to practice their righteousness, which is the very thing that the prophet is going to say they actually failed most to do. So the disconnection between what is affirmed on one hand and what they do on the other is the heart of the critique. Now this is not an unusual critique in the Bible, it's not a surprise to, not least, to God that we fail to do what we say. That's not the surprise. The surprise is that the people of God, the people of Israel are meant to be the people for whom that is less and less the case. The trajectory of our lives is the trajectory of what we say and what we do is meant to become more and more of a piece and if we regularly come to God and fail to enact a life that

2. Isa 58:1–9 NRSV.

looks like the God that we worship, that in this context it's Isaiah's indictment, God's indictment through Isaiah, that in fact this is the bankruptcy of their worship. So it turns out God does measure our worship, but he doesn't measure by whether or not our worship gives us a certain sort of worship buzz, whether we've used a certain particular liturgical form, whether or not we've had a certain kind of mental or emotional or social experience; it's measured by whether it actually transforms our character in such a way that it gets demonstrated in real time in the world. Do we, in other words, actually live our worship? Is it evident by how we actually live as God's people in the world, that we belong to the God whose righteous character we claim to seek? Now, the God of the Bible, I think, is not holding us up to some kind of impossibly high standard as though, somehow, unless we practice it with absolute perfection, it's as though it's rags. That's not the indictment. I think it is frankly much more crass and basic than that; it's just saying at the most basic level the things that you do. It's not that you fail in the 99th point to get to 100, it's that somewhere down the 50, 60, maybe 40, 30 percentile we haven't made the energy to actually bring these themes together. That's, I think, the heart of the indictment. And yet we protest that God doesn't answer our prayers, this is the cry of Israel to God. "Why do we fast, but you do not see? Why humble ourselves, but you do not notice?" In other words, Israel's holding God accountable for not being the God that they want him to be. We cry to you, but you don't hold up your part of the bargain. We have the right to call you on your unrighteousness, is really what I think the heart of their questioning is. We ask you why look and God's response to that is "Look, you serve your own interest on your fast day." I mean it's just an immediate counterpoint just saying this is actually the nub of the crisis. The crisis is that your worship claims to be about me, but when I look at your life it demonstrates that your life is no more or no less about you than it ever was. And when your life simply looks like it's a reflection of the same self-interest that it's always been, then it's no great surprise that the context of that leads me to suggest, I think in God's language, leads me to suggest that your worship is really not about me, God might say, but really about you.

"You fast only to quarrel and to fight and to strike with a wicked fist. Such fasting as you do today will not make your voice heard on high. Is such the fast that I choose, a day to humble oneself? Is it to bow down the head like a bulrush, and to lie in sackcloth and ashes?" The assumption is that there's a connection for the God of Israel, between the worship that we practice and the life that we live in the social sphere where relationships, ordinary relationships are measured by whether or not they reflect the righteousness, justice, and mercy of this God. And when they fail to do that, it's a worship problem, it's a worship crisis. This is a worship war worth having. This is a dramatically different worship war than the worship war over the aesthetics of the liturgical form of worship, the instrumentation of worship, all of which has its own place somewhere in the pantheon of concerns in the life of the church, but certainly those concerns, I would argue based on this text, would not be a first order concern. It's whether or not our worship creates a life that actually mirrors the character of God. So when we show God's glory, we do so not by as some contemporary worship I think is particularly vulnerable to, simply raising your head and hands toward Heaven and saying the word 'glory' as if that is what brings God glory. Instead of actually living a life that demonstrates that we mirror the glory of God, we're a reflection of the reality of God in the world. That's, I think, the convergence of where worship is meant to lead. And therefore the benchmark of our worship is not what happens in the service *per se*, it's what happens in the social sphere when, in fact, we actually live or fail to live a life of authenticity that reflects the character of the God that we actually claim to say that we honor.

A few years ago I was at an event where I was speaking and the lights were so bright on the stage that I really could see no one that I was talking to, but what I could see were two video monitors. There was one here that had a large image of me and then there was another video monitor over here that had a very large image of me and then there was me. And I thought this is sort of the post-modern trinity. There's me, and me, and me. Everywhere I look, it's all about me, all the time. This is the world I was made for, this is the world I've always looked for, this is the place I've longed to be in where it's all about me all the time. That's the culture that we're all a part of, this endless trinity of self and here Isaiah would say "that is actually the worship crisis." So in the end we protest, we claim, we make affirmations, we do it alone, we do it together in the community, even against God. We even hold God to a righteous standard, but we fail to hold ourselves to the same standard and we fail to actually ask, "what is our worship actually producing in the world. Is it actually enabling a life that is actually not principally centered in ourselves but really centered in communion?" A communion that has got a reflection of God's own communion with Israel, with creation, with reality of a world of suffering and need. And it seems to me this is the direction to which the next portion of the text goes.

> Is not this the fast that I choose: to lose the bonds of injustice, to undo the thongs of the yoke, to let the oppressed go free, and to break every yoke? Is it not to share your bread with the hungry, and bring the homeless poor into your house; when you see the

naked, to cover them, and not to hide yourself from your own kin? Then your light shall break forth like the dawn, and your healing shall spring up quickly.[3]

See, what's described in verses 6 through 7 is really this amazing language of the intimacy of communion that is being recreated by the character of a worshiping life that actually shows up in the world to be committed to the kind of restoration of human communion in a world of mercy, and justice, and righteousness that God intends. "Is not this the fast that I choose: to lose the bonds of injustice." What is injustice? Could be variably described, but among the many ways that we could describe injustice is simply that it's a disordering of power, it's an abuse of power. Every form of injustice is in some way or another, an abuse of power. Is it not what worship should do to reorder the way in which power exists in the world. Relationships that are now redefined by the capacity to reorder power to lose the bonds of injustice, to stand against what would violate it, and abuse a person in the context of some use of power.

"To undo the thongs of the yoke," again this sense of both the enslavery and the control that keeps us from being able to be actually the people who labor in freedom, who offer our lives in dignity, and instead of being abused. To let the oppressed go free, to break every yoke. In each of these cases, all similar and parallel in this form of poetry, is really simply an exploration, it seems to me, of relationships, of life that is meant to be reconstituted as we worship the God of righteous power who is just, who is merciful, who is gracious, that God rewrites our character and our actions in such a way that our actions shows up in a world then begins to reflect this reordered power, this reordered concern for human dignity for the purposes of creation, for human communion with one another, and certainly ultimately with God.

And then it becomes even more personal it seems to me in the next verse. "Is it not to share your bread with the hungry, and bring the homeless poor into your house?" So this is not just something that you might say happens in the broad public sphere, it's actually something that comes all the way into that imagery of Middle Eastern hospitality, of relationship, of communion, of sharing in the breaking of bread.

Having just been briefly in Palestine a couple of weeks ago being very aware of the intensity of Middle Eastern hospitality. "When you see the naked, to cover them, and not to hide yourself from your own kin." These images are profoundly personal images that are going to say that at the very core of our relationship with one another, we step toward the vulnerable,

---

3. Isa 58:6–8a.

we step toward the naked, we step toward our kin. We're part of restoring communion.

What's the work of worship? It's really an experience of being in communion with God which then spills over in reconstituted communion with those that are around us. And the evidence of faithfulness of our worship is a connectedness between all those things and that means that not only do love God with all our heart, mind, soul, and strength, but we also love our neighbor as ourselves. It's this language of integral connectedness that, it seems to me, is part of what a faithful worshiping life looks like.

"Then your light shall break forth like the dawn, and your healing shall spring up quickly; your vindicator shall go before you, the glory of the Lord shall be your rear guard. Then you shall call, and the Lord will answer; you shall cry for help, and he will say, here I am."

Now, the initiative of this is not principally about Israel because as the text will go on to say this is about Israel reflecting what God is doing, it's not about Israel making something happen which God is impartial and passive about. This is about us participating in a work that God is doing.

> If you remove the yoke from among you, the pointing of the finger, the speaking of evil, if you offer your food to the hungry and satisfy the needs of the afflicted, then your light shall rise in the darkness and your gloom be like the noonday. The Lord will guide you continually, and satisfy your needs in parched places, and make your bones strong; and you shall be like a watered garden, like a spring of water, whose waters never fail. Your ancient ruins shall be rebuilt; you shall raise up the foundations of many generations; you shall be called the repairer of the breach, the restorer of streets to live in.[4]

Now all of this language, it seems to me, and we could go on in so many other texts in Isaiah especially, but other prophets as well, that make this same sort of case. God is in a process of a deep work of recreation and the people of God are meant to be the exemplars of the demonstration of that and then the enactment of that for the sake of the world. This is where our worship is so integrally connected, then, to our sense of mission. It isn't worship separate from mission or worship even in a certain measure even distinguishable from mission. It's worship as mission, mission as worship. Not because it all becomes bland and indistinguishable, but because they are so integrally connected that it's only a function of language that actually makes the distinctions as opposed to the reality itself. If we live in the reality that is God's life than it is to worship God, to be in restored communion with

4. Isa 58:9b-12.

God and if we are in that kind of restored communion with God, then in an inseparable way it leads us into restored communion with the people that are around us. That will take work, that will take sacrifice, that will be labor, that will be sweat, that will be sacrificial effort. This is not a portrait of a kind of non-sweaty Presbyterian worship, this is really sweaty worship. This is worship that's really close, that's tactile, that involves a real engagement in a community, it involves stepping close to the needy, and the vulnerable, and the places where the needs are really great. We offer our food to the hungry, we stop pointing the finger. We start instead loving and enacting the reality and mercy and justice of God in a very tangible and pragmatic way.

Now all of this is mirrored to me in a very interesting moment in the gospel of Matthew. And again, we could look at many but I just want to point to this one particular place, which I think brings these themes together. At the end of the Sermon on the Mount as you know, Jesus tells this well-known parable:

> Everyone then who hears these words of mine and acts on them will be like a wise man who built his house on rock. The rain fell, the floods came, and the winds blew and beat on that house, but it did not fall, because it had been founded on rock. And everyone who hears these words of mine and does not act on them will be like a foolish man who built his house on sand. The rain fell, and the floods came, and the winds blew and beat against that house, and it fell—and great was its fall!" Now when Jesus had finished saying these things, the crowds were astounded at his teaching, for he taught them as one having authority, and not as their scribes.[5]

The parable is an amazing conclusion to the sermon to suggest, as I think Isaiah has been saying, that if you really hear these words of mine and are actually prepared to do them then you're actually enacting the life of worship, the life that loves God with all your heart, mind, soul, and strength, your neighbor as yourself. It's enacted. If you don't choose to enact it then it really is as though you've chosen to simply build your house on sand and not on rock. Now, having said that, the text makes the observation that all were astounded at his teaching, and where he taught them, he taught as one having authority. And my understanding of that word in this context and as it appears in several other places in Matthew is the sense that in Jesus there's a connectedness, a deep authority that comes—that what he says and what he does are the same thing and they are so distinctively and even truly uniquely bound together, that in fact the authority of Jesus is not just his

---

5. Matt 27:24–29.

identity, it's actually this authority that comes from this connection between word and act.

Now, having said that, that's what makes, then, the opening verses of chapter 8 so astounding. Now Jesus said, on the mount that you need to exceed the scribes and Pharisees, you must do what it is that I've actually taught, this is the life that's going to look like the character of the Kingdom of God, and then in chapter 8 we come immediately to these two sections:

> When Jesus had come down from the mountain, great crowds followed him; and there was a leper who came to him and knelt before him, saying, "Lord, if you choose, you can make me clean." He stretched out his hand and touched him, saying, "I do choose. Be made clean!" Immediately his leprosy was cleansed. Then Jesus said to him, "See that you say nothing to anyone; but go, show yourself to the priest, and offer the gift that Moses commanded, as a testimony to them."[6]

It would be hard to think of any more emblematic next move in the Gospel according to Matthew than this particular next move. So, having said that your righteousness must exceed that of the scribes and Pharisees, Jesus comes down from the mountain and the very first person he encounters is this emblematic representation of ritual impurity and the one who is most to be avoided. Now we have to ask ourselves, so what does the Kingdom look like? Are you paying attention, are you paying attention? What does the Kingdom look like? What does worship look like? Does it look like what you do on the mountain? Does it look more like what you do when you come down from the mountain? I think was Matthew's argument. What happens to our worship when we come down from the mountain? And Jesus encounters this leper and the exchange, the honoring, the healing, the acknowledgment, the touch all demonstrate what I think Isaiah 58 is really demonstrating, which is simply to say, this is what real, authentic, integrity, spiritual theological integrity, worship and mission actually looks like. It means we actually encounter the other and we engage touch and respond to the other and that's where the reality of the Kingdom that Jesus has been affirming in five through seven actually gets lived out. This is a demonstration of building house on rock not on sand and it would be hard to come up with any one symbol that's more dramatically that then this issue of Israel's purity. Then in the next section it's stepped up as though one through four isn't enough, then Matthew immediately moves on to this text:

---

6. Matt 8:1–4.

> When he entered Capernaum, a centurion came to him, appealing to him and saying, "Lord, my servant is lying at home paralyzed, in terrible distress." And he said to him, "I will come and cure him." The centurion answered, "Lord, I am not worthy to have you come under my roof; but only speak the word, and my servant will be healed. For I also am a man under authority, with soldiers under me; and I say to one, 'Go,' and he goes, and to another, 'Come,' and he comes, and to my slave, 'Do this,' and the slave does it." When Jesus heard him, he was amazed and said to those who followed him, "Truly I tell you, in no one in Israel have I found such faith. I tell you, many will come from east and west and will eat with Abraham and Isaac and Jacob in the kingdom of heaven, while the heirs of the kingdom will be thrown into the outer darkness, where there will be weeping and gnashing of teeth." And to the centurion Jesus said, "Go; let it be done for you according to your faith." And the servant was healed in that hour.[7]

If the leper represents the chief ritual purity challenge then this section seems to represent the chief political challenge. A centurion—that representation of Roman oppression, the enemy, the political social enemy—actually arrives and Jesus again, just like with the leper not only engages and responds to the leper's cry, but now here, hears, receives, and affirms that the centurion's faith is real, more real, more tangible, more demonstration, it seems in the enduring kingdom of heaven, he says, then in fact those who claim to be in the bloodline of Israel, but who may actually be found in the outer darkness. There's those now who seem to be in the outer darkness are those who may actually be found in the household. It's an amazing demonstration. And again, in both of these two texts it seems to me that Jesus is underlining this is the character of the kingdom of God. It comes in unexpected ways from unexpected people; it comes from those that are the outsiders, the oppressors, the unclean, and the oppressor. Those may be the people that are actually in the kingdom of heaven. And those that think that they're in the kingdom of heaven may be those that are actually found in the outer darkness.

I think this is extremely uncomfortable and very important to grapple with, because what it actually underlines again as Isa 58 did is that the people of God who may so confidently believe that we have it right may actually be those who have it wrong. And those who may seem to have it wrong are those that actually might be those that have it right. Now this is a reversal that I think is salty and uncomfortable and awkward especially, I

---

7. Matt 8:5–13.

think, in a culture of our own denomination in which we often have built up such accretions, that are thicker and thicker and thicker layers of distancing ourselves from the essence of this kind of exchange with Jesus. Then you come through all of that back to this kind of exchange and think "Oh, my gosh this is not asking the questions of ecclesiology that we would ask. This isn't asking the questions of church form and structure and polity." These are asking questions that I would say are much more of the essence of this communion that is meant to be the most characteristic distinctive of the people of God. Where is the evidence that we actually demonstrate the unexpected character of the God of Israel, the God now made known in Jesus Christ? That is a very awkward thing and it involves in part our engagement with the unclean, it involves in part our engagement even with the oppressors.

We've tended to be, I think, a better denomination doing other things than these things. And yet when I read Isa 58 and I think about the ecclesiastical industrial complex of the church it's hard, I think, to find the evidence as much as I would wish of Isa 58. And it's even harder to find the evidence of what is given here in Matt 8. Where are the places where the people of God are showing up with peculiar acts of faith, of risk, of courage that actually ventures into this salty territory where in fact God is re-creating communion. That's the identity of the church, that's the work of the church in the world. But so many conversations about the church are really about the ecclesiastical industrial complex, about the kind of nature of the function of the institution. And all those things have their own appropriate place, but they do not have the place that these things have. This is, to me, much more about the essence of what the church is meant to be and the essence of what practice of the people of God is meant to be in the world that is the enactment of the character of God and the enactment of the character of the kingdom that Jesus came saying has come at hand.

It will require more of us. It will not be able to be as contained. It will not be able to be as managed. It will not look neat and tidy. It will not be easily formatted and turned into a book of any particular kind. It will be a story of an unfolding experience of seeking to follow God in places where the complexity of that and the struggle and challenge of that will be sometimes great, and where the risks will need to be real.

I remember over the course of the years that I was at Berkley, the number of times having conversations with people who in hearing themes like this would be surprised and I remember this one particular person who had been in our church for a number of years and he said, "I'm really liking this, but this is a little more uncomfortable for me than I'm used to being, not least in a Presbyterian church." I said, "Say more." He said, "Well, I think that what you're wanting, I think what you're saying is we're supposed to actually be the church." It's like "yeah, actually that would be a good way of summarizing it." That is what I'm trying to say and what I'm trying to say about what the church is, is something like what I've tried to just describe from Isaiah 58 and Matt 8. Much, much more can and would need to be said, there's many different ways in which one holy catholic apostolic church needs to be understood. But if at the core, whatever those things mean, doesn't land us in the kind of space that we're talking about so far this morning, it seems to me that we're actually missing what the point of that whole exercise is about and we may be caught in a pattern of, what I've come to think of, as thick church. Thick church, that's like a crust, a crusty thick layer that surrounds the gospel itself and the dynamic life of the kingdom of God. And part of that—what these texts call me back to is a sense of trying to ask, what I think of is actually first order questions about the nature of the church and its mission. And, at least for me, these texts are provocative in that way.

14

Mutual Transformation in Mission

Heidi Worthen Gamble

It is indeed good news that the church is growing into a deeper missional identity. At the very time of Christendom's recession in the West, a new and compelling vision has emerged that has sparked the imagination and given us all fresh hope and new life: *missio Dei*, the mission of God. Since the advent of Darrell Guder's book *Missional Church: A Vision for the Sending of the Church in North America* in 1998 there have been countless articles and books published on how to live into this theological paradigm shift of understanding *missio Dei*, in which God sends us out to participate in God's redemptive reign of the peaceable kingdom on earth. Rather than an appendage, a "side dish," or an occasional good deed that we do as followers of Jesus, God's mission becomes our reason for being, the center of our church life and the reorienting of our identity and self-understanding of what it means to be church.[1] Ministry on the margins is moving into the center. This is cause for great rejoicing.

At the same time there are truths being revealed within mission circles about the mission outreach of the church itself, and some of it painful. One of the most poignant is that our primary posture for mission—as a relationship of benefactor/beneficiary—is in need of its own paradigm shift. Although churches continue to do great good in mission, we have also done considerable harm, not because of ill intentions but because of underlying assumptions of moral, religious, cultural and class superiority that have planted themselves deep within us. Whether our mission has been primarily evangelical or charitable, international or local, we have been culpable of

---

1. Kreider and Kreider, *Worship and Mission*, 53.

operating out of a framework that has been at times patronizing, disempowering, hurtful and ineffective to those we meant to help. We did not intend to do this. As an old Southern saying goes, "If the devil can't make me do wrong, he'll make me do right wrong!"

In conversations about worship and mission in post-Christendom I invite us to honestly examine how we lead people into mission through worship and how we shape and form a deeper understanding of our mission work as worship. This paper will outline current missiological writings on the problem with North American missions; propose a reframing of our understanding of mission; and propose ways worship can shape a more just, compassionate and transformational missiology.

I'll begin with my own story. My call to ministry came out of a seminary internship with the homeless in Sacramento, California. I was invited to be a "minister of presence" to homeless guests of a large nonprofit, and it transformed my life to accompany people on the streets as their pastor and friend. Since that formational experience I have served as co-pastor in a village church in Alaska; director and pastor of a drop-in center for the homeless in Washington; and currently as the Mission Advocate for Hunger, Poverty and Peacemaking Concerns in Los Angeles, California, where I have been organizing and facilitating domestic and international mission opportunities. I am absolutely passionate about what it means to follow Jesus and to participate in the *missio Dei* of redemptive justice and peace. I love the work I have been called to do. However I am no less culpable than anyone else of cultural and class dominance in mission, and I continue to learn valuable lessons in my own journey, all of which I hope to share freely here.

In recent years there has been a growing body of literature about the problems of the American church's mission activities. Steve Corbett and Brian Fikkert in their book *When Helping Hurts: How to Alleviate Poverty Without Hurting the Poor . . . and Yourself* write candidly about what happens when we attempt to help the poor without the disciplines of spiritual formation, education and reflection, specifically in the area of poverty alleviation.

> One of the biggest problems in many poverty-alleviation efforts is that their design and implementation exacerbates the poverty of being of the economically rich—their god-complexes—and the poverty of being of the economically poor—their feelings of inferiority and shame. The way that we act toward the economically poor often communicates—albeit unintentionally—that we are superior and they are inferior. In the process we hurt the poor and ourselves. . .this dynamic is likely to be particularly strong whenever middle-to-upper-class, North American

Christians try to help the poor, given these Christians' tendency toward a Western, materialistic perspective of the nature of poverty.[2]

One of the major premises of their book is that "until we embrace our mutual brokenness, our work with low-income people is likely to do far more harm than good."[3]

Our culturally dominant approach to international mission has become even more urgent to address because of the shift happening in the practice of mission itself: the classical mission model of the church sending missionaries on the denomination's behalf has shifted towards short-term mission trips, with congregations now engaging in mission themselves. As Hunter Farrell, Director of PC(USA) World Mission, describes,

> In recent decades, a seismic shift in how we understand and practice mission has led to direct involvement of U.S. Presbyterians at unprecedented levels . . . Millions of Americans participate in short-term mission trips each year . . . But is all that mission activity necessarily effective? Is there adequate broad cross-sector coordination in order to address these critical global issues . . . Christian leaders across the global south are saying that while short-term missions and partnership are important, their people are struggling with life-and-death issues. They are asking for our help to address them. Based on what World Mission had heard from global partners and our mission workers, there is a feeling that, in many ways, Presbyterian churches are less than effective in mission.[4]

As co-pastor in a mission church in Alaska, my husband and I hosted short-term mission groups in our home. As time went on we struggled to continue to find work projects for these groups, and we began to ask whether it wouldn't be more beneficial to create jobs in the village rather than mission projects for church groups. In a village primarily on welfare because jobs were scarce, this would have been a worthy mission indeed. However we had no context for how to address this and were grateful for the church groups' time and expense to come to Alaska and serve, so we simply kept finding things for the mission teams to do while the people in the village would stand and watch. I myself have been someone culpable of lack of education and reflection in the mission church I served.

---

2. Corbett and Fikkert, *When Helping Hurts*, 62.
3. Ibid., 61.
4. Taylor, "Dallas II."

As Americans, we are a consumer-driven society saturated with materialism, and we are one of the most powerful economic and military forces in the history of the world. Yet even though we might be able to recognize and name these qualities easily about ourselves, when we enter into cross-cultural mission our materialism and cultural dominance become unintentionally manifest, and we have a hard time seeing is how destructive it can be. There are church groups who have created whole neighborhoods of beggars by randomly distributing goods out of a bus to children on the street and water wells built by outside groups that go unused and become symbols of a recipient community's lack of self-agency and low self-esteem. These are not isolated incidences but rather dramas that play themselves out repeatedly by mission senders and recipients. It is far too easy to think we have done good when we may have done precisely the opposite.

As Mission Advocate in Pacific Presbytery in Los Angeles, California, I've been facilitating an international partnership facilitated by a Nicaraguan ministry and PC(USA) Mission Co-Workers, and have been humbled many times by what it means to truly engage in a long-term partnership of mutuality, accompaniment and self-determination in addressing root causes of poverty. It is a spiritual and cultural discipline and it is labor intensive, because we have so much to learn and unlearn. It is pure joy to be in a relationship of mutual transformation however. We have developed deep friendships with the people in our partnership. Yet because we are not giving away material goods or building something concrete and visible it is difficult to translate that we are "doing" anything to help the poor. Despite several years of interpretation, formation and countless presentations on partnership model and mutually transformational mission, the benefactor/beneficiary model for mission continues to be the dominant model most people defend.

This is not only a problem with our mission work internationally but also here at home. A few years ago a controversial book emerged by a Presbyterian and lifetime minister to the urban poor, Robert Lupton, titled *Toxic Charity: How Churches and Charities Hurt Those They Help*. He describes the "compassion boom" in our own country in recent years. Nearly every church, business, and organization is giving to some kind of service project, largely for the purpose of boosting their image, while the outcomes of all of these charitable acts go almost completely unexamined. Then he adds, "And religiously motivated charity is often the most irresponsible. Our free food and clothing distribution encourages ever-growing handout lines, diminishing the dignity of the poor while increasing their dependency . . . Giving to those in need what they could be gaining from their own initiative may well be the kindest way to destroy people."[5]

The drop-in center where I served as director and pastor served meals and emergency services and yes, during my years there I was certainly culpable of fostering dependencies! Many of our homeless guests were chronically homeless and/or marginally housed with severe mental illnesses, who truly cannot provide for themselves, and I know many families who depend on food banks not because they cannot provide for themselves but because they do not have jobs that pay a living wage. However, we could have done more to empower those we served.

Mission is dangerous and messy. There is no way around it. Even if our church outreach appears innocuous—an occasional canned food drive, supporting a missionary overseas—it is most certainly treading controversial and murky waters. To be sure, we will all make mistakes, and mistakes are necessary and important part of the process. Making mistakes is not the problem; it is our inability to admit to our mistakes that is the problem. It is our inability or unwillingness to see and hear that we have hurt others and our fear of facing up to this truth that is the problem.

Mission is not about us: it is not about improving our church's image, it is not some kind of magic bullet for church growth, and it is not about sharing a bit more of our material abundance. The mission to which we are called is God's redemptive mission in Jesus Christ who brings good news to the poor, release to captives, and sets the oppressed free. It is about living into the kingdom that Christ proclaimed. It is love in action; the kind of love inaction that Fyodor Dostoevsky describes: "love in action is a harsh and dreadful thing compared to love in dreams."[6]

Mission is not a list of things we do; it is a posture, an orientation. It is being with relationship with those who suffer and being willing to sacrifice on their behalf. Although it can be deep and powerful joy, mission is not a feel good fix; rather, it is a humble emptying of oneself that disorients, disturbs, and confuses us. It demands reflection, humility, deep listening, self-examination, and questioning our assumptions. Missional Christianity, describe the Kreiders, is living in "a constant, question-asking, liminal, restless state—a kind of holy restlessness that comes from loving people and the gospel."[7]

5. Lupton, *Toxic Charity*, 4.
6. Dostoevsky, *Brothers Karamazov*, part 1, book 2, chapter 4.
7. Kreider and Kreider, *Worship and Mission*, 187.

As we emerge more fully into post-Christendom we have an opportunity to reframe our self-understanding in ways that can deepen our missiology. If we can name what is happening to our church today within the framework of journey and bewilderment, humility and instability; if we can identify our grief and pain and admit we are in need of God's redemptive mission we will be further on the way to understanding mission in humility and equality with our brothers and sisters experiencing poverty. Remember Fikkert and Corbett's foundational message, that until we embrace our mutual brokenness, our work with low-income people will do far more harm than good. We have an opportunity, in our brokenness, to really begin to understand mutually transformational mission.

What is dangerous is to prop up Mission Dei as another kind of panacea for post-Christendom woes. Scott Halsey writes in *Cultivating Sent Communities: Missional Spiritual Formation*, "We must be careful not to let missional movement create the illusion of cultural agency through the production of new initiatives, which keep the church from recognizing its exilic instability and vulnerability."[8]

How do we begin to articulate a vision for mission in the church that moves us from the power paradigm of donor/recipient into one that is mutually transformational? We simply cannot get there without intentional spiritual formation in worship. If a missional identity is central to who we are, worship is the central gathering place that nurtures us in this new identity. Conversations between the two historically separate fields of mission and worship is critical. We need deep, intentional missional spiritual formation in worship today. We need worship to be the place where the vision of the reign of God is proclaimed with vitality; where we are trained in right ways of being and thinking in mission; where our imagination is renewed and creativity is elicited; where we are sensitized to recognize the inbreaking of God's kingdom invitation in our own lives. We need worship to help us tell the truth and dream dreams. Alan and Eleanor Kreider write,

> Worship can name the institutions that cast God in our own image and whose unwitting instruments we would be if it were not for worship. When we say Jesus is Lord and bow at his feet we radically resist the worth we ascribe to Caesar. And as people who are freed from the thrall of false gods, we respond by giving thanks to God, by praising God and by committing ourselves to live in light of God's mission so that we flow with it and not impede it . . . This is God's mission—to bring right relationship in every area of life, to make multidimensional shalom. We cannot

8. Haigle, "Exile on Main Street," 72.

participate in God's mission without worship. We are not strong or clever enough.[9]

Glorifying God. Worship can start by reframing our understanding of what it means to glorify God. Passages such as John 13:35 can instruct us in new ways; when, at the moment his betrayal, arrest, torture and death is put into motion by Judas Jesus proclaims, "Now the Son of Humanity is glorified and God is glorified through him." Jesus completely reverses what it means to glorify God. Instead of proclaiming God's glory through pew-based worship it is to live into the way of the cross, to speak truth to power, live a life of mercy and compassion and to live it with intention about what this means the world will do to you as a result. If glorifying God is primarily proclaiming God's attributes without God's missional story of love in action; an act of proclamation with our lips but not also with our lives; understood exclusively as belonging in the sanctuary and not also on the streets then we are not proclaiming the whole truth. While proclaiming with our lips who we worship is central, the Word was made flesh and the Word without flesh is vague and meaningless. "As we attune ourselves to God's mission and align ourselves with God's purposes we ascribe worth to God," write the Kreiders.[10]

Love in action. In the verses following Jesus says, "I give you a new commandment, that you love one another as I have loved you" Let us become scholars in how to love! To love God and neighbor is our primary task as followers of Jesus—it is our penultimate task in worship and mission. I often hear the message to love others proclaimed in worship but rarely do I hear it described. What does it mean to love? What does it look like? To love one another the way Jesus loved us is risky, dangerous, messy, difficult, heartbreaking and unglamorous. It is also powerfully real and redemptive and mutually transformational. Far more important than what we do in mission is how we relate to others. I have witnessed how redemptive it is for someone on the streets to experience another person's loving interest in them as a human being and a child of God rather than an object of their scorn, guilt, embarrassment or pity. How much more important this is than giving them socks!

But we need to be nurtured and trained in love. Our global partners in Nicaragua call it "the love that is justice":

> The love that is justice is not the same as creating the love that feels comfortable. If we could ever get out from under the baggage of

---

9. Kreider and Kreider, *Worship and Mission*, 34.
10. Ibid.

our Westernized psychological distortion of love, within which we have to check out frequently our subjective feelings as if they were some dependable law to be obeyed, we might discover a love that is "caring" beyond our comfort level . . . It is always "in process," never finished. It may or may not "feel good" for those who do it (that is why they have to sing a lot) . . . It is not a veneer to cover desperation. It is not a "hand-out" to make anyone feel better temporarily. It is the never-ending arduous task of catalyzing sustainable human community development, fostering self-determination, self-sustenance and self-respect, and enabling all, especially the poor and the marginalized, to fulfill their greatest potential. It is the work of the Church.[11]

The Kreiders write that glorifying God and sanctifying humans is the role of worship in post-Christendom.[12] How might worship be a place to strengthen us in the love that is justice?

Confession and Liberation. The confession cycle is a place of so much potential but in my experience confessing a sin that was written by someone else does not lead to authentic self-reflection and honesty. Neither does it model how to admit when we are wrong. Even if collective cultural sins such as arrogance and pride are named in a confession cycle it gives people no road map for recognizing when that behavior manifests in their own lives, let alone give them the necessary tools for changing the behavior. How can worship shape and form us in a posture of confession that, rather than imparting guilt, identifies what we need to be set free from? What hurts others kills our own souls too. Identifying a crisis of meaning as the poverty of the West might be a place to start. As Jonathan Bonk describes, "The great purpose of modern life is to move from birth to death as comfortably as possible"[13] which keeps us shackled in our materialism and addiction to comfort, which is what feeds our problematic assumptions in mission. We need to be set free from apathy, grumpiness, anxiety, hopelessness, cynicism, isolation and meaninglessness. Hurt people hurt people; transformed people transform others. We worship a most liberating God in Jesus Christ who reaches down and liberates us!

Mission as Worship. David Livermore in his book *Serving with Eyes Wide Open: Doing Short-Term Missions with Cultural Intelligence* suggests we see an event like short-term mission trips not as a penultimate act of discipleship, but rather as "another expression of a seamless life of missional living

---

11. *Covenant Relations Manual*, 50.
12. Kreider and Kreider, *Worship and Mission*, 141.
13. Jonathon Bonk, as quoted in ibid., 86.

that includes giving and receiving" where our primary task is to learn.[14] I really like this. We proclaim God's mission as our primary center, not the acts we do. Understanding our collective and individual mission work as an extension of our worship, and all of it having equal value and worth—whether it is holding the hand of someone in a nursing home down the block or traveling halfway around the world to hold the hand of a brother and sister of a vastly different culture—will level the playing field within our worshipping communities and help keep us humble. Jesus says in Matt 6:3, "When you give to the needy do not let your left hand know what your right hand is doing." When mission becomes the center of our identity and Christian spiritual formation is robustly and creatively taught, our various manifestations of mission will become no big deal. When we commission and pray for those going overseas in worship we can use these as moments of inspiration to be reminded of everyone's calling as the body of Christ.

Witness and being. The Kreiders suggest it is our witness and being that will be the most powerful response to the atheism, cynicism, and bad press of the church today.[15] In my experience of churches worshipping in congregations who incarnate a compelling transformational missiology in urban Los Angeles, they have reached out deeply and intentionally in relationship in their neighborhoods, welcome and embrace all in worship, and continue to be transformed by their context. They are communities of faith who understand themselves to be on a journey. They are always experimenting and cultivate a culture of flexibility and humor in their congregations. They are intentional about including and loving the other, so much so that their congregations are filled with diversity across class, race, language and culture. Mission Dei is what they do, who they are, and who they are constantly becoming: the beloved community.[16]

Although our the dominant framework out of which we understand mission work is need of reformation, I believe that reincorporating it into the strong theological foundation of *missio Dei* in worship that is honest and humble, critical and self-reflective will go a long way to set us aright. We are invited to enter into God's epic missional story of love and redemption ourselves and live into the mystical flow of God's Spirit. May we engage in the intentional communal process of growing in our relationship with God

---

14. Livermore, *Serving with Eyes Wide Open*, 148.
15. Kreider and Kreider, *Worship and Mission*, 180, 181.
16. The congregations of United University on USC Campus and Immanuel Presbyterian Church, both in Los Angeles, California.

and becoming conformed to Christ through the power of the Spirit for the sake of the world.[17]

And for the sake of the world, let us act now.

Bibliography

Corbett, Steve, and Brian Fikkert. *When Helping Hurts: How to Alleviate Poverty without Hurting the Poor . . . and Yourself.* Chicago: Moody, 2009.

Covenant Relations Manual: Guidelines for Partnership. Managua, Nicaragua: CEPAD, 2010.

Dostoevsky, Fyodor. *Brothers Karamazov.* http://www.online-literature.com/dostoevsky/brothers_karamazov/9/.

Guder, Darrell L., ed. *Missional Church: A Vision for the Sending of the Church in North America.* Grand Rapids: Eerdmans, 1998.

Hagley, Scott J. "Exile on Main Street: Reframing Short-Term Mission." In *Cultivating Sent Communities: Missional Spiritual Formation*, edited by Dwight Zscheile, 56–80. Grand Rapids: Eerdmans, 2012.

Kreider, Alan, and Eleanor Kreider. *Worship and Mission after Christendom.* Harrisonburg, VA: Herald, 2011.

Livermore, David A. *Serving with Eyes Wide Open: Doing Short-Term Missions with Cultural Intelligence.* Grand Rapids: Baker, 2006.

Lupton, Robert. *Toxic Charity: How Church and Charities Hurt Those They Help (and How to Reverse It).* New York: HarperCollins, 2011.

Taylor, Judson. "Dallas II October Consultation to Create a Collective Impact for Mission." Presbyterian News and Announcements, April 16, 2012. https://www.pcusa.org/news/2012/4/16/dallas-ii-october-consultation-create-collective-i/.

Zscheile, Dwight. *Cultivating Sent Communities: Missional Spiritual Formation.* Grand Rapids: Eerdmans, 2012.

---

17. Zscheile, *Cultivating Sent Communities*, vii. This is Dwight Zscheile's definition of Christian spiritual formation. I liked it so much I incorporated it as the benediction.

15

A Praxis of Worship and Witness

Allen Permar Smith

The Gospel according to Matthew reads, "Suddenly Jesus met them and said, 'Greetings!' And they came to him, took hold of his feet, and worshipped him. Then Jesus said to them, 'Do not be afraid; go and tell my brothers to go to Galilee; there they will see me.'"[1]

This passage, at the end of the first gospel, established a link between worship and witness. Mary Magdalene and Mary encounter the risen Christ. Their immediate response was to worship their Lord. Then, Jesus commands them to witness by saying " . . . go and tell . . ." It can be argued that worship and witness is the foundation of the Christian faith.

The *Book of Order* of the Presbyterian Church (USA) echoes the above idea in the great ends of the Church: the proclamation of the gospel for the salvation of humankind; the shelter, nurture, and spiritual fellowship of the children of God; the maintenance of divine worship; the preservation of the truth; the promotion of social righteousness; and the exhibition of the Kingdom of Heaven to the world.[2] This is the work of Christian faith.

In considering the relationship between worship and witness one might specifically remember three of the above: the proclamation of the gospel for the salvation of humankind, the maintenance of divine worship and the exhibition of the Kingdom of Heaven to the world. The church is called to worship. It is call to witness to the world through proclamation and exhibiting the Kingdom of Heaven to a broken world. To a great extent, the

---

1. Matt 28:9–10.
2. *The Book of* Order, F-1.0304.

Christian community knows *what* to do—what is considered here is one aspect of the *how* of doing it.

Definitions

To better understand the terms of worship and witness simple definitions may be helpful. Worship can be defined as ascribing worth. For Christians, we ascribe worth—the ultimate worth—to God the Father, Son and Holy Spirit. Historically, corporate worship was divided into four parts: gathering in the name of God, reading and proclaiming Scripture, the celebration of Communion and sending the community into the world to practice and proclaim our faith to others.

The Reformed tradition holds to a similar construction. Worship is centered on the word of God. The community gathers around the word, prepares to hear the word, proclaims the word, responds to the word, seals the word and takes the word into the world.

As the Reformed tradition of worship progressed, an ordered and formal structure emerged. For many in the worshipping community, the order and structure of worship provided meaning to life and the expression of faith.

At the same time, the order of worship finds its power and direction in the Holy Spirit. In the preparation and presentation the community calls upon and looks for the power of the Holy Spirit. The Holy Spirit calls those who participate into an experience of profound change. As Jane Rogers Vann writes,

> . . . the real presence of Jesus Christ made known in word and sacrament comes to the Christian community as they gather to hear scripture proclaimed and to share the holy meal, to share their lives with one another, and to share the Gospel with the world. In the worship the common place actions of everyday life are represented and encountered in ways that intensify their meaning and invest them with both the promises of God and the hopes and needs of humankind. Congregations do not just "go through the motions" of accustomed Christian worship. By the grace of the Holy Spirit, the presence of God is mediated through their words and actions in communal participation.[3]

Worship, through the presence and power of the Holy Spirit, is at its core transformational.

---

3. Vann, *Gathered Before God*, 23.

It is also important to emphasize that worship is an act of community in community. This moves the discussion to the importance of witness in the Christian life. The church gathers because of the gospel of Jesus Christ. The Christ event has changed lives. Therefore, all are welcomed to the church with the authentic hope that the gospel will change lives. It is a community filled with the grace of Jesus Christ. The community is a way into a new identity and understanding of life. Rowan Greer notes that at its beginnings, Christianity and its worship offer a way into transformation:

> If we were to seek for one way of describing the experience of early Christians, it would be to point to a representation of victory like the Jonah story. Christ's victory by his death and resurrection is found in Jonah's deliverance from the whale, Daniel's deliverance from the lions' den, the three young men's deliverance from the burning fiery furnace, and above all in the deliverance of Israel from bondage in Egypt. What did the victory mean to the early Christian? In one sense, it was a way out. The social, political and economic evils that make up a large part of life in late antiquity would all be left behind as the Christian passed through death to life. And the new age is pictured as the obverse of this life. A banquet would replace the hunger and poverty of the present. Peace and rest would replace toil. But in another sense, the victory was a way in. For many early Christians the Church provided for the first time a place to belong, a community of hope in what must often have seemed a hopeless world.[4]

Professor Greer observes the early Christian community was an act and experience of belonging and inclusion. Christians attempt to include people by witnessing to the good news of Jesus Christ.

The term witness can be understood as an attestation of a fact or event—a witness is one that gives evidence and one who has a personal knowledge of something.[5] In sum, to witness is to proclaim an event or fact that a person has individual knowledge of. Put into a Christian context, a witness for Christ is one who proclaims the gospel of salvation because she has a personal experience of it.

Worship and witness in the Christian context are intertwined in such a way that one does not work without the other. Worship and witness are two sides of the same coin. When we worship, we offer witness and when we witness we are pointing to the ultimate worth in our lives and in the lives of others.

4. Greer, *Broken Lights*, 21–22.
5. http://www.merriam-webster.com/dictionary/witness.

Our Society

Clearly the Christian community has engaged in both of these practices from its foundation. As a movement, Christianity has been very successful no matter how one chooses to measure it. Yet, at the beginning of the twenty-first century, many are questioning the viability of the Christian movement. Christianity is in decline and the PC(USA) has lost millions of members over the last forty years. Experts who crunch numbers have made the uncomfortable prediction that if our denomination declines over the next forty years at the same rate it has declined over the last forty, the community will be a community less than forty thousand members.

The Post-Christian World

Christianity's decline of numbers and influence has been labeled post-Christian. Many have been told that they are living in a post-Christian society. In a very basic sense, this term may be defined on an individual level and on a societal level. The individual post-Christian is one who chooses to live and is influenced by the teachings of Jesus as she understands them. However, she chooses to distance herself from the Christian community. Her experience of Christ and his teachings are not mediated through the church. A post-Christian society is a society that follows the same pattern as an individual. The society structures itself around the moral teachings of Jesus, but the church is not seen as the arbitrator or keeper of these ideas. In both cases, the church has less authority, participation and prominence in the community.

There are many notable exceptions to this trend. A number of church communities have increased. Some congregations have moved into the realm of the mega-church[6] attracting thousands of members each Sunday to ever larger buildings and worship spaces.[7] In different parts of the world, Christian communities are on the increase. This poses and interesting question with an allusive solution: is the church in decline or is a certain type of church declining?

---

6. A mega-church can be defined and a church community that exceeds a membership of 2000.

7. See for example First Baptist Church of Dallas, Texas. This community has just completed a $150 million building project, which they claim to be the largest church-building project in history.

The Project

This short introduction brings the essay to the point of the project. How can the church work today? The good news of Jesus Christ changes individuals. Therefore, how do Christians translate this Gospel to our world? Christians who believe are not post-Christian—their faith is current. In fact, one would venture to say that the faithful are very present Christians looking to the future. In the following, this essay would like to offer one possible direction that may help stimulate some communities. It involves, of course, the interplay between worship and witness and a small church in Asheville, North Carolina.

The Community

Kenilworth Presbyterian Church was founded eighty years ago in a neighborhood near the center of the city. In the mid-1950s, the size of the congregation swelled to more than five hundred members. To meet the needs of the growing community, a large facility was constructed that included an expanded sanctuary, Sunday school rooms, a fellowship hall and office space. Despite the impressive building the church followed the pattern of decline noted above. By the year 2010, the church membership was thirty-five. The sanctuary, at one time a powerful symbol of worship and influence in the community, became an overwhelming responsibility to the small group of Christians who gathered for worship each Sunday morning.

Like all churches, Kenilworth wanted to grow. On one level, their hopes were modest. The congregation wanted to gain enough members to keep the doors open. They had no illusions of being a congregation of four or five hundred. The building still had a high steeple but the members did not believe they would ever be a "high steeple" church again. On another level, their hopes were great because they believed that no matter how modest the number in the community, the community could and would make a difference. Kenilworth Presbyterian Church believed it could have a profound impact in the community and the world. In short, the members still believed they could "do church."

The Process

Over the last four years the church has attempted, along with the assistance of Presbytery, a process of revitalization and renewal. The two terms sounded impressive, and it was an easy way to talk about where the church was when asked. "We are in a process of revitalization and renewal at Kenilworth," so the statement went, "and we are looking forward to what God has in store for us."

On a deeper level, Kenilworth Presbyterian Church struggled to understand what this meant. What was renewal? What does it mean to be vital again? How is this accomplished, and how will it change the identity of the community? Overall, the members were open to change in all aspects of church life. However, they, like so many, did not know what change was or what it could be. Naturally, the process brought with it success, set-backs and second guessing. Long-time members left and new members joined. The membership remained the same.

A Possible Direction

Quite by accident the committee members stumbled onto the illusive good idea. It started with a discussion about one element of worship: the offering—specifically how offering should be collected. The discussion was started during a vision meeting. One member felt that taking up the offering with offering plates or baskets sent the wrong message to visitors. She believed that passing a plate down each pew was a type of pressure that turned people off. "Many of my friends," she stated, "do not have a lot of money and they do not carry cash with them. When the offering is taken during worship, they have nothing to put in the plate. People are embarrassed. It seems to me that the last thing this church wants to do is embarrass someone during worship." She further went on to express her concern that people may not come back to the church or may not attend church altogether because they have no money.

This made sense. Did the church need to pass a plate to collect the offering? After further discussion, it was agreed that the offering would not be collected during worship. Instead, a basked would be placed in the narthex and, as people left the church, they could place their offering there. This simple suggestion proved to be a great insight into what it means to worship and witness.

The first Sunday this was started, the congregation collectively entered a process of praxis. Praxis can be understood to be action followed by reflection followed by action and so on. It could be argued that the church participated in what can be called a "praxis event." This is the moment when a congregation as a whole "clicks" and understands that an action they have taken is working. This was change, and this was the church working in the present. Not collecting the offering during the service was so unique to the church that they began discussions about what an offering to the church truly means.

As the Sundays progressed, the time for collecting the offering transitioned unto a time of reminding the community that an offering was more than money. The focus of tithing to the church itself took second place. The message to the congregation was to give first to those in greatest need and then give to the church. The narthex now holds three containers: one for 5 cents a meal, one for donations to a local food pantry and a basked for church offerings.

The above actions, it can be argued, brings together the two key themes of this essay: worship and witness and their relationship to one another. Refocusing the understanding of offering *focused* the understanding on how the church worshiped and witnessed. The power of the event for the congregation was found in its' simplicity. A simple action was taken by the faith community. The action was clear and the action could be understood. The offering was theological and expressed how the members understood God and how God understands the world. In the end, it was a very practical theology.

The Results

The results have been modest and encouraging. The membership has increased to fifty-five. The church budget is balanced and benevolences have increased from 5 to 15 percent. The numbers are promising. However, the true success of the church is not measured in this way. The true success of Kenilworth Presbyterian Church is the belief that the members have nothing to lose and everything to gain. One member proclaimed: "I would rather fail by doing the right thing than be successful while doing it wrong." No matter the case, it is clear that the grace of Jesus Christ is moving the community into an exciting future.

Bibliography

The Constitution of the Presbyterian Church (U.S.A.), Part II, Book of Order. Louisville: The Office of the General Assembly, 2013.

Greer, Rowan. *Broken Lights and Mended Lives: Theology and Common Life in the Early Church*. University Park: Pennsylvania State University Press, 1991.

Vann, Jane Rogers. *Gathered Before God: Worship-Centered Church Renewal*. Louisville: Westminster John Knox, 2004.

16

Newbigin House of Studies
An Experiment in Missional Theological Education

SCOT SHERMAN

During my final year of seminary I received a momentous invitation. A new church was being started on Manhattan's Upper East Side and I was asked if I wanted to help out. To be honest, I wasn't that interested in church planting, but I was game for weekends in NYC so I took the train and lent a hand. Before long I had fallen in love with this rapidly growing church and was ordained to serve on a multi-staff team. A few years later I planted the church's first daughter congregation in Greenwich Village. The course of my life's ministry—new church development in urban contexts—was set.

This was a wonderful ministerial destination, but the ride was unnecessarily bumpy. I left seminary loaded with information, with what I thought were *answers*. When I arrived in New York, in a missional context of thoughtful skeptics and spiritually curious seekers, I quickly found that my scripted answers were *to questions no one was asking*. To borrow Lessing's famous phrase, there was "an ugly great ditch" between the shape of my ministerial formation and the realities of ministry. In the years that followed it was the city that became my seminary—a classroom made up of rich stories, diverse people, neighborhoods and cultures—these apprenticed me into the wisdom and skills that I needed for an engaged life of ministry.

I like to think that it has all worked out OK, that I've become a fairly decent pastor. But I wish my journey had less of a Johnny Knoxville/Jackass "five feet short of a ten-foot jump" quality to it. I do not blame seminary for all my mistakes, but it would have been better for me (and the church) if I had been more carefully prepared for pastoral leadership.

Nowadays I regularly interact with influential church leaders who openly disdain seminary education. Most of them have their own "ugly great ditch" story. As far as they are concerned today's seminaries are ineffective, at best producing chaplains for static or declining "one hundred attender" congregations, or—to put it more starkly—a dying Christendom. Of course, they insist that the church needs leaders that are theologically educated. This outcome is not a matter for debate; rather, at issue is whether seminaries, as they currently exist, are the best model for training and developing pastors who can lead the church in mission. Are there other leadership development models that are more effective?

"The seminary cannot exist without the church," says Daniel O. Aleshire, executive director of the Association of Theological Schools (ATS). He is simply doing the math. If there are no faith communities sending students to seminary or congregations that want to hire seminary graduates, then seminaries will, in Aleshire's words, "wither and die like cursed fig trees." That is sober logic, but Aleshire is nonetheless optimistic about the future of seminaries. They need to focus on what they do best, what they were designed to do. They are good at formational learning, theological teaching and scholarly research. The ones that survive will be the ones that get *better*. Seminaries are institutions that have an incredible capacity to endure, and while some may close or merge, others will successfully adapt and develop new ways of offering effective theological education.

This is why I am participating in one of these adaptive strategies, a partnership between a *historic seminary* and a *teaching church* (Western Theological Seminary and City Church San Francisco). We are building a bridge between the two, a mediating structure enabling each partner to bring their particular strengths to the ministerial formation process. The hybrid entity we've created is called Newbigin House of Studies.

Newbigin House of Studies

The name honors Lesslie Newbigin (1909–98), the British missionary-theologian whose life legacy was a call for the church to re-engage in mission. Newbigin taught that "the church *is* mission," "the magnet between Christ and the world." He frequently quoted Emil Brunner's famous dictum, "the church exists by mission as a fire exists by burning." According to Newbigin, spiritual renewal will only happen when "local congregations renounce an introverted concern for their own life, and recognize that they exist for the sake of those who are not members, as sign, instrument and foretaste of God's redeeming grace for the whole life of society." Newbigin is iconic for many of us who think that the crucial need of the church in the West is for leaders who are capable of planting new mission-shaped churches or revitalizing churches in decline.

Newbigin House of Studies began in 2009, as the brainchild of myself, the Reverend Fred Harrell, the founding pastor of City Church San Francisco, and Dr. Chuck DeGroat, the founder and director of the City Church Counseling Center. Fred and I are passionate about mentoring church planters. Chuck is a therapist with previous experience as director of the Spiritual Formation program for Reformed Theological Seminary. He is devoted to issues of pastoral health and sustainability.

We are presently involved in two primary projects at Newbigin House: first, the Newbigin Fellowship, a yearlong discipleship program for laypersons with a strong emphasis on issues of faith and work; and second, the partnership for the Distance Learning Master of divinity (MDiv) offered by Western Theological Seminary. I'd like to tell the story of these two projects and how they've come about.

City Church San Francisco and the City Classis

City Church San Francisco was planted in 1997 by Rev. Fred Harrell. When he and his family moved to San Francisco the previous year, the person who recruited him gave him a list of contacts with only three names—one was a confident Christian, one was confidently not a Christian, the other was somewhere in the middle. Those three belief demographics were the roux City Church began with and have characterized it ever since. After a networking period of six months public worship began in February 1997 with around thirty adults. Today, City Church is multisite congregation of 1700 people with 1,000 in weekly attendance. City Church currently gathers for worship at locations in lower Pacific Heights and the Mission district, and—eight times a week—in San Francisco County Jail! A new worship site will launch this Fall in the Tenderloin. The facility is currently in development in this community of deep need, a project of City Hope, the social justice subsidiary of City Church. With a mission to renew the city, City Hope equips and pastors hundreds of volunteers weekly to provide support to non-profits, schools, hospitals, jails, social enterprises and faith-based organizations throughout San Francisco.

From its earliest days, City Church has sought to be more than just a church. The founders wanted to be the catalyst for a movement of new churches and ministries that would renew the city spiritually, socially and culturally. City Church has catalyzed twenty-six new church starts during the last seventeen years in cities around the country, and locally in Marin, Berkeley, and Silicon Valley. Beyond this, City Church has been instrumental in the creation of the City Classis, a new missional structure within our denomination, the Reformed Church in America (RCA). With a goal of creating healthy and reproducing urban churches, City Classis has extended to Los Angeles, Denver, Chicago, Philadelphia, and New York. Essentially, these are churches and church plants that are focused on ministry in large urban centers.

The Newbigin Fellowship: The First Program

When Newbigin House was launched, the initial focus was on the need for theological training for existing and future cultural leaders in various professional fields—technology, media, business, government, academia, and the arts. This was an important emphasis for Newbigin himself; the *whole* people of God must be equipped for mission, discipled and supported for public life: "If the gospel is to challenge the public life of our society, it will only be by movements that begin with the local congregation in which the reality of the new creation is present, known and experienced, and from which men and women will go into every sector of public life to claim it for Christ."[1]

Our response was to launch the Newbigin Fellowship, a yearlong intensive training program providing theological, spiritual, and relational foundations for meaningful and sustainable integration of faith and work. More than 100 people have participated in the program. There are thirty fellows in the program this year, with cohorts in San Francisco, Berkeley and Sacramento.

The vision we cast for the Fellows program is one that sees every vocation as a kingdom activity, and the city as the best place to stay and live into one's vocation. It's a vision to fill San Francisco with influential followers of Jesus, with what Newbigin liked to call "subversive agents of the kingdom." I realize that's a loaded and provocative phrase! But he wasn't calling for culture war or revolution; rather, for a faithful presence that engages our culture and brings gradual transformation, what he termed "challenging relevance." The Fellows come to see that the church is simultaneously for and against culture. On the one hand, opposing idolatry and distortion of the creator's intentions; on the other, bringing new meaning to cultural

1. Newbigin, *Gospel in a Pluralist Society*, 232–33.

expression through the power of the gospel. N. T. Wright articulates the vision well:

> Our task as image-bearing, God-loving, Christ-shaped, Spirit-filled Christians, following Christ and shaping our world, is to announce redemption to a world that has discovered its fallenness, to announce healing to a world that has discovered its brokenness, to proclaim love and trust to a world that knows only exploitation, fear and suspicion . . . The gospel of Jesus points us and indeed urges us to be at the leading edge of the whole culture, articulating in story and music and art and philosophy and education and poetry and politics and theology and even—heaven help us—biblical studies, a worldview that will mount the historically-rooted Christian challenge to both modernity and postmodernity, leading the way . . . with joy and humor and gentleness and good judgment and true wisdom.[2]

I think it's important to say that the Fellows have given back as much as they've received. (I'm not just referring to cool things like inviting me to lunch at the decadent employee cafeterias of Lucasfilm and Google)! I mean that when theology is done by people who are deeply engaged in the life of the broader society, when the voices of cultural leaders in other spheres participate in the conversation, then theology is simply better, more fertile, sumptuous and worthwhile. Martin Kähler observed that in the first century theology was not an academic institutional luxury, but something developed out of missionary necessity. Mission was the "mother of theology." The Fellows program has given me a taste of what I think he meant. These folks are hungry for wisdom to live faithfully, to connect the true story of the world revealed in Scripture to the issues and challenges of life in what is arguably the most secular city in the country.

Western Theological Seminary

Newbigin House began with a desire to actually start a new seminary, a West Coast RCA seminary, there currently being seminaries on the East Coast and in the Midwest. But as we did our research we quickly saw that astronomical costs would be involved in a start-up, and that many existing seminaries are finding it difficult to sustain themselves economically. So we began to look for other creative ways to get involved in theological education. We learned from the President of the GTU, that ATS has a designation for what we were trying to do— "House of Studies," i.e., a partner

---

2. Wright, *The Challenge of Jesus*, 184.

organization in the theological education process that comes alongside the seminary; the seminary is solely responsible for and grants the academic degree, but the house of studies is a partner in providing something unique and distinctive that does not exist within the seminary. We realized, "that's what we want to be, a house of studies," then proceeded to search for a seminary that would be a good fit.

We approached Western Theological Seminary (WTS) in Holland, Michigan, because of our denominational ties through the RCA. We quickly saw that we had ties that were even stronger than those of denominational affiliation: WTS was laser-focused on becoming a recognized center for training women and men who could lead the church in mission. The president, Dr. Timothy Brown, was passionate about church planting and urban church revitalization. We also learned that WTS had been a leading provider of accredited distance learning education for more than a decade. But most importantly for us, we found partners who valued what *we* could bring to the table, and immediately and enthusiastically welcomed the conversation. The President and the academic dean, Dr. Leanne Van Dyk, worked tirelessly with us to develop a partnership plan, and to bring the various stakeholders—the denomination, the faculty, the trustees—on board with the vision. We eventually settled on a contract model for the partnership: Newbigin House is a ministry of City Church and is governed as such; our obligations to WTS, and theirs to us are guaranteed by contract. Most importantly, there is an *entente cordiale*, a commitment towards one another to a deepening relationship of trust-confidence. We are bound together by shared values and vision, and awareness that we really need each other for the mission to succeed.

The WTS-Newbigin Distance Learning MDiv

This MDiv has been developed to train women and men for ministry in urban and secular contexts. It is for those who want to revitalize struggling congregations, launch new ministries, or plant new churches in cities. It includes coursework, mentoring and spiritual formation with a focus on urban ministry, and internship placements in a variety of urban settings. Newbigin House is for those who want to apprentice for ministry in the city, but also for those who want to be apprenticed by the city for ministry.

The Educational Model

This degree brings together some of the best of WTS's coursework with courses taught by the Newbigin House faculty. It is offered via distance learning technology, along with face-to-face instruction and mentoring within a cohort community. The students participate in three, one-week intensives per year: two are held on campus at the seminary, in October and May; in July they come to San Francisco. The mentoring takes place primarily in years 3 and 4 during their embedded urban internships (see description below).

The Faculty

Our small faculty are designated as "Senior Fellows" at Newbigin House, and "Newbigin Faculty" at WTS. Two of us are based at City Church, three others are involved in either City Classis churches or urban churches in our network. Beyond this, the entire pastoral staff at City Church is engaged with the program in various respects. City Church has committed itself through and through to becoming a "teaching hospital," a center for hands-on training in urban and missional ministry. All of the Senior Fellows/Newbigin Faculty have ongoing responsibilities for ministry within their respective churches. This is an essential commitment for our team, for all to keep some ministry "skin in the game" to keep our edge sharp.

The Students

Our cohorts are small, twelve to fifteen students per year. They have not been recruited fresh from college campuses. Most of them are late twenties, early thirties, and already engaged in ministry in various cities around the country. Some were actually converted within the church they now serve. Some are recognized as a key talent that the church does not want to loose. Some serve on church staffs, some are already church planters credentialed as "Commissioned Pastors" within a Reformed denomination, such as the PC(USA), RCA or CRCNA. Some are pastors within other networks that lack traditional Protestant ordination requirements, "PDEs" (Post-Denominational Evangelicals),but they come to us with a recognition of their need for theological education. They are hungry for it and teachable.

Feedback on the educational model has been very positive. What we've heard from these students is a clear preference for distance learning combined with face-to-face intensives, over other educational models that feature classes on nights and weekends traveling to a regional seminary extension site. And they love the camaraderie that comes with being in a community of city loving entrepreneurs and church planters.

Two-Year Embedded Urban Internship

At the heart of this program is a two-year embedded internship in years three and four in the context of an urban church, church plant or mission-shaped congregation. During the summer prior to the beginning of the embedded internship, students undergo an Urban Ministry/Church Planting Assessment as part of the course, "Introduction to Urban Church Planting." The Assessment process is designed to accurately and objectively gauge the developmental level of the student in light of a competency model in order that the student might best understand how to grow in leadership. The assessment indicates areas of weakness and strength measured according to core competencies, dimensions and characteristics of effective church planters. The students develop learning contracts with their coaches informed by the findings of the assessment process. The coach works with the director of the Urban Church Planting Center at Newbigin House, who oversees the embedded internship process. This team (director/coach) access progress and growth in these crucial areas of ministry competence at the end of each semester and give a report to the student.

Curriculum

Courses taught by Newbigin Faculty include: The Urban Christian; The Urban Church; Urban Church Planting; The Urban Pastor; Gospel, Culture, and Church; Systematic Theology (with a strong missional emphasis); The Missional and Ecumenical Theology of Lesslie Newbigin; The Practice of Worship and Preaching.

I'd like to take a few moments to talk about that last course (it's one that I teach!), because this is a key component to our program, and it deals with a core ecclesiological question that brings us together for this conference: what is the connection between liturgy and mission?

As the leader of Newbigin House, I am strongly committed to the project of missional theology. I believe worship cannot be an exception to the rule that we must rethink all of our theology in light of the *missio Dei*.

Missional Liturgics at Newbigin House

I currently chair the Commission on Christian Worship for the RCA, and I've had over twenty years of experience leading and shaping worship in congregations where I've served as pastor—as a church planter in Greenwich Village, then helping a "praise band" church in downtown Atlanta embrace some of the riches of the liturgical spirituality, and now in San Francisco at City Church. During that time, I've seen scores of churches "pick up" liturgical practices that they experienced when visiting our worship service. City Church follows the lectionary and church year closely, and celebrates the eucharist weekly. We kneel, we light candles, we make the sign of the cross, we follow a lectionary. Most of the churches and church plants within the City Classis do the same. Why? Because the planters have seen the missionary wisdom embedded in the ancient patterns developed by the greatest missionaries of all time, the early Christians! They've come to see the liturgy as a gift for the church's mission, and our seminarians at Newbigin House are of a similar opinion.

There are two questions I'd like to address here: First, what is missional worship? Second, in what ways can liturgical worship be missional?

In his book *Cadences of Home: Preaching among Exiles*, Walter Brueggeman argues that preaching must, on the one hand, be thick enough to form identity of exiles in Babylon. I would add that liturgy also needs to meet this "thickness" critieria, and that the identity that needs to be formed is a missional identity. But, says Brueggeman, this preaching is also meant to be overhead by Babylonians among whom the exiles live, and whom God desires to bless. This is the challenge and opportunity of missional worship. It is worship that is thick enough to form missionary disciples and *at the same time* comprehensible enough for outsiders to overhear.

My church planting mentor in New York, Dr. Timothy Keller, puts it this way: "To reach this growing post-Christendom society in the West will obviously take more than what we ordinarily call an evangelistic church: it will take a missional church. This church's worship is missional in that it makes sense to nonbelievers in that culture, even while it challenges and shapes Christians with the gospel."[3]

So what is the connection between missional worship, defined this way, and the liturgy? I propose this: missional worship is *shaped by* and *engages the world* with the *biblical story*. And the historic liturgy is nothing less than a covenantal narrative expression of the biblical story, and an application of that story to our own, so that it becomes our story. Let me unpack this . . .

---

3. Keller, *Center Church*, 141.

Shaped by the Biblical Story

In the words of theologian James K. A. Smith, "to be restored is to be re-storied with the story." Newbigin calls it "reliving the story":

> The community of the Christian Church understands itself and the human and cosmic history of which it is a part in terms of the biblical story. Its being and life are incomprehensible apart from that story. Its liturgical actions are the *reliving of this story* ... The gospel, the account of God's actions for the creation and redemption of the world, is always in narrative form.[4]

It is this reliving of the story that grounds the church in its missional identity and vocation, bearing witness in word and sacrament to the risen and returning Lord Jesus, to his inauguration of God's kingdom, and to the mission of God into which we are called to share.

According to Newbigin, this "reliving" happens in what he calls the "painful tension . . . between the 2 embodiments of God's people." On the one hand, we are members of our cultural communities, shaped by our cultural stories. But we also part of a new humanity shaped by the biblical story. Worship is a drama of living at the crossroads of these two stories. The great missionary theologian, Andrew Walls, describes this dialectical tension as an "indigenizing principle" and a "pilgrim principle." Christianity can be at home everywhere, even as it is at home nowhere.

> Not only does God in Christ take people as they are: He takes them in order to transform them into what He wants them to be. Along with the indigenizing principle which makes his faith a place to feel at home, the Christian inherits the pilgrim principle, which whispers to him that he has no abiding city and warns him that to be faithful to Christ will put him out of step with his society; for that society never existed, in East or West, ancient time or modern, which could absorb the word of Christ painlessly into its system.[5]

The wisdom of the historic liturgy becomes apparent in light of this tension. Thick identities require deep grounding in the narrative of Scripture read and preached, and the covenantal renewal of sacramental life at font and table. We need to be re-storied with the story.

---

4. Newbigin, *Proper Confidence*, 52.
5. Walls, *The Missionary Movement*, 7.

Engaging the World with the Biblical Story

I recently read that T. S. Eliot loved vanilla ice cream with chocolate sauce. He was eating it in a restaurant once and a man opposite said, "I can't understand how a poet like you can eat that stuff." Eliot, with hardly a pause, said, "Ah, but you're not a poet," and went on eating.

This reminds me of the several conversations I've had about the experience of the liturgy over the years—both with longtime Christians and those exploring the Christian faith. The churches I've planted or led have been "liturgical" and, by God's grace, they have been effective in introducing people to faith in Jesus Christ. I have found seekers, whether skeptical or mildly curious about faith, on the whole, to be poets who recognize the poetry. They find the silence refreshing; the hospitable explanation of unusual acts such as confession of sin to be immensely helpful and practical. I don't remember a month when someone hasn't decided to come forward and take communion as their act of conversion. (This regardless of how clearly communion was explained!) But I don't mind. They want to be part of the story that is unfolding before them.

But there are those who do not hear the poetry, or perhaps a more charitable thing to say would be, who prefer other poetry. Every critical comment I've ever encountered about a liturgical element of worship—a responsive psalm, confession of sin, passing the peace, weekly eucharist, Lenten observance, etc.—every single one has come from a long-time Christian, someone who has been traditioned in another pattern of worship.

I recently read article by the popular biopsychologist Nigel Barber arguing that religion is becoming obsolete and can no longer compete with what he calls "rival feel-good products" such psychotherapy, anti-anxiety drugs, movies and sports. "However hard religions struggle to be modern, relevant, and entertaining, they seem destined to fall behind in the sense that attending church has become an exercise in self-imposed tedium." Based on what we're seeing in our church plants in the City Classis, he couldn't be more wrong. In the midst of a world of competing narratives that tell people who they are, how they should feel, what they should buy, what they must achieve, in short—what they should love—in the liturgy we hear and see enacted before us the true story of the world, the only story that can enable any of us to truly understand ourselves. When worship is led and the sacraments celebrated with even a modicum of missionary sensibility and skill, the nations overhear. Congregants begin to trust the leaders with what is being offered, and they bring their friends.

In Newbigin's classic work, *The Gospel in a Pluralist Society*, he asks this question: "how is the life of Christ, the life which is a true foretaste of the kingdom, continued in the period after the ascension"? He gives this answer:

> It will be in the life of a community which remembers, rehearses, and lives by the story which the Bible tells and of which the central focus is the story told in the New Testament. The remembering and rehearsing will be through the continual reading of and reflection of the Bible and the continual repetition of the sacrament of baptism and eucharist.

Our strong conviction at City Church, within the network of churches of the City Classis, and at Newbigin House, is that liturgical worship, rightly modeled and taught to the students and pastors who lead and will lead the church in its mission, is uniquely suited to shape the church with the biblical story, and at the same time engage with world with its true story.

Conclusion

Newbigin believed that for ministers to be effectively trained there had to be changes to the structure, content and method of theological education. Classical seminary education took its shape in the context of Christendom when the church had lost its missionary character and was "entirely conceived in terms of pastoral care of existing congregations." The future shape of theological education lay in answering this question: "what kind of ministerial leadership will nourish the Church in its faithfulness to the gospel in a pluralist society?"

This is the primary question we are wrestling with at Newbigin House. We have more questions than we do answers, but we're pretty confident that one of the ways to scale the "ugly great ditch" is by bringing the seminary and the church together in the formation process, rethinking the content and context of theological education, assessing for and nurturing essential ministry competencies.

I began writing this article during the holidays shortly after watching my favorite British sci-fi drama, *Dr. Who*. At a dramatic moment when the building that the Doctor and his companions are in turns into a spaceship, he is forced to act on the spur of the moment. As the building begins to take off, his companions shout in panic asking him what to do. The Doctor calls over his shoulder, "Do what I do—hold tight and pretend it's a plan!"

That image has stayed with me as I think about the experience of launching Newbigin House. This is an experiment in faith. The uncertainty of what lies ahead is a bit unnerving, but I'm holding tight. Thankfully, I don't have to pretend. This plan reflects my deepest convictions about the future of theological education: seminary and church in partnership, serving the mission of God together.

Bibliography

Brueggemann, Walter. *Cadences of Home: Preaching among Exiles*. Louisville: Westminster John Knox, 1997.

Keller, Timothy. *Center Church: Doing Balanced, Gospel-Centered Ministry in Your City*. Grand Rapids: Zondervan, 2012.

Newbigin, Lesslie. *The Gospel in a Pluralist Society*. Grand Rapids: Eerdmans, 1989.

———. *Proper Confidence: Faith, Doubt and Certainty in Christian Discipleship*. Grand Rapids: Eerdmans, 1995.

Walls, Andrew F. *The Missionary Movement in Christian History: Studies in the Transmission of Faith*. Maryknoll, NY: Orbis, 1996.

Wright, N. T. *The Challenge of Jesus: Rediscovering Who Jesus Was and Is*. Downers Grove, IL: InterVarsity, 1999.

17

From the Palace to the Streets

STEVEN TOSHIO YAMAGUCHI

Christendom's Decline: A Range of Coming to Terms

In my work as a Presbytery Pastor and Executive, I serve fifty-six churches and fellowships as each one is wrestling with what it means to live faithfully in a post-Christendom world. Some eagerly face the change, alert, experimental and excited. Some have little understanding of the sea change happening around them. And some fight desperately to maintain the passing privilege of Christendom, fearful, grieving, and angry over the loss that threatens what they have loved.

For the purpose of this colloquium, as the theme of Christendom's impact has been developed throughout these colloquia, I am not going to take time to try to define Christendom further. I am assuming that by now we understand adequately what we mean by Christendom, that favored status the church enjoyed with state and society, a favor tracing back to Constantine.[1]

Our presbytery's bounds contain a fascinating mix of Christendom's remnants along with many people who never knew Christendom. The presbytery bounds include 5.2 million people—2.2 million of us live in a corner of Los Angeles County along with the 3 million who live in all of Orange

---

1. While there is much written about the shift from a Christendom world into post-Christendom, I particularly appreciate Guder, *The Continuing Conversion*; Stuart Murray's assessments of Christendom as treated in Pietersen, *Reading the Bible*. Also helpful is Bolger, *The Gospel After Christendom*.

County. Our presbytery's population teems with diversity. Our "Little Saigon" is the largest Vietnamese population in the world outside of Vietnam. We include similar concentrations of immigrants from India, Cambodia, Korea, China, and many Latin American and African nations. "They" are "we." Religious and spiritual practices of all kinds spawn and grow and become movements within our bounds, outside the church. For many older folks who enjoyed the heyday of the church's Euro-centric Christendom privilege, it is painfully obvious that Christendom's reign has passed. Our L.A. neighborhoods are the home of gangster rap and urban density that show little regard for Christendom. On the other hand, our younger people have no memory of that Christendom privilege so they feel no pain for that particular loss. We are a mixed bunch.

Still, for some within our presbytery's bounds, especially in Orange County, the dream of Christendom holds fast. At my office in Anaheim, I sit less than twenty minutes from: the mother church of Calvary Chapel; the mother church of the Vineyard; the Crystal Cathedral (or what's left of it); the Evangelical Free Church of Fullerton where Chuck Swindoll preached; the TBN broadcasting center; and Saddleback Church with Rick Warren. Plus there are many other less known but still large churches like Mariner's Church in Irvine with over thirteen thousand members. They create a force field. And much of it helps sustains a vision and longing for the church as "palace."

Life in the Palace

A palace is a grand residence for royalty and officials. It takes its name from the *Palatium*, the hill in ancient Rome that housed the imperial residence. Across Europe the palace also came to be the residence of aristocrats. Eventually, palace also became the official residence for the church's bishops and archbishops. A bishop's palace was a clear expression of the Christendom church's benefit of popular favor and status. But the place of the palace in our society has changed. Many palaces have been repurposed and become public spaces for museums, government and amusement. But the palatial vision persists in parts of the church.

It is difficult for many of our longtime church members to grasp or accept the loss of societal favor their church once had. I find that comparing the idea of "palace" church to missional church sometimes helps bewildered church members begin to understand what is happening to their church and world. They have a mental model of what a palace is. That can help them, by contrast, to form a new mental model of what a missional church must not be.

Palatial life is not simply one of various random positions in society. It is a peculiar position of privilege with resources and power. It can insulate the palace dweller from the struggles of the world outside the palace, and it can deafen the palace dweller to the gospel's persistent prophetic calling to justice and love for our neighbor. The palace gig appears to be lovely and desirable, but while a delight to the eye it can be a peril to the soul.

Some old-time churchgoers remember wistfully a time gone by when the laws of the land and social pressure encouraged church attendance, when Christian church folks received preferential treatment in government and business, when those who expressed disbelief or other beliefs were treated as second class. While some view nostalgically that cozy relationship between the church and Caesar as a heyday for a "Christian America," that wedding of church privilege with state and societal power can also be viewed as a "religious totalitarianism" as Miroslav Volf discusses in *A Public Faith*.[2] The wedding of the church with the world's power tends not to nurture a servant church who lovingly and humbly bears salt and light in the world, giving itself away so as to love neighbor. The power of the palace readily forges heavy handed, well-intended inflictors of palatial values. The palace is seductive and powerful. It has shaped the Christian church in the West for centuries.

Training Matters

How did we learn to be palatial Christians? Only by training. You have to be trained through long practice and modeling and socializing. The training happens persistently even while the trainees are not aware they are being trained. They are simply experiencing life, doing what seems normal in their palace world. It is a persistent training, nonetheless, a training that shapes a soul. This question thus haunts me: Is it a training that can be unlearned? Can a church born and bred in the palace be retrained to live among the people, to thrive on the streets outside the palace?

Stories of trading places between palace and poverty, like Mark Twain's *The Prince and the Pauper*, remind us that people must be trained for their place in society. Simply transplanting a person from one world to the other, even if the dress and costume are perfect, does not immediately change the mind and heart and language and practice. The behaviors, world view, and mental model must be transformed through training. And some deeply

2. Volf, *A Public Faith*.

imbedded mental models can only be changed with deep pain and great transformational cost.

Nineteen years ago my spiritual director, Father Pat, a Vincentian priest, was trying to help me understand that I needed retraining in my spiritual life. I understood the ideas. I affirmed the spiritual truths and insights. But Father Pat knew I needed more than knowledge and even understanding. I needed training. So he told me the story of his experience in a jet fighter flight simulator at the military base. His brother arranged this for him as a birthday present. Father Pat was paying close attention to the instruction he was receiving with its warning that he will crash if he is not absolutely devoted to his training. "Because," said the Top Gun instructor, "in the moment of crisis you will not rise to the occasion. You will default to your training." Father Pat continued in his spiritual training with me for years. I came to experience the truth of his wisdom again and again: In our moment of crisis we do not rise to the occasion. We default to our training.[3]

A church that has lived in the palace for generations, yea even for so many centuries, has been trained in the ways of privilege. It has not been trained in street smarts. A church that is trained to count on the protection of the state is not trained to fend for itself on the streets. So when state and society withdraw their special favor towards the church, it is a very rude awakening for the palace trained church. It is disorienting and painful. It can lead to despair and anger, denial and blaming, and selective memory and a nostalgic sentimentalism that overglorifies the "good old days."

How can a palace-trained church learn to live among the people, with the people, for the people, out on the streets? How does a privileged palace church learn street smarts? It takes training.

Retraining?

In Exodus we watch Israel freed from slavery under Pharaoh. Had they been immediately transplanted into the Promised Land, they would still have acted and thought like slaves. That would have been their default. It was what they were trained to do. So God trained them through years and generations of wandering. During that time they became a people. They began learning to trust God rather than Pharaoh for their daily bread. They received a name. They received a law. Their identity was forged. They learned of God's unspeakable name. Did they wander for so long because

---

3. See the story of the priest and the jet fighter pilot: http://www.youtube.com/watch?v=XIovOzJGHXU.

they lacked GPS? No. They were not lost. God was leading them. They were being trained, by God's grace.

The New Testament talks about our need for training. In Titus 2:11 Titus is told that God does the training: "For the grace of God has appeared . . . training us to renounce impiety . . . to live lives that are self-controlled, upright, and godly."[4] In 1 Tim 1:4 Timothy is warned against being occupied by myths and speculation rather than "divine training."[5] In 2 Tim 3:16 he is told "All scripture is inspired by God and is useful for . . . training in righteousness."[6] In 1 Tim 4:7–8 he is told, "Train yourself in godliness"[7] which is of value in "both the present life and the life to come." These references to training are nuanced by different Greek expressions for training. Training is important. Paul insists that training matters. Training must be deep and persistent; it is of eternal consequence.

Centuries before Christendom raised its head, followers of Christ needed that training in godliness, training to renounce impiety, training in righteousness and justice. All the more today, followers of Christ trained in the palace and now spurned by Caesar need new training for life after the palace, lest they default to their training in palatial ways. Who can train a palatial church desiring to change its ways? Who can teach the ways of God and the ways of the people on the streets?

I suggest two sources where we can find the trainers we need. The first is the immigrants and aliens already among us. The second is our Reformed liturgy.

Trainers for the Palace Church: The Center Needs the Edges

The palace church suffers today because of its palatial instincts. It needs to be trained by people who do not have palatial instincts. These will most likely be people who have never lived in the palace. Where better to find

---

4. Training as παιδεύουσα in Titus 2:12. "Ἐπεφάνη γὰρ ἡ χάρις τοῦ θεοῦ . . . παιδεύουσα ἡμᾶς, ἵνα ἀρνησάμενοι τὴν ἀσέβειαν" from παιδεύω.

5. Training as οἰκονομίαν in 1 Tim 1:4. "μηδὲ προσέχειν μύθοις καὶ γενεαλογίαις ἀπεράντοις, αἵτινες ἐκζητήσεις παρέχουσιν μᾶλλον ἢ οἰκονομίαν θεοῦ τὴν ἐν πίστει" from ἡ οἰκονομία.

6. Training as παιδείαν in 2 Tim 3:16. "πᾶσα γραφὴ θεόπνευστος καὶ ὠφέλιμος πρὸς διδασκαλίαν, πρὸς ἐλεγμόν, πρὸς ἐπανόρθωσιν, πρὸς παιδείαν τὴν ἐν δικαιοσύνῃ" from ἡ παιδεία.

7. "Trained" as γύμναζε in 1 Tim 4:7. "τοὺς δὲ βεβήλους καὶ γραώδεις μύθους παραιτοῦ. Γύμναζε δὲ σεαυτὸν πρὸς εὐσέβειαν" from γυμνάζω; 1 Tim 4:8, "ἡ γὰρ σωματικὴ γυμνασία πρὸς ὀλίγον ἐστὶν ὠφέλιμος," "training" from ἡ γυμνασία.

such people than among the immigrants in our midst? Or among those who have long been systematically excluded from the palace. These people know how to thrive in the world among the people, on the streets, outside the palace walls. They may be awkward inside the palace and lack palace manners, but they have street savvy. Within the Presbyterian Church we have faithful Reformed brothers and sisters who come from other lands and they are not a part of American palace life. They have learned to thrive in business, in living communities, and in churches, but they are off the radar of the palace church. As a denominational staff person and leader, I acknowledge that the palace church's institution has at least tried to engage the streets. In 1998 the PC(USA) General Assembly adopted the "Racial Ethnic/Immigrant Church Growth Strategy"[8] with a goal of increasing our "racial ethnic" church membership from 4 percent to 20 percent by the year 2020. This past December, General Assembly Moderator Neal Presa reported to the church, "We in the PC(USA) have goals for a truly multicultural church, yet membership statistics tell us that in the last forty years racial-ethnic membership has not grown as a percentage of the total membership over this same period." I fear that for the palace church, the desire to have a more diverse looking church is, for all practical purposes, a more decorative than missional project. Kevin Park at Columbia Theological Seminary calls this "Ornamental Multiculturalism"[9] and thoughtfully critiques what can be the shallowness of diversity efforts by, what I would call, the palace church.

When I think of that 1998 General Assembly resolution, I wonder if those who voted for it were thinking, "Wouldn't it be swell if our life in the palace looked more like the streets and we had some more of those lovely people of color among us here in our palace?" I think the better question would have been, "Who can liberate us from our captivity in this damned palace?" Perhaps, ironically, that may also actually be the easier question to answer.

It has been hard for the "majority" church in the PC(USA) to appreciate and receive the gifts that immigrant churches have to offer. Traditionalists easily criticize newcomers with stereotypical criticisms such as: they don't respect time; I can't understand their English; their records are a mess; they don't follow Robert's Rules. The criticisms get more personal: their food smells; they smell; they huddle in cliques and only talk with each other. The failures to connect are many and obvious. This failure happens easily when the cultural values of the palace are used to assess the worth of the cultural values of the streets. What if we could appreciate street smarts for what they

---

8. *Racial Ethnic/Immigrant Church.*
9. Park, "Ornamental Multiculturalism."

are? If the church finds itself no longer protected by palace walls but now surrounded by Philistines and giants, perhaps the palace's values and tools are more like Saul's heavy armor, when our rescue may rest in the hands of nimble shepherds who know how to brave wild beasts with smooth stones and a sling.

The palace church tends to engage its extra-palace neighbors as objects of "mission" projects or as people who can cook exotic and savory foods and dance and sing for their church programs. But rarely has the palace church looked to their immigrant brothers and sisters as trainers for the church's future strength. Our immigrant churches have generations of experience living on the edges, displaced from the center, as more than survivors. But is the palace church open to receive training from them?

True Story: A "Palace Church" Is Being Retrained

It is delightful to see how this is happening in, of all places, the Church of England through its ecumenical Fresh Expressions movement.[10] It is a liberating movement in which the church moves into the streets and neighborhoods and dwells among the people, listening and learning and loving neighbor rather than automatically imposing the traditions of the palace. In their case, the most important support for this movement literally came from the palace. Lambeth Palace is the London residence of the archbishop of Canterbury. Archbishop Rowan Williams for a decade lent his full support to this movement. He regards Fresh Expressions as the one thing he wants most to be remembered for in the Church of England, "the thing that's most cheered me and encouraged me in recent years."[11] In full support he walked the streets, hanging out with tattooed and pierced young, new Anglicans who love him and know him and call him Rowan. The movement has flourished and grown ecumenically. Thousands of Fresh Expressions of church have been birthed in neighborhoods throughout the UK, at least half of them are other than Anglican, and the movement is spreading around the world, even here among us. The move from the palace to the streets is possible. It is happening. Now.

---

10. For the beginnings of the Fresh Expressions movement that flowed ecumenically out of the Church of England, see the seminal work in the report from the Archbishop of Canterbury's Council on Mission and Public Affairs, *Mission Shaped Church*. For an assessment of the movement after eight years of dynamic growth, change and learning, see Moynagh, *A Church for Every Context*.

11. Williams, "Rowan Williams on Being Remembered."

Thus my first recommended resource for training for life after the palace is the very people who have long been excluded from, or have gladly eschewed, life in the palace. The immigrants and those we consider alien among us can be our teachers. This will require great humility and great listening. But the Presbyterian Church has this treasure among us if we can suspend palatial judgment and receive these gifts that come from outside the palace walls.

Reformed Liturgy as a Trainer

My second recommendation as a resource for training for the missional life outside the palace is our Reformed liturgy. Our practice over time is our training. The newly proposed draft for revising the Directory for Worship in the *Book of Order* contains these wonderful lines:

> W-5.0301: The Church's Mission in the World
> God sends the church in the power of the Holy Spirit to join the mission of Jesus Christ in service to the world. The church's mission and worship are deeply connected. The church's mission springs from its worship, where we glimpse the reality and the promise of God's eternal realm. The church's mission flows back into worship as we bring to God the joy and suffering of the world.[12]

The worship we experience together can train us in humility and submission to our sovereign God. It can make tender our hearts for the world God loves. And it can send us into that world grateful and renewed by God's saving grace. Or it might not. What passes for worship can become a liturgy of palace values that reinforce the comfort and privilege of palace life. In the

---

12. From a copy of the draft received from its editor, Dr. David Gambrell. The draft is a revision of the Directory for Worship in the *Book of Order* of the PC(USA). The 217th General Assembly (2006) recommended that the Directory for Worship be revised to be shorter and better organized. On February 7, 2014, the Presbyterian Mission Agency Board voted "That the draft of the proposed Directory for Worship be sent to the 221st General Assembly (2014) as a study document and that the General Assembly forward it to the church for study and comment in consideration of submitting it to the General Assembly for approval in 2016."

I am enthusiastic about this revision and was privileged to participate in consultation on the revision. David Gambrell says this about the revision: "We hope that new worshiping communities will be able to find clear guidance and teaching on the basics of Reformed worship; that existing congregations will be able to find fresh inspiration for vital, vibrant worship and that multicultural communities and new immigrant fellowships will find encouragement to teach the church new patterns of prayer and praise." May it be so!

strange and fantastic mall of religious mega-experiences where I live and serve, what is presented as worship can be reduced to "songs and a talk." By contrast, the cosmic drama of the divine-human interaction enacted in our Reformed liturgy can provide a disciplined engagement with the awesome and just redeeming creator come to us in grace in Jesus Christ. But the palace is filled with idols who would usurp the throne. So our liturgy can be a helpful trainer only to the extent that we are disciplined to use the fullness of the liturgy's interactions, and faithful to worship the God who invades and disrupts our world to make it right. Our worship cannot help us if we bow before the gods of the palace, gods whom we choose for how they reinforce our palatial comfort.

Our worship can help us only if we keep the right God as the center of our worship. Psychologist Kelly Flanagan wrote this to his son in anticipation that he would someday marry:

> Many people are going to tell you the key to a happy marriage is to put God at the center of it, but I think it depends upon what your experience of God does for your ego. Because if your God is one of strength and power and domination, a God who proves you're always right and creates dividing lines by which you judge everyone else, a God who keeps you safe and secure, I think you should keep that God as far from the center of your marriage as you can. He'll only build your ego-wall taller and stronger.
>
> But if the God you experience is a vulnerable one, the kind of God that turns the world upside down and dwells in the midst of brokenness and embraces everyone on the margins and will sacrifice anything for peace and reconciliation and wants to trade safety and security for a dangerous and risky love, then I agree, put him right at the center of your marriage. If your God is in the ego dismantling business, he will transform your marriage into sacred ground.[13]

In our worship, which God we worship will determine whether the liturgy can actually train us for life outside the palace. But can a palace-trained church even detect when the palace's false gods are usurping the throne? Might not palace life inure us to its own perversities. Here, again, I would argue that those who have lived and trained outside the palace have the best tools for sniffing out the foul odors of the false gods that inhabit the palace.

---

13. Flanagan, "A Dad's Letter."

Cross Training: When Edge and Liturgy Reform Each Other

There is a third exploration for another time, and if we had time now I could rhapsodize until my feet lifted off the floor about the intersection of these two trainers—the aliens among us and the richness of Reformed liturgy. What we have to gain by seriously integrating these gifts is a whole world of discovery that we have barely begun to explore.

Keep It Real: No Fantasy Needed

One caveat here is that I must not romanticize life outside the palace. I am not trying to suggest that the immigrants and aliens among us are somehow better or have fewer problems than palace dwellers. I am plenty Reformed to believe that all our communities stand equally in need of absolute grace. Nevertheless, I am trying to say that people trained in different life locations will have different sensibilities, and we as the church post-Christendom need all the sensibilities we can garner to make sense of life in a world where the palace was once home for so long for so many in the church, but the palace offers such sanctuary no more. As we seek to learn from each other, we need to maintain a respectful and vibrant hope and imagination while avoiding the easy slip into exoticizing and objectifying one another. It's not always easy, it requires great attention and listening, but it does happen and it is so worthwhile.

Trainers from Surprising Places

I do fear that if our mental model of home and identity is the palace, then our missional enterprise, as "sent" as we try to be, will remain limited to forays out of Christendom's palace into the non-palatial world, but at the end of the day, continually returning to or longing for retreat to the palace. How shall we be trained to behave and think differently? Really trained to live differently, not simply acquire more insight into the issues? Who shall train us to eschew the palace for the freedom of the people in the streets—the messy, broken mix, the rich and lovely mix of all that humanity hungry for God on the streets—streets filled with God—streets we learn to love, streets we learn to call home, streets whose people become "we people," no longer "those" people?

The PC(USA)'s palatial instincts are killing us. Our worship instincts, our mission instincts, have been too long shaped by palace life. But there are those who are not spoiled by palace. Their instincts are sometimes different in profoundly simple ways—simple, yet inconceivable and unimagined for the palace dweller. My grandfather was like that. He never lived in a palace, and that shaped him. I share this story about him as an example of how being free of the palace's values can produce a completely different, unimagined way forward.

My grandfather, whom we call *Ojichan*, which is like "grandpa" in Japanese, was a truck farmer and my mom was a junior high girl in Harbor City, Los Angeles, in the spring of 1942. One April day notices were posted in their neighborhood that in two days all people of Japanese ancestry would have to report to be shipped to internment camps. They could bring only what they could carry in their arms, which explains why many families like ours have no family heirloom furniture. Japanese American farmers tried to sell their possessions for cash. They received pennies on the dollar. Some women chose to shatter their own china rather than feel exploited by their neighbors offering a pittance. My Ojichan owned a houseful of family possessions, a barnful of farming tools, a truck, a tractor and a car. His crops were ripening in the field. Rather than cash out his possessions, as seemed wise to the rest of the world, my Japanese immigrant grandfather gifted all his possessions to the family's beloved Mexican immigrant farmhand, Pedro, whom he called "Pi-do-ro" in Japanese fashion. My mother remembers that she loved the kind young man, Pi-do-ro. Rather than suffer the financial loss and humiliation of scrambling to cash out, Ojichan saw a way of grace and redemption and dignity. He earned the inestimable satisfaction of helping Pi-do-ro's family start a new life. That experience shaped my mother for a life of grace and generosity. I hope it has in some small way also shaped me. Ojichan's instincts and insights were so completely foreign to the values of the palace. My point is that we need the Ojichans to train the church. We need trainers unspoiled by the palace, fit to live on the edges of a wild new world. Smiling and thriving, that was always my Ojichan. And today's "Ojichans" are not only old Japanese farmers. They are also young and hungry app developers, organic urban farmers, holistic healers, environmental activists, entrepreneurs, labor organizers, and artists. They come in all kinds of colors. They live in intentional communities. They have just never bought into the palace.

Can Leaders Formed in the Palace Really Be Retrained?

It is one thing for someone who has never lived in the palace to have those non-palace instincts. But can someone who has been formed by palace life be changed? For this I look to Victor Hugo and his Bishop Bienvenu in the novel *Les Misérables*.[14] In the popular musical version, which I love, the recently paroled Jean Valjean steals the bishop's silverware while a houseguest. But the bishop cleverly averts reincarceration for Jean Valjean by telling the arresting police that the silver was not stolen, but was a gift from the bishop. Reinforcing this act, the bishop takes the most valuable silver candlesticks from the table and hands them to the thief, singing, "You forgot I gave these also; would you leave the best behind?"[15] The police depart, and Jean Valjean's world is turned upside down by this act of grace. It is a profound moment in the story, as the musical tells it. For twenty-five years I wondered, "Wow! Could I be so clever a pastor in a moment like that?" I marveled at the bishop's quick thinking. Then the new movie version of the musical came out last year and I wept again, this time determined to learn the full story. In the novel, this Bishop Bienvenu, appointed by Napoleon himself, arrived at his bishopric of Digne and immediately began divesting himself of the privileges of the bishop. Upon seeing the splendid bishop's palace next to a small, crowded and cramped hospital, he quickly decided to give the spacious and airy palace for the care of the many sick, and he took the small hospital building to be his living quarters. He gave his bishop's stipend to provide for the poor. He walked so he could give his transportation and carriage allowance for the care of others. He wore his robes to tatters so he could spend for those in need. He eschewed the palace to walk the streets, living among the people, touching them, knowing them, loving them. His integrity earned him the love and respect of many and he became adept at getting the wealthy to give money for the poor. He gave away all his family's possessions until the only personal possessions of value remaining were his family's silverware and candlesticks. Then in the moment of crisis, he gave them away freely and instantly.

 It was then, while reading the novel, that it struck me. The bishop did not at all "rise to the occasion." He defaulted to his training. He had been training for this moment so persistently for so many years that when presented with this opportunity to show mercy to a thief, he could do no other. This was not just a trick pulled on the police or the quick thinking of a clever

---

 14. Hugo, *Les Misérables*. Hugo uses almost all of the first twenty-seven chapters to develop the Bishop's rich character. Jean Valjean is not mentioned until the chapter 15. Hugo provides a clear story of the Bishop's "training" for the "moment of crisis" with Valjean and the police.

 15. From the musical *Les Misérables*, original French lyrics by Alain Boublil and Jean-Marc Natel, English-language libretto by Herbert Kretzmer. English lyrics copyright ©1986 by Alan Boublil Music Ltd. (ASCAP) c/o Joel Fadden & Co. Inc., New York.

bishop. This act flowed naturally from who he had become. He defaulted to his training.

Today in real time, life imitates art and I am inspired by Pope Francis. From his palaced privilege he actually lives the grace which Hugo wrote into Bishop Bienvenu's character. I do believe that if a Pope today can actually do this, even Presbyterians can do it. Trained by God's grace, we are doing it. It is happening; the movement is already begun. Because of what is happening at the edges in our most creative faithfully Reformed worship and mission, I am more excited about life in the Presbyterian Church than I ever have been. The edges are vibrant and it is thrilling and fun. My lingering worry is for our palace life at the center of privilege and power.

Holy Mischief

Inspired by Hugo's Bishop Bienvenu, I still hold this hope that we "inside" the church system might be trained to respond with the instincts of Jesus rather than the instincts of the palace court. When Bishop Bienvenu welcomed Jean Valjean to his home and table, Valjean was uneasy and confused by the Bishop's ease with him, ease even after Valjean revealed that he was a paroled convict. At this moment, before eating together, before Valjean stole the silverware, hear these words of Bishop Bienvenu, a name that literally means "welcome":

> The Bishop, who was sitting close to him, gently touched his hand. "You could not help telling me who you were. This is not my house; it is the house of Jesus Christ. This door does not demand of him who enters whether he has a name, but whether he has a grief. You suffer, you are hungry and thirsty; you are welcome. And do not thank me; do not say that I receive you in my house. No one is at home here, except the man who needs a refuge. I say to you, who are passing by, that you are much more at home here than I am myself. Everything here is yours. What need have I to know your name? Besides, before you told me, you had one which I knew." The man opened his eyes in astonishment. "Really? You knew what I was called?" "Yes," replied the Bishop, "you are called my brother."[16]

If mischief is behavior that causes discomfiture or annoyance in another, then holy mischief is afoot. Thanks be to God. The Spirit is at work and I have never been more hopeful, never been more excited, and never been more daunted by the challenge facing the church of the palace. But

16. Hugo, *Les Misérables*, 67.

just over a year ago, from a real palace, from Lambeth Palace, Archbishop of Canterbury Rowan Williams said this about the church he served, with a twinkle in his eye:

> . . . mainstream presences were carrying on more or less alright, with only the average levels of decline. But around it, so much else seemed to be going on. And something that I've always believed in theory was quite clearly happening in practice. And what I've always believed in theory was that the church gets renewed from the edges, not the middle. What do you think of it? The world itself was renewed by Christ from the edges, not the middle. There's nowhere more edgy than on the hill of Calvary.[17]

To the edges! To the streets! May God bring mercy and transformation to the people of the palace.

Bibliography

Archbishop of Canterbury's Council on Mission and Public Affairs. *Mission-Shaped Church*. London: Church House, 2004.

Bolger, Ryan K. *The Gospel after Christendom: New Voices, New Cultures, New Expressions*. Grand Rapids: Baker Academic, 2012.

Boublil, Alain, and Jean-Marc Natel. *Les Misérables*. English-language libretto by Herbert Kretzmer. New York: Joel Fadden, 1986.

Directory for Worship—Draft of Proposed Revision. http://www.presbyterianmission.org/ministries/worship/rdfw-chapter-five/#W503.

Flanagan, Kelly. "A Dad's Letter to His Son (About the Only Good Reason to Get Married)." http://drkellyflanagan.com/2014/01/29/a-dads-letter-to-his-son-about-the-only-good-reason-to-get-married/feed/.

Guder, Darrell L. *The Continuing Conversion of the Church*. Grand Rapids: Eerdmans, 2000.

Hugo, Victor. *Les Misérables*. Translated by Isabel F. Hapgood. New York: Thomas Y. Crowell, 1887.

Moynagh, Michael. *A Church for Every Context: An Introduction to Theology and Practice*. London: SCM, 2012.

Park, Kevin. "Ornamental Multiculturalism 1: Kimchi, Korean Boy Band, and Costco." February 23, 2011. https://www.pcusa.org/blogs/faith/2011/2/23/ornamental-multiculturalism-1-kimchi-korean-boy-ba/.

Pietersen, Lloyd. *Reading the Bible after Christendom*. Milton Keynes, UK: Paternoster, 2011.

Racial Ethnic/Immigrant Church Growth Strategy. Louisville: General Assembly Council of the Presbyterian Church (USA), 1998. http://www.pcusa.org/site_media/media/uploads/immigrant/pdf/growth-strategy.pdf.

Volf, Miroslav. *A Public Faith: How Followers of Christ Should Serve the Common Good*. Grand Rapids: Brazos, 2011.

17. Williams, "Following the Missionary Spirit."

Williams, Rowan. "Following the Missionary Spirit." Conference, London, November 22, 2012. http://www.freshexpressions.org.uk/missionaryspirit/rowanwilliams.

———. "Rowan Williams on Being Remembered." Transcript. October 1, 2009. http://www.freshexpressions.org.uk/news/rowanwilliams-beingremembered.

18

Testificar
A Call to the Presbyterian Church (USA)

RUTH-AIMÉE BELONNI-ROSARIO

Consistent with the spirit of offering a reflection on the church as a worshipping/witnessing community, I would like to examine this topic through a different lens. The lens through which I see the Church allows me to see a gathered community, and in gathering, a community that is compelled by the worship experience to witness beyond the walls of the building. Being an ordained minister who is also an immigrant and having served several immigrant congregations of Latino, African, and West Indian origins informs my hermeneutical perspective. From this perspective I suggest that a careful and attentive examination of the life and ministry of immigrant churches can offer the PC(USA) an opportunity to redefine, or better yet a rediscover, the roots of our Reformed understanding of ecclesiology and of the mission of the church. According to the Brookings Institute, approximately 40 million people in the United States are foreign born.[1] According to the Pew Institute, 68 percent of immigrants in the United States are Christians.[2] Latinos and Latinas comprise the third larg-

---

1. "What Percentage of U.S. Population Is Foreign Born?" http://www.brookings.edu/blogs/brookings-now/posts/2013/09/what-percentage-us-population-foreign-born.

2 "The Religious Affiliation of U.S. Immigrants: Majority Christian, Rising Share of Other Faiths." http://www.pewforum.org/2013/05/17/the-religious-affiliation-of-us-immigrants/#affiliation.

est immigrant group in the Presbyterian Church, making up over 40,000 members and 330 congregations.[3]

In this paper I want to share three arguments and observations.

1. At the heart (foundation) of the worship practices of immigrant congregations lay the concepts of *familia* and *testificar*, which are critical to their understanding of worship and Christian community. The presence of this unique perspective means that the communities seek to actively extend the effectiveness of the visible church beyond the physical church walls into the community.

2. These immigrant communities are not able to fully realize their own unique practice of "church" because often their resources, be they financial or time investments, are dedicated to maintaining a building or to fulfilling the requirements of Presbyterian polity. This often leaves church members with inadequate time and money to extend their understanding of witness outside of the church walls in praxis.

3. Finally, I want to suggest that there is an ironic relationship between mid-governing and high level structures of the PC(USA) and its many immigrant communities. Immigrant communities within this church are committed to adhering to and following Presbyterian polity, even willing to assimilate into "American Presbyterian culture" in order to be viewed as legitimate members and congregations. However, the PC(USA) should be open to what immigrant communities are already offering to this church and to the witness of Jesus Christ. I suggest that this denomination, in the midst of a decline in its numbers, will benefit from adopting that which is unique in the ethos of immigrant congregations. I want to suggest that the whole church should follow the example of immigrant congregations in shifting the focus from a rigid, and often legalistic, adherence to church polity to a greater focus on a commitment to the concept of Church as *familia*.

The two overall questions I ask you to consider are:

- Has the PC(USA) adequately addressed the concerns of immigrant communities, allowing for honest space for their unique approaches to witnessing to the Gospel?

---

3. "Hispanic/Latino-a Congregational Support: About Us/Sobre Nosotros." http://www.presbyterianmission.org/ministries/hispanic/about/.

- Has PC(USA) seriously examined how its immigrant communities might help inform its strategy for reforming the denomination, and be willing to be infused by the vibrancy of the worship and witnessing of these communities in light of the PC(USA)'s current decline?

Testificar and Familia

According to the *Dictionary of the Royal Academy of the Spanish Language*, the term *testificar*, to testify, means to declare, affirm or prove some belief. It also means action. *Testificar* means to be the evidence, to be the proof, or to demonstrate a belief. Contextually, *testificar* has an important meaning in the life of the Latino/a, African, and West Indian immigrant churches. It is not only within the walls of the church building where worship takes place and where a gathering to witness takes place. Within these communities, within their social constructs, political life, and religious devotion, there is great importance given to gathering, worshipping, and experiencing the religious community beyond the physical church walls. For immigrants, *testificar* is an invitation that derives from a conviction to *compartir*, to share the good news of the love and forgiveness of Christ, and to be intentional in becoming and being *familia* with each other and with others outside the formal church community as a way of witnessing and offering testimony.

In his book *Can I Get a Witness?*, Blount invites readers to consider the distinction between the terms *witness* and *testimony*. Blount's biblical support for his position comes from the book of Revelation. He explains that the Greek word for witness has been transliterated to *martyr*. As a result, when many of us read the word martyr in Revelation we associate the term with someone who dies for a cause. However, Blount argues, "witnessing, not *dying*, was the goal John (in the book of Revelation) sought out for his hearers and readers." Thus, "witnessing was the ethic by which he wished them to live."[4]

These two words—witness and testimony—come together in the definition, implication, and invitation to action in the word *testificar*. *Testificar* motivates and drives communities of faith in the Latino/a, African, and West Indian communities to live out and share with others outside the church, what Jesus has done for them. *Testificar* describes the manner by which they articulate their life of faith and worship in praxis outside the church building.[5]

4. Blount, *Can I Get a Witness?*, x.

5. For the purpose of this paper I am limiting use of the term immigrant to describe the populations of Latino/a, African, and West Indian congregations, as I have

Elizabeth Conde-Frazier in the book she coauthored, *Latina Evangélicas*, describes the fundamental reality and complexity of immigrant churches: "For people that make up congregations shaped by the realities of immigration, the congregation, *la iglesia, la congregación*, is a place to remake *familia* and to achieve a sense of stability and community in their 'new' and often unsought life within America. The church congregation is *familia*. And as *familia*, congregations enjoy the same gifts and challenges any family shares. The congregation becomes to many immigrant Christians (in the United States, and throughout the world) the best choice of an extended *familia*. The congregation becomes a system (and for some the only system) through which to live and journey in the realities of immigration."[6]

The church, *la iglesia*, becomes "the place to remake *familia*" and an "extended *familia*" for immigrant churches. I suggest that the church, the congregation, becomes their house, their place of familiarity, their "sanctuary" as explained by Martell-Otero in *Latina Evangélicas*. There are no rigid rules or stipulations to which those seeking a sanctuary and a collective experience of God with compassionate others must adhere. Their desire for sanctuary presumes a difficult and oppressed reality, a reality from which persons want to turn away to experience comfort, peace, and *familiaridad*. This is what the church represents to immigrant churches. It is a place of hope and new beginnings, a place where the message being preached is one that helps build self-worth and encouragement for the person and for the community, a place where that message compels all its members to be in solidarity with one another, always seeking each other's well-being, and by doing so, also extending the same experience to those in the larger community.

Immigrant churches are often formed by people who have been oppressed, and whose experiences with social order and political structures have kept them at the margins. Their experience with rules and regulations has not been one of gaining access to mainstream rights and privileges of the rest of society. More fundamentally, they feel excluded from a true feeling of being an integral part of something. The only place where they can attempt to achieve this sense of belonging is the church. What drives the worshipping immigrant community is to know themselves as being loved by a powerful God who loved them so much that in sending His Son, all barriers are broken, even death, and that through the power of the Holy

---

served congregations composed of these communities. To extend the analysis beyond these two groups would require more study.

6. Elizabeth Conde-Frazier, "Ecclesiology: A *Dabar* Church," in Martell-Otero et al., *Latina Evangelicas*, 90.

Spirit they too can share in this same love and grace. The community is convinced that the only thing to do is to share this compelling story with the world, not only with words but witnessing, *testificando*. The worship experience is not meant to be personal nor self-serving. The worship experience is a firm invitation to live out the incomparable story of the Gospel in and with the community.

Importance of the Eucharist to Forming Community: Ordained Ministers

This attempt to achieve a sense of belonging becomes real, particularly during the Eucharist. The invitation to the table is important to the Christian identity and provides a sense of equality for members of immigrant churches. At the table there is no social order that excludes them from a blessing, from access, from belonging, from being an equal part with the rest of the saints throughout the world. Immigrant churches from all Christian traditions, regardless of their denominational theologies, treasure that moment. At that place, the immigrants experience a sense of transcendence of belonging to God without the fear of a rigid stipulation getting in the way of such understanding. Sadly, this feeling is tarnished when, due to limited financial resources, many of these immigrant churches cannot have an ordained pastor installed and constantly available to administer the sacraments.

I do not want to suggest that the immigrant concept of ecclesiology is new. I do, however, feel that it has been, perhaps, forgotten. The Reformed tradition, and therefore PC(USA), adheres to John Calvin's understanding of ecclesiology, which, among other things, affirms that "the marks of the true church [are] that the Word of God be preached and the sacraments be rightly administered."[7] According to Calvin, "members of the visible church are those who by confession of faith, by example of life, and by partaking of the sacraments profess the same God and Christ." In our tradition, preaching the Word, and particularly administering the sacraments rightly or properly, requires the presence and administration of a duly ordained minister. Moreover, a body that, by and large, is foreign to the needs and struggles of immigrant communities stipulates seemingly unchanging ordination standards, without taking into account the changing nature of the membership of the church, and the diversity of cultural realities already in it. Conversely, many immigrant congregations affiliated with the PC(USA) accept the letter (as opposed to the spirit) of the ordination requirements without protest, seeking to adhere to the requirements of its ecclesiastical authority. In doing

---

7. Calvin, *Institutes*, IV.1, 9.

so, they strive and work very hard to follow the necessary rules in order to be recognized as congregations in good standing. Nevertheless, the reality is that many immigrant congregations do not have the financial and educational resources that are required by the larger church readily available to them. Many leaders in immigrant congregations who feel called to ordained ministry in order to be of service to their communities struggle, for years, in trying to fulfill these requirements imposed seemingly from outside their life and experience.

I served as a pulpit supply minister for an immigrant congregation in Queens, New York. Most of the members of this congregations where African and West Indian. They had their regular pastor. This pastor was the one who visited their sick, who celebrated the birth of a new child, who celebrated graduations, who counseled them through difficult situations, who helped them navigate a new place, and who taught Bible study. This pastor was the one who this congregation called and acknowledged as pastor. He was a member of their family, their *familia*. However he was not ordained through the PC(USA). Therefore every first Sunday of the month, in order to comply with the requirements of the PC(USA) with regard to administering the sacraments, an outsider, I, not a member of their *familia*, came to rightly and properly administer the sacraments. PC(USA)'s adhering to their polity in this regard is not new. Blount reminds us that the practice of Church leaders sending pastors and preachers sanctioned by the ruling denominations traces back to practices throughout the history of the American churches. For instance, Churches in the American North and South dispatched approved clergy to minister to African Americans so that they might experience church the "right way," albeit not consistent with their unique cultural identity. Eventually, these communities rejected these ministers because these ministers did not understand their particular social challenges, and were not part of their *familia*.

Today, immigrant congregations like those during the developing history of the church in the United States, in seeking an ultimate sense of belonging—to experience a sacred connection with God, with one another, and with the larger community through communion—must ultimately have this experience led by a stranger in order to comply with the rules and regulations of a rigid interpretation of Presbyterian polity. The result is that the continuity of community is interrupted. Congregants cannot fully experience—they are not allowed—this sense of sacred connection led by a member of their *familia* during the Eucharist. This results in yet another reminder to them of their migrant condition; a condition and experience from which they look to find relief in the Eucharistic rite.

Learning from Immigrant Communities to Shift the Tide of Denominational Decline

I am not arguing that PC(USA) eliminate the requirement that ordained ministers administer the sacraments. In addition, I commend the initiatives that the PC(USA) is taking to providing pastoral resources to immigrant congregations through the commissioning of ruling elders, and in the encouragement of new ways of being the Church through the worshipping communities initiative, even though these do not fully address the realities and challenges of the immigrant presence in our Church, nor of its decline. My goal is to bring to this conversation a piece that is missing from the larger conversation on ecclesiology—an alternative form of conversation that focuses not on numbers but on building community. My observations are based on my experience as an immigrant itinerant preacher and pastor. Immigrant congregations can offer the larger church an insight into how it might better enhance the feeling amongst its members of being the body of Christ, *la iglesia, una familia*, who *testifica* to the story of the gospel with the same fervor outside in the community in daily life as they do inside the church walls. However, for this to happen there has to be a Church-wide conversation and actions about reforming this Church beyond its idolatry of rigid rules and regulations. Presbyterian immigrant communities want to contribute a gift of reform to their denomination. They seek to have a greater voice, to be taken seriously as full members of the PC(USA), concerned with the future of this Church and of the Christian witness.

Yet, it seems (and it feels) that the Presbyterian Church (U.S.A.) does not take seriously the perspective of its immigrant presence, even as the PC(USA) claims to live up to its heritage of being open to reform. There is little evidence that the PC(USA) recognizes the experiences and perspectives of immigrant communities provide a compelling model of witnessing communities in the true spirit of the Reformed tradition. It appears to me that the reason behind PC(USA)'s lack of awareness of the contributions that immigrant churches are bringing and could provide to the Church stems from a rigid position of what is a "traditional" Presbyterian Church— that of the English tradition, or the Scottish tradition. This myopic approach to a definition of the Church affects PC(USA)'s ability to recognize and learn from the immigrant church's understanding of how to witness to the Gospel, and to welcome this wonderful presence already within this church. Further affected is the capacity of the church to allow this presence to change and transform its life, to allow immigrant *testimonios* to shed light into the PC(USA)'s understanding of the Reformed tradition, ecclesiology, and mission.

In some circles of American Presbyterianism the dominant understanding of church seems to have moved away from Calvin's definition of the visible church. The focus seems to be increasingly articulated with a focus on the church building, polity, and rigid requirements for admittance and access to the body of Christ. Today, buildings are taking a significant amount of the financial resources as well as time and energy of already struggling congregations. Throughout my pastoral work, I have seen how many of these immigrant churches are either renting space (not hosted, renting) to another congregation, therefore requiring them to spend energy on securing and hoping for their own space, or they have inherited a building that is deteriorating. In these situations, congregations must shift their focus from work in mission and outreach to gathering the limited resources they have into fixing or securing a building. The never-ending focus on the immediate seems not to allow creative time and space to deal with polity and with fulfilling the expectations of the Presbyterian culture to be a true church, and trumps the need, desire and call to *testificar*, to witness to God's love in Christ through the Holy Spirit.

Conclusion

It is time to be still and listen to the *testimonio* of immigrant churches. It is time to stop treating immigrant congregations as if they were church welfare cases or mere objects of missionary projects and good public relations. We are called to intentionally call and engage immigrant Presbyterian congregations in helping the PC(USA) form a new reformed message that speaks to the core of what we have been assembled here to discuss as the mission of this Church. Immigrant congregations, based on my experience, have a genuine and deep desire to serve God, to witness to God's unconditional love, and to foster a community dedication to care for each other.

I believe immigrant churches are longing for, yet have been passive in demanding to be recognized and have their voices heard as full members of American mainline Christianity; to be acknowledged as "true" churches. As soon as the powers that be become aware of immigrant understanding and practices to being a true and faithful church, and welcome these understandings fully within the life of the American Church, and of American Presbyterianism, we will reap the benefits of their contribution to Reformed theology and ecclesiology.

Conversely, respecting immigrant identities in this ecclesial space will allow immigrant congregations to welcome without *sospecha*, without suspicion, the organizing paradigms and structures of the Church. This will challenge the whole of the Church, but particularly those who hold fast to constitutional documents as a way to control and manage the affairs of the Church, to the exclusion of other voices. The desire to control and to manage is the result of a fear of change. In the moment this fear is acknowledged and allowed to be dealt with, the Holy Spirit will show us—in us, through us, and beyond us—the wonders of God at work every day in Christ's Church and in the world. True community—of welcome and engagement with who the person is, to what the person or congregation should be—is where God is present.

In his *Introduction to Ecclesiology*, Kärkkäinen reminds us that ecclesiology "is the freedom to belong to God, to worship God exclusively, and it is the freedom to participate in the divine agenda without selective hindrance from other human beings."[8] Therefore, I decided to bring the voices of those whose voices seem to be continually unheard in our Church. There is a lot of talk about the decline of mainline American Christianity, and of the PC(USA). But I am here to say that there is vibrancy in immigrant congregations that is lacking in mainstream Presbyterian congregations. What drives this vibrancy, what compels immigrant Christians, is the gospel story. As Conde-Frazier puts it, "Christ's love compels us. The verb compel (synecho) is 'to hold together,' to surround, not to allow to escape, and to hold together so that it does not fall apart."[9] Immigrant congregations are calling the Presbyterian Church, USA, and American mainline Christianity to be compelled by the power of the gospel which is experienced in worship through liturgy, a gospel and a worship life which is encouraged to be lived outside as witnesses sent out into the world. The church, according to immigrant congregations, is a community of believers compelled to live out, to witness, to *testificar* the gospel story to all.

May we do so, together, "holding each other together, so we do not fall apart." Let's take seriously the invitation in the Lord's Supper to welcome all regardless of any impulse to impose a human sense of order. Let us be and act as the body of Christ, the church, *la iglesia, la comunidad*, in the world.

---

8. Kärkkäinen, *Introduction to Ecclesiology*, 44.

9. Elizabeth Conde-Frazier, "Ecclesiology: A *Dabar* Church," in Martell-Otero et al., *Latina Evangelicas*, 92.

Bibliography

Blount, Brian. *Can I Get a Witness? Reading Revelation through African American Culture.* Louisville: Westminster John Knox, 2005.

Calvin, John. *Institutes of the Christian Religion.* Edited by John T. McNeill. Translated by Ford Lewis Battles. 2 vols. Library of Christian Classics. Philadelphia: Westminster, 1960.

Kärkkäinen, Veli-Matti. *An Introduction to Ecclesiology: Ecumenical, Historical and Global Perspectives.* Downers Grove, IL: InterVarsity, 2002.

Martell-Otero, Loida I., et al. *Latina Evangélicas: A Theological Survey from the Margins.* Eugene, OR: Cascade, 2013.

19

From Blueprint to Foretaste

Worship, Mission, and Multiculturalism in Reformed Congregations

Corey Widmer

Recently I traveled to a large city in the United States to attend a conference that focused on renewing the missionary impulse of the PC(USA). After arriving at the airport, I took a subway train from the far southern point of the city where the airport was located, all the way north through the city center in the direction of the large church campus where the conference was being held. As we rode the train, I observed many different people getting on and off. The diversity of cultures and ethnicities represented was at times staggering. Most of the time I was a minority on the train; in several cases my companions and I were the only white travelers in the entire car. I saw multiple nationalities and heard numerous languages. I was struck freshly by the growing diversity of our American cities and the reality that the nations are increasingly represented in our metro areas.

Throughout the conference, I was moved by the passion among the attendees to see our declining denomination renewed. Many leaders from the platform called for a return to our biblical roots and the reclamation of our Reformed heritage, one that is marked by the sovereignty of God and the supremacy of God's Word and gospel. There was also much attention given to missions, evangelism, and church planting. Leader after leader called for the church to reclaim its missional identity and to adopt a missionary posture toward our now post-Christian culture. Overall the experience was energizing and inspiring.

Yet I could not stop thinking about my experience on the train. Looking around the large sanctuary, where nearly 1000 church leaders were gathered, only a small handful of non-white participants were present. I could not help observing the irony of the fact that as we called for a renewed mission to the people of the surrounding society, the people gathered in this particular room did not reflect the growing majority of that society to which we believed we were sent. I could not help but wonder if our commitment to return to the traditional roots of our Reformed denominational heritage would only serve to further isolate ourselves culturally from the growing diversity around us. I left with gratitude but also with a sense of profound dissonance between the call to an evangelical Reformed renewal and the call to mission to a society in which the cultural pillars of that Reformed tradition are less represented than ever before.

This experience illustrates the dilemma that lies before not just our denomination but nearly every congregation and denomination in the United States that values their theological heritage, most of which have been formed in the Western European theological traditions. Within the last one hundred years, seismic changes have occurred in the religious and cultural landscape in North America that have altered the church's relationship to the broader culture. Among the most dramatic of these changes is the influx of cultural diversity in environments that were once culturally monolithic. Because of travel, migration and media, people can experience the cultural differences that have traditionally separated communities, and in many cases those differences are manifested within a single local environment as people come together in common neighborhoods and cities. This diversity is manifesting itself in multiple levels of society such as education, government, military and business. As early as 1993 *Time* magazine bore the lead title, "The New Face of America: How Immigrants Are Shaping the World's First Multicultural Society."[1] The most recent U.S. Census Bureau figures predict that by 2042 whites will be a "minority majority" within the United States.[2]

Yet despite this reality, the American church remains generally unresponsive to this new environment. The American church persists as a surprisingly homogenous institution, with only 7 percent of churches qualifying as multiethnic congregations.[3] Among American Reformed

---

1. "The New Face of America."
2. http://www.census.gov/main/www/access.html.
3. The generally accepted definition of a "multi-ethnic congregation" is one in

congregations, the percentage is even smaller. Despite the rapid diversification of our culture, the ethnic composition of the church remains generally unchanged among the majority of American congregations in traditional denominations.[4]

I believe that at the heart of this situation is a crisis of the church's mission. Scottish missiologist Andrew Walls calls this moment in history of the United States an "Ephesian moment," referring to the unprecedented opportunity in the current chapter of the North American church to translate the Christian gospel into the lifeways of the world's cultures, even within a single local congregation.[5] Even a cursory read of the New Testament reveals that one of the most powerful demonstrations of the truth of the good news about Jesus Christ was the inexplicable diversity of new Christian communities in which there was neither "Jew nor Greek" (Gal 3:28).[6] Cultural diversity in the local congregation is a mark of its missionary identity, a demonstration that the body is taking seriously its call to bring together diverse and divided peoples under the new Kingdom realties of Jesus Christ. If the church is going to be serious about it missionary identity in the twenty-first century, it must be serious about forming diverse and multiethnic congregations. A failure to germinate such congregations is a failure of mission, indeed a failure to embody the church's central identity as a missionary people.

So what is preventing this from happening? There is certainly no lack of interest in diversity in the PC(USA). There is much talk about diversity

---

which no one ethnic group makes up more than 80 percent of the congregation. See Davis, "Multicultural Church."

4. The PC(USA) is currently 90.2 percent white in its membership. Though this statistic reflects that 9.8 percent of membership is non-white, the percentage of multiethnic congregations is of course much smaller. Even among the membership, most gains in the racial ethnic share among PC(USA) members have resulted from declines in total white percentage, not increases in the racial ethnic one. The 1999–2008 shift from 6.4 to 8.6 percent racial ethnic membership happened partly because of a net gain of 15,000 racial ethnic members, but mostly because of a net loss of 233,000 white members. See http://www.pcusa.org/media/uploads/research/pdfs/gofigureaug10.pdf.

5. Walls, "The Ephesian Moment."

6. One of the most striking examples of a missional multi-ethnic congregation in the New Testament is the church of Antioch as recorded in Acts 11:19–13:3. Acts 13:1 lists the five leaders of the church of Antioch who represented three different continents and four racial groups. Remarkably, it is at Antioch that "the disciples were first called Christians" (Acts 11:26). Here was a new religious phenomenon that could not be attributed to any one particular culture, so the public named them instead by the person they followed.

at national assemblies, conferences and seminaries. In 1998 the General Assembly committed to increasing its "overall ethnic membership" to 20 percent by 2010. The PC(USA) created The Mission of Multicultural Congregational Support with a full time director, staff support, grants and significant web resources. Yet despite all this, demographics of local congregations remain relatively unchanged. The reasons for this are innumerable and reach deep into the hegemonic and colonial past of American Presbyterianism.[7] But for the purposes of this paper, I'd like to focus on one reason why congregations remain unchanged: an incomplete ecclesiology that manifests itself in our worship.

Many congregations fail to see the connection between worship and mission. As one example, recently I was asked to review a mission study of a PC(USA) downtown congregation in Richmond that was beginning a pastoral search process. The mission study group wrote a wonderful mission study, one that was clearly influenced by the best of missional theology. They wrote descriptively of their changing urban neighborhood, of the many diverse cultures present, of the many unchurched and never-churched people surrounding their parish. They wrote of their passion to be a missional, hospitable congregation that reaches out and welcomes their neighbors. They spoke boldly of their willingness to change and adapt for the sake of mission and do whatever it takes to become a more culturally diverse congregation. Yet after all this, they included this brief but significant statement: "To fulfill our mission, the Session and the congregation need to embrace fundamental change—*not in our theology or style of worship*, but in our understanding of what God's call requires of us."[8] The statement represents an inability or unwillingness to see the dichotomy between the expressed vision and the actual theology and worship practices of the church. There is embedded within this statement the idea that the theology and worship of the church are invariable and even a-cultural, even while there is an admission that mission requires change.

I have found a helpful metaphor to describe this perspective on ecclesiology, what Nicholas Healey calls "Blueprint Ecclesiologies." Healy characterizes "blueprint ecclesiologies" as those attempts to encapsulate in tight theological descriptions the most essential characteristics of the

---

7. See Alvis, *Religion and Race*, and Washington, *Anti-Blackness*. The history of racist practices in the American Presbyterian denominations are extensive. Despite the fact that few contemporary Presbyterian congregations manifest explicit racist practices, our current traditions are built on centuries of discriminatory practices that have woven themselves into the very fabric of our ecclesial rhythms.

8. "Grace Covenant Presbyterian Church Mission Study Report," 10; emphasis mine.

church.⁹ Such methodology tends to form normative systematic and theoretical forms of the church that are often not reflective of its everyday life, thus representing an idealized account of the church rather than one that embodies its true identity and context.¹⁰ Although Healy acknowledges the occasional usefulness of such models especially in academic theology, he concludes that this ecclesiological approach is not ultimately helpful to the church because it lacks robust consideration of the church's present practices, institutions and environment. According to Healy, the impression that this heavily deductive approach offers is "that theologians believe that it is necessary to get our *thinking* about the church right first, after which we can go on to put our theory into practice. It is as if good ecclesial practices can be described only after a prior and quite abstract consideration of true ecclesiological doctrine."¹¹ This is ecclesiology in a vacuum rather than a living, missionary ecclesiology that is always taking account of the church's surrounding mission.

It is my belief that many Reformed congregations operate with this "blueprint" metaphor in the background when it comes to its lived ecclesiology. There is a blueprint of what the church is, what it should be and how it is deemed faithful. Some of this has to do with theology, but much of it has to do with worship practices. Some of the blueprint is articulated clearly in places such as the Directory of Worship, while some of the blueprint is inherited and inculcated tacitly through repetition. The blueprint is embedded in our hymnbooks, our instrumentation, our orders of worship, even the way we speak when we are in the pulpit. The underlying narrative functions as a standard by which we discern our faithfulness to our heritage. Taking a musical metaphor, the blueprint functions like a sacred musical score, one that cannot be altered from the composer's trust, and the congregation is the symphony that practices hard so as to get every note right.

But there is a problem with the score. It is a rich, robust, and beautiful score, but one that was written for a different time and for a different mission. It is one that is born out of our rich theological heritage, but also one that is laden with our heritage of white privilege, a heritage that failed to see the way that privilege has conditioned our theology and practices. It

---

9. Healy, *Church, World and the Christian Life*, 26. An example of this in our own tradition would be the definition of the marks of the church as right preaching and right administration of the sacraments. With such a definition a congregation could be deemed faithful even if it is completely disengaged from its surrounding community.

10. Healy cites Avery Dulles' book *Models of the Church* as an example of this, although Dulles does warn against attempting to identify a "supermodel" of the church to relativize all others.

11. Healy, *Church, World and the Christian Life*, 36.

is a score that does not take account of where we currently find ourselves as a church, in a post-Christian, culturally pluralistic land. And ultimately the score suggests that the church is not a community of people in mission but an idea of the past that contemporary people can simply rehearse and memorialize for the present.

But the church is not an idea, it is a witnessing community. Healy calls it a *concrete, apostolic agent.* "If we begin with what the church does," Healy writes, "one of the things we must say about it is that is has been entrusted with the apostolic task. The church's responsibility is to witness to its Lord, to make known throughout the world the Good News of salvation in and through the person and work of Jesus Christ."[12] With this calling in view, Healy argues that it is the task of ecclesiology not to formulate theoretical images for the church, but is "to reconstruct its concrete identity so as to embody its witness."[13] The church of every age finds itself in ever shifting contexts that deeply challenge its members to bear truthful witness to its entrusted message. Unlike so many forms of ecclesiology that pay little attention to the church's context and focus on describing its theological essence, Healy insists that the main purpose of ecclesiology is to equip the church to *understand and respond to its context*, both how it has been corrupted and infected by it, and also how it is called to bear witness faithfully within it as apostolic agent. "We can assess any ecclesiological proposal by how well it helps the church respond to its context," Healy writes.[14] The standard for ecclesiology is not just faithfulness to the past but also orientation toward how it will be faithful to the gospel in its present and ever changing context.

Given all this I would like to suggest a supplemental metaphor for Reformed congregations to bring greater balance to our ecclesiology, a balance that I believe can help us more faithfully respond to our diverse environment. This is not a new metaphor; in fact, it is one that is replete in our theology and Reformed heritage yet often goes neglected. It is the metaphor of *foretaste*. The metaphor of foretaste suggests that the calling of the church is not simply to be faithful to a blueprint written in the past, but also is called to be an anticipatory foretaste of a new and coming future. There are many examples in the PC(USA) *Book of Order* that speak to this metaphor:

> The Church is to be a community of hope, rejoicing in the sure and certain knowledge that, in Christ, God is making a new creation. This new creation is a new beginning for human life and

12. Ibid., 6.
13. Ibid., 22.
14. Ibid.

> for all things. The Church lives in the present on the strength of that promised new creation.[15]
>
> The congregation reaches out to people, communities, and the world to share the good news of Jesus Christ, to gather for worship, to offer care and nurture to God's children, to speak for social justice and righteousness, to bear witness to the truth and to the reign of God that is coming into the world.[16]
>
> The church in its worship and ministry is a sign of the reign of God, which is both a present reality and a promise of the future. The church's worship and service do not make the Kingdom of God come. In an age hostile to the reign of God, the church worships and serves, with confidence that God's rule has been established and with firm hope in the ultimate manifestation of the triumph of God.[17]

Much of this rich theology borrows from the neo-Calvinist tradition that acknowledges the reign of Jesus Christ over all of creation and the redemptive intention of God to restore all things. It is grounded in a soteriology that envisions salvation not just as the salvation of individual souls but also as the reconciliation of a broken creation.[18] To that end, it is the calling of the church to bear witness to that comprehensive reconciliation here and now, embodying in its practical and social expressions fragrances and foretastes of the coming reign of God. As Reformed missiologist David Bosch puts it in his masterful work *Transforming Mission*, "The church is a proleptic reality, the sign of the dawning of the new age in the midst of the old, and as such the vanguard of God's new world. It is simultaneously acting as pledge of the sure hope of the world's transformation at the time of God's final triumph and straining itself in all its activities to prepare the world for its coming destiny."[19] As such, the worship of the church is germane to the mission of the church, because in worship the people of God express their identity as present carriers of the future Kingdom. The gathered congregation is the social embodiment of the coming Kingdom that bears witness to Jesus Christ.

If classical music is representative of Blueprint Ecclesiology, then a musical representation for foretaste ecclesiology is jazz. In his book

---

15. *Book of Order*, F-1-0301.
16. Ibid., G-1.0101.
17. Ibid., W-7.600.
18. See Wolters, *Creation Regained*.
19. Bosch, *Transforming Mission*, 169.

Resurrection City, Peter Heltzel unpacks jazz as a metaphor for the kind of "faithful improvisation" that is needed for the church today. Jazz essentially takes old tunes and plays them in new ways. "While the blues is about the world that was, jazz is often about the world to come."[20] Jazz is fitted by the constraints of its musical heritage but is always improvising toward new possibilities. Hetzel writes, "Like jazz, Christian thinking and acting exemplify a dynamic of constraint and possibility. Constrained by the norm of God's Word, Christians seek to creatively engage their world in light of the Word. In their work and witness, Christians use the materials at hand . . . to creatively riff for justice, love, and shalom in the present and thereby open up a new future."[21] This is "faithful improvisation." Building on the old tunes but yearning and experimenting toward the possibilities of a new future. Foretaste Ecclesiology is always surveying the new environment and new mission to which the church is called, and looking to see what new changes and improvisations may be required to embody faithful witness. In the "Blueprint Ecclesiology" approach, change or experimentation in the church's patterns and practices can be seen as a threat or a distortion of the church's true essence, a pollution of its pure form.[22] But in "Foretaste Ecclesiology," change and adaption can be a sign of missionary faithfulness, as a congregation strains to bear witness to the reign of God in the ever shifting contexts in which it finds itself.

So how does this relate to worship and multiculturalism in the church? If a local congregation embraces a Foretaste Ecclesiology, it will always be looking at how, given its theological heritage, it can built on that heritage for faithful expression of the gospel in the new diverse environment to which it is called. It will be looking to how, given the people in its parish and the kind of community that surrounds it, the congregation might embody a foretaste of the coming Kingdom in its worship and ministry practices in order to give expression to that Kingdom in the here and now. But it will not do so by discarding its heritage; just as Jazz must improvise out of the rich library of its musical roots, so the local congregation improvises while staying faithful to its biblical and theological foundations.

Let me offer a concrete example from my own congregation of how this might work. East End Fellowship (EEF) is located in an urban neighborhood of Richmond, Virginia, that for several decades has been marked

---

20. Heltzel, *Resurrection City*, 17.

21. Ibid., 21.

22. But in doing so the church assesses its faithfulness according to its own closed theological templates, rather than according to its living Lord who calls the church to bear witness to Jesus Christ in ever changing contexts.

by intense blight and poverty, yet is now showing signs of renewal and gentrification. The neighborhood is made of up mostly black and white populations, and those populations are diverse educationally and socioeconomically. Richmond itself is marked by abiding suspicions and segregation between the black and white communities, and our neighborhood bears the wounds of that historic struggle. Given these realities, our church's mission is to be a community of reconciliation that demonstrates the power of the gospel to bring together divided peoples. We believe that we are called to do in a segregated city what is not possible without the grace and Spirit of God. Everything in our congregation is oriented around this mission of reconciliation: how we choose our leaders, how we do discipleship, and most certainly, how we worship. Our journey of six years as a congregation has been one long improvisational experiment, seeking to be true to the gospel, Scripture and the Reformed heritage, yet constantly experimenting as we gather the diverse peoples of our community. It is a highly contextual mission that simply would not make sense in any other context but our own.[23]

This has resulted in some fresh and life-giving improvisations. Here is one example. In the Reformed tradition we value the Psalms as central to the worship of God. For centuries Reformed congregations have used the Psalms to guide us in worship, taking our cues in song and prayer from the Word of God. My first experience of using whole Psalms in worship was in the chapel at Princeton Theological Seminary, in which a cantor led the congregation through an entire Psalm antiphonally.[24] It was a beautiful and moving experience, and my love of the Psalms deepened because of it. However, later as I began to lead this new congregation in the diverse urban context of Richmond, I knew that the musical form of Psalmic worship in the PTS chapel would have no resonance within the context of the inner city. But rather than discard the Psalms as a tool for worship, our team asked, "How can we improvise on this theological heritage and lean into a new future, one that gestures to our particular community that the Kingdom is for them?" So we began to experiment with poetry, hip hop and spoken-word, and resulted with forms of antiphonal Psalmic worship that articulates the groans and yearnings of many urban youth.[25] It is a remark-

---

23. Our congregation was highlighted recently through the PC(USA) 1001 New Worshipping Communities initiative. To see the two-minute video, visit http://vimeo.com/42228240.

24. To see the wonderful fruit of Martin Tel's labor from years of using the Psalms in worship, see Borger et al., *Psalms for All Seasons*.

25. To listen to our antiphonal form of Ps 27, follow this link: https://arrabon.bandcamp.com/track/whom-shall-i-fear-ps-27-feat-alex-mejias-shad-e.

able thing to see a young black hip-hop artist serving as a cantor, slinging Psalm-drenched rhymes as the congregation joins in with the repeated antiphon. We are carrying on the Reformed tradition of Psalmic worship, yet improvising in such a way to embody something new as we anticipate a Kingdom of reconciliation together.

Can the PC(USA) and other traditional denominations become more reflective of the growing diversity in our society? Yes, but I believe this will not come through edicts and GA resolutions, but must come through local congregations taking their missionary identity seriously. It will take an apostolic movement that sees our diverse neighbors not as diversity projects but as people to whom we are called and sent. It will come through a renewed missionary ecclesiology that does not just look backward to perpetuate our theological heritage, but also looks forward to anticipate the coming Kingdom, a Kingdom in which all nations are gathered around the throne of God (Rev 7:9). And it will take an adaptive posture that welcomes change in worship and ministry practices not for change's sake, but to embody faithful witness to our changeless Lord. May it be so for our church, may it be so for us.

Bibliography

Alvis, Joel L., Jr. *Religion and Race: Southern Presbyterians, 1946–1983*. Tuscaloosa: University of Alabama Press, 1994.
Borger, Joyce, et al., eds. *Psalms for All Seasons: A Complete Psalter for Worship*. Ada, MI: Brazos, 2012.
Bosch, David. *Transforming Mission*. Maryknoll, NY: Orbis, 2002.
The Constitution of the Presbyterian Church (U.S.A.), Part II, Book of Order. Louisville: The Office of the General Assembly, 2013.
Davis, Ken. "Multicultural Church Planting Models." *The Journal of Ministry and Theology* 7 (2003) 114–27.
"Grace Covenant Presbyterian Church Mission Study Report." Richmond, VA. 2012.
Healy, Nicholas. *Church, World and the Christian Life: Practical-Prophetic Ecclesiology*. Cambridge: Cambridge University Press, 2000.
"The New Face of America: How Immigrants Are Shaping the World's First Multicultural Society." *Time*, November 18, 1993.
Walls, Andrew F. "The Ephesian Moment." In *The Cross-Cultural Process in Christian History: Studies in the Transmission and Appropriation of Faith*, edited by Andrew F. Walls, 72–81. Maryknoll, NY: Orbis, 2002.
Washington, Joseph R., Jr. *Anti-Blackness in English Religion*. New York: Mellen, 1984.
Wolters, Albert M. *Creation Regained: A Biblical Basis for a Reformational Worldview*. Grand Rapids: Eerdmans, 1985.

20

A PC(USA) Reflection on an Ecumenical Understanding of Ecclesiology

ROBINA WINBUSH

I would like to share with you three different experiences related to questions of ecclesiology and ecumenical relationships to which the PC(USA) is called.

Following more than forty years of Lutheran/Reformed dialogue, the PC(USA) entered into a full communion relationship with the Evangelical Lutheran Church in America, the Reformed Church in America and the United Church of Christ in 1999. It was a relationship in which we recognized each other as church, recognized the baptisms of our churches members and recognized the ordination of each other's pastors/ministers/ teaching elders and made provisions to share in ministry and engage in theological dialogue over those issues that confronted our churches with the potential to divide us again. Unlike the ecumenical agreements of the midtwentieth century that ga ve birth to united churches, this agreement offered the possibility of entering into a relationship of mutuality while retaining our particularities. We were not required to give up any of our organizational structures or radically change our own ecclesial self-understandings. We mutually agreed to recognize the legitimacy of each other's ecclesiology and the subsequent implications.

Shortly after I began working as the Director of Ecumenical Relations for the PC(USA) in 2000, one of my colleagues in World Mission brought to me a challenge from one of our global partners in Brazil. We were being asked why we were willing to recognize the ordinations of ministers in the Evangelical Lutheran Church in America, but were not willing to automatically recognize the ordination of Presbyterian churches in Brazil, churches that we had founded through missionary efforts, seminaries that we supported and whose polity and theology in many ways mirrored our own. There wasn't an easy answer. The fact of the matter is that constitutionally we did recognize our global partners as church and subsequently their ordinations; however, there was the expectation that ministers coming from our partner churches were still required to meet all the academic requirements of PC(USA) ordained ministers. While it may not have been the intent, we created tiers of ecclesial recognition and acceptance amongst our ecumenical partners. These tiers were not unaffected by the legacy of racism and paternalism within the PC(USA).

The second scenario, I would like to share with you is from a visit of a PC(USA) delegation to the Pontifical Council for Promoting Christian Unity in the Vatican. The occasion for this delegation visit was to present to Pope John Paul II the PC(USA) response to his encyclical *Ut Unum Sint* inviting consideration of a new situation in which the Bishop of Rome might serve the aspirations of many Christians for unity. Professors Anna Case Winters and Lewis Mudge drafted our response in the paper "The Presbyterian Understanding of the Successor to Peter." As you might imagine, there were significant differences in our reading of the biblical texts and Christian Tradition that led us to very different understandings of how the community of faith is ordered and governed. Nevertheless, we struggled to find points of agreement and ways that we might give visible expression to that agreement. In addition to acknowledging that the language related to the Roman Catholic Church in some of our Confessions was problematic and inconsistent with our current understandings, it also became evident that there was not a constitutional category of ecumenical relationship in which we clearly acknowledged the Roman Catholic Church as church. The delegation report sent the following request through the General Assembly Committee on Ecumenical Relations to the 213th General Assembly (2001): "The General Assembly Committee on Ecumenical Relations recommends that the 213th General Assembly (2001) acknowledge the Catholic church as part of the body of Christ and that the assembly instruct the General Assembly Committee on Ecumenical Relations to form the appropriate language to describe the character of this relationship." The Ecumenical Advisory Delegate from the United States Conference of Catholic Bishops spoke passionately before the General Assembly about the necessity of approving this recommendation. The Assembly approved the recommendation. Interestingly, it was during this same period of time that the Congregation for the Doctrine of the Faith issued the declaration *Dominus Iesus* in which the Roman Church reiterated its exclusive ecclesiological claims.

> Those churches which do not accept the Catholic doctrine of the primacy of the bishop of Rome remain united to the Catholic Church by means of the closest bonds, that is, by apostolic succession and a valid eucharist. Therefore, the church of Christ is present and operative also in these churches, even though they lack full communion with the Catholic Church. On the other hand, the ecclesial communities which have not preserved the valid episcopate and the genuine and integral substance of the eucharistic mystery are not churches in the proper sense; however, those who are baptized in these communities are in a certain communion, albeit imperfect, with the Catholic Church. Therefore, these separated churches and communities as such, though we believe they suffer from defects, have by no means been deprived of significance and importance in the mystery of salvation.[1]

While this was not a new doctrine, it did raise questions about what if any ecumenical progress had been made in how we view and mutually recognize each other as church.

The third example I would like to share comes from the 24th General Council of the World Alliance of Reformed Churches meeting in Accra Ghana. A significant part of the General Council meeting was a visit to the Elmina and Cape Coast slave dungeons. We took the extremely painful journey through the slave dungeons, we moved through the dungeons that held male and female people who were being enslaved, we peered into the cell where male captives were thrown so that they may be starved to death in the midst of others who had died. We stood in the courtyard where enslaved women who refused to be the sexual play toy of their captors were made to stand naked in the hot sun with a ball and chain around their ankles, to the small enclosed room of no return, to the Reformed chapel that had been built on top of the female slave dungeon, because the Dutch Reformed Church felt they could not worship in the Catholic chapel left by the Portuguese slave traders that had preceded them. It was in that place the ludicrousness of our ecclesiastical squabble and divisions were evident. The sixteenth- and seventeenth-century ecclesiastical division between Christians was more concerned with delegitimizing each other, than they were with the atrocity of slavery and their participation in the dehumanization and exploitation of God's people. I stood in that Reformed chapel in existential conflict—a daughter of those who had been enslaved and a minister in the tradition that had enslaved them. My friend and colleague, the Reverend Dr. Moiserale Prince Dibeela, immediate past General Secretary of the

---

1. John Paul II, "Dominus Iesus," chapter 4.

United Congregational Church of Southern Africa, reflecting on his experience in the dungeons, talked about the ambivalence of being a Christian. He described it as wrapping oneself in a flea-infested blanket: knowing you need the warmth it brings, but having to endure the painful bites.

It has been said that the ecumenical challenge we face is as much within churches as it is between churches. Struggles within national and regional churches as well as within global communions and traditions beg for the clarification of what does it mean to be the church in our generation and what will we leave for future generations to resolve. How might the global ecumenical conversation on ecclesiology inform local context and what are the questions, experiences and critiques local context bring to the global conversation.

Even before the World Council of Churches came into existence, the World Conference of Faith and Order (the predecessor to the WCC Commission on Faith and Order) wrestled with questions of ecclesiology. Following the pain and devastation of World War II, the World Council of Churches was formed in 1948 as a fellowship of divided churches seeking to find a way to express their oneness in Christ. The Commission on Faith and Order has been instrumental in both providing a forum for church theologians to address together doctrines that both divide and unite the churches as well as offering the churches studies to challenge and deepen their own understanding and responses to God's calling on their lives. The Commission on Faith and Order understands its primary purpose is "to serve the churches as they call one another to visible unity in one faith in one Eucharistic fellowship, expressed in worship and common life in Christ, through witness and service to the world, and advance towards the unity in order that the world may believe."[2]

One of the most notable studies, "Baptism, Eucharist and Ministry (BEM),"[3] became a foundational offering to the churches that shaped bilateral and multilateral agreements and informed how churches engaged their internal studies related to BEM. It was a convergence document that allowed churches to articulate agreement and clarify points of divergence or further study. Of significance was the identification of several ecclesiologicalthemes that needed further study. In 1998, "The Nature and Purpose of the Church: A Stage On the Way to a Common Statement"[4] was published and sent to the churches for responses. Based on the comments and responses of the churches, a second study, "The Nature and Mission of the Church: A Stage

2. "By-laws of the WCC Commission."
3. "Baptism, Eucharist and Ministry."
4. "The Nature and Purpose of the Church."

on the Way to a Common Statement"[5] was published in 2005 and again sent to the churches for response. Earlier this year, the WCC forwarded to the churches, "The Church: Towards a Common Vision"[6] as a culmination of the churches engagement in the previous studies and as a prayerful hope of what we might say together about what it means to be the church.
Clearly, there are things we can affirm and reflect much of what has been heard to yesterday and today in our discussions about ecclesiology.

1. God's intention is for humanity to be in community/in relationship with God and one another. Sin breaks the God's intended relationship both between God and humanity and humanity with itself and the rest of created order. God acts through the incarnational life and liberating actions of Jesus, the crucifixion and resurrection of the Christ to restore that which sin had broken. Jesus the Christ invites us into a community of disciples to both be his witnesses in the world and to continue the mission of God through Christ in the world. The Holy Spirit empowers the community of believers with all that is needed to carry out the mission of God in the world.

2. The Church is a community of action and relationship. As was reiterated yesterday, the Church is both personal and communal. (In an age of individualism and a Western epistemology that is rooted in the individual, to be called into community can be revolutionary)

3. The Church has its origins in the activity of the triune God and does not exist for its own sake or security but is to be SENT as the Son and the Holy Spirit have been sent for the salvation/liberation/healing/transformation of the world.

4. Christian unity is important for the mission and nature of the Church. Early Christian communities had to resolve tensions that threatened to divide Christians and distract from their witness. Contemporary Christians are also called to resolve modern tensions and seek the unity of the Church so that we may be credible witnesses and effective instruments in God's mission.

5. We claim what the Creed of Nicea-Constantinople calls the "one, holy, Catholic, apostolic Church" and would understand that our oneness and holiness are rooted in the Oneness and holiness of the

---

5. "The Nature and Mission of the Church."
6. "The Church."

triune God and we are called to reflect that oneness and holiness. We understand our catholicity to be experienced in the abundant goodness of God and the wideness of God's mercy that extends to all who will receive reaching beyond the confines of our particularities. We can claim the apostolic tradition as we walk in the tradition of the apostles who had been sent by Christ, empowered by the Holy Spirit to continue the mission of the triune God in the world.

6. We can claim the Church is "an eschatological reality, already anticipating the [reign of God], but not yet fully realizing it. We are constantly in a state of ever-becoming, or in more familiar language, always being reformed.

7. We can claim that the Sacraments of baptism and the Eucharist/Lord's Supper both give birth to us in the community of faith/the Church and nurture our development in faith, creating for us a bond of unity and commissioning us to ministry in the world.

8. We understand that all through their baptism are called to ministry and the ordaining of persons to particular ministries is to enable the whole Church to be faithful in fulfilling its apostolic ministry. We have significant differences over authority, expressions of personal, collegial and communal exercise of ministry.

9. We understand that Church is seen in local, national and global expressions and there is a relationship between all expressions of the Church.

10. We understand that the Church engages the society in which it exists. The form of that engagement differs. For some the Church stands outside of society/civil society as its critic. For others, it stands as a moral conscious within society/civil society and for others it remains "neutral."

11. As Christians in the United States, we recognize that we are in a world with people of many faiths and no faith. We are called to proclaim the good news of Jesus Christ as we respect the humanity of those who hold other beliefs and their freedom to hold other beliefs. We resonate with the ecumenical struggle to understand the fullness and limits of salvation.

There are questions I would like to lift up from the study in light of the questions that I raise at the beginning of this discussion. The study acknowledges that a critical issue in quest for visible unity is the capacity to recognize in each other the marks and signs of the Church.

> Ever since the Toronto Declaration of 1950, the WCC has challenged the churches to "recognize that the membership of the church of Christ is more inclusive than the membership of their own church body." . . . "How can we identify the Church which the creed calls one, holy, catholic and apostolic?" "What is God's will for the unity of this Church?" "What do we need to do to put God's will into practice?"[7]

> Currently, some identify the Church of Christ exclusively with their own community, while others would acknowledge in communities other than their own a real but incomplete presence of the elements which make up the Church. Others have joined into various types of covenant relationships, which sometimes include the sharing of worship. Some believe that the Church of Christ is located in all communities that present a convincing claim to be Christian, while others maintain that Christ's church is invisible and cannot be adequately identified during this earthly pilgrimage.[8]

My first question is centered on what is the underlying force that leads us to sit in seats of power that attempts to legitimate or delegitimate Christian expressions and traditions that differ from what we know and practice? As "The Church: Towards a Common Vision" appropriately notes, this struggle for determining legitimacy can be seen in the very birth of the Christianity. The radical teachings of Jesus were questioned and tested for their orthodoxy and found lacking by religious establishment. The early disciples were continuously proving their authenticity and Paul stood before tribunals telling his story and claiming the faith. Whether it was the inclusion of Gentiles or the eating of food offered to idols or the form of baptism or questions of circumcision, new realities and questions emerged that called the community of believers to clarify boundaries. Clarification came in different forms. For instance, we recall the words of Gamaliel: ". . . if this plan is of God or undertaking is of man it will fail, but if it is of God, you will not be able to overthrow them. You might even be found opposing God" (Acts 5:38b–39). Or possibly the letter of the Jerusalem Council to the Gentiles outlining expectations for their acceptance (Acts 15). Or the Apostle Paul's letter to the Church at Corinth questioning their divisions

---

7. Ibid., 8.
8. Ibid., para. 10.

and proclaiming power of the crucified and resurrected Christ as the source truth. These three instances demonstrate that for early Christians there was a need to define the marks and boundaries of faithfulness.

As the Christian communities grew in power and position, ecumenical councils attempted to resolve differences. When they were unable to do so, schisms emerged and centuries evolved in which Christian communities were defined by their differences not by what they shared in common. Definition by difference was as much informed by social and geopolitical realities as it was theological beliefs. Anathemas and schisms often served to cement a tradition's particularities and differences over and against others. Ecumenical dialogue and engagement have sought to heal some of these rifts and schisms, but this is often only after the underlying social and geopolitical tensions no longer hold the same power they once did. We must be careful that we avoid the dynamic that is too often seen in ecumenical engagement in which some believe they can determine the legitimacy of Christian communities/churches and other Christian communities/churches beg for the acceptance and approval of other Christian communities/churches. Another way of framing the question may be is our ecclesiologies rooted in what we hold in common or defined by our differences? Do we have faith sufficient to see in another tradition the Lordship of Jesus the Christ and the movement of the Holy Spirit? This is not for the power or glory of any one tradition, but for the mission of God in the world today. This requires a genuine spirit of humility; trust in the counsel of the Holy Spirit and the wisdom of Gamaliel. The quest for unity is not dependent upon our remaining in our comfort zones, but daring to be led by the Holy Spirit into those places where we may be least comfortable.

> Ecumenical dialogue has repeatedly shown that issues relating to ordained ministry constitute challenging obstacles on the path to unity. If differences such as those relating to the priesthood of the ordained prohibit full unity, it must continue to be an urgent priority for the churches to discover how they can be overcome.[9]

> Significant steps towards convergence on authority and its exercise have been recorded in various bilateral dialogues. Differences continue to exist between churches, however, as to the relative weight to be accorded to the different sources of authority, as to how far and in what ways the Church has the means to arrive at a normative expression of its faith, and as to the role of ordained ministers in providing an authoritative interpretation

---

9. Ibid., 26.

of revelation. Yet all churches share the urgent concern that the Gospel be preached, interpreted and lived out in the world humbly, but with compelling authority. May not the seeking of ecumenical convergence on the way in which authority is recognized and exercised play a creative role in this missionary endeavour of the churches?[10]

My second question is similar to the first. "Why do we continue to become divided over issues of authority and ministry?" For over sixty years, the Presbyterian Church (USA) has engaged ecumenical dialogue around the office of bishop or episcope in the Consultation on Church Union and Churches Uniting in Christ. Our bilateral dialogues with the Roman Catholic Church and the Episcopal Church have given significant attention to this subject. It has been noted that within the Reformed tradition as a whole there is often not the same angst seen in other Reformed churches outside of Scotland and Ireland towards bishops as there is within the Scots-Irish Presbyterian tradition. Scots-Irish Presbyterianism is informed and heavily influenced by the geopolitical relationship of England to Scotland and Ireland and the subsequent relationship of the Church of England and their bishops.

We were able to enter into full communion with the Evangelical Lutheran Church of America and the Northern and Southern Provinces of the Moravian Church because we were clear that differences in ordered ministries were not historically or currently church dividing. However, a significant component of these agreements is centered on developing procedures for the "orderly exchange of ministers." Have we become some focused on the "professionalization" of the church, that we ignore the "mission and witness" of the church?

Struggles within international communions (e.g., Anglican Communion, Lutheran World Federation, World Communion of Reformed Churches) in recent years have focused on the ordination and/or election of women and/or LGBT Christians as ministers and/or bishops. It is particularly curious that even though the 24th General Council of the World Alliance of Reformed Churches adopted the "Accra Confession: Covenanting for Justice in the Economy and the Earth" in 2004, churches have threatened to break relationships with others churches in the World Communion not over issues of economic or ecological justice, but over issues of ordination standards.

Within the Presbyterian Church (USA) our most recent struggles and divisions have come over the ordination of women, and the full inclusion and ordination of lesbian, gay, bisexual, transgendered Christians. While

10. Ibid., 29.

many have claimed the issue of biblical and confessional faithfulness as grounds for separation and division, it has been repeatedly noted that there is often inconsistency or selective faithfulness to biblical mandates.

It is as though we are developing an ecclesiology that is rooted in the power to exclude. How is this related to the distribution and exercise of power? How does this relate to the call of faithful discipleship of Jesus the Christ and being his witnesses in the world? How does this relate to the baptismal calling on Christians that is foundational for all expressions of ministry?

> Ecumenical dialogue at the multilateral and bilateral levels has begun to sketch out some of the parameters of the significance of moral doctrine and practice for Christian unity. If present and future ecumenical dialogue is to serve both the mission and the unity of the Church, it is important that this dialogue explicitly address the challenges to convergence represented by contemporary moral issues. We invite the churches to explore these issues in a spirit of mutual attentiveness and support. How might the churches, guided by the Spirit, discern together what it means today to understand and live in fidelity to the teaching and attitude of Jesus? How can the churches, as they engage together in this task of discernment, offer appropriate models of discourse and wise counsel to the societies in which they are called to serve?[11]

In a recent interfaith dialogue, we were discussing the teachings of each of our traditions about how we are called to shape and influence society. As Christians we read from the Prophets and the Gospel teachings of Jesus. Our partners read from their sacred text. However, as we explored the application of these teachings, we had to acknowledge the ways in which each of our traditions had fallen short of these aspirations. We acknowledged that as our traditions moved from the peripheral to the center of power in society, they were more likely to be shaped by the society than to have any significant influence on the world in which they lived.

Churches must first be willing to exam how their traditions have been shaped and influenced by the societies in which they were formed. This requires a painfully honest introspection and even more painful confession. The annihilation of Indigenous peoples, the enslavement of Africans, the genocide of non-Aryans, internment of Americans of Japanese descent, subjugation of women, the colonization and exploitation of peoples, the impoverishment of communities were all acts of society that were biblically

---

11. Ibid., 35–36.

justified and blessed by churches and Christians. It is humbling to remember that Jesus reserved his harshest words of criticism, not for those on the margins of life, but for those who sat in seats of religious power and attempted to pass judgment on others while waddling in hypocrisy.

Are churches able to disentangle themselves from the societies in which they exist, confess their own complicity in the sins of the society and speak a word of liberation and grace on those issues with which society wrestles? Will the world in which we live even listen or care? Is it possible that there might be movements in communities outside of the church that are messengers of God's liberation and grace for the church and faithful Christians?

As I reflect on the three scenarios at the beginning of this paper, I realize that as the largest expression of the Presbyterian tradition in the United States, as we consider what does it mean to be the church at this moment in history, we must wrestle with questions of privilege and power, inclusion and exclusion, acceptance and rejection, and ways we may have been complicit in the brokenness of the world in which we live. In humility we know that God is still reforming us and we remain open to God's healing and transformative power.

Scripture and the PC(USA) Constitution (both our *Book of Confessions* and *Book of Order*) offer us key insights as to our nature and calling. "The Church: Towards a Common Vision" offers us an ecumenical lens through which to both see ourselves and engage other Christian communities. We are challenged by its offering, recognize that we have much to learn from others, trust that we have gifts to bring to the others and know that apart from our sisters and brothers in Christ we remain incomplete. It seems appropriate to close with these words from the Foundations of Presbyterian Polity in the *Book of Order*.

> Unity is God's gift to the Church in Jesus Christ. Just as God is one God and Jesus Christ is our one Savior, so the Church is one because it belongs to its one Lord, Jesus Christ. The Church seeks to include all people and is never content to enjoy the benefits of Christian community for itself alone. There is one Church, for there is one Spirit, one hope, "one Lord, one faith, one baptism, one God and Father of all, who is above all and through all and in all." (Eph 4:5–6)
>
> Because in Christ the Church is one, it strives to be one. To be one with Christ is to be joined with all those whom Christ calls into relationship with him. To be thus joined with one another is to become priests for one another, praying for the world and for one another and sharing the various gifts God has given to each

Christian for the benefit of the whole community. Division into different denominations obscures but does not destroy unity in Christ. The Presbyterian Church (USA), affirming its historical continuity with the whole Church of Jesus Christ, is committed to the reduction of that obscurity, and is willing to seek and to deepen communion with all other churches within the one, holy, catholic, and apostolic Church.[12]

Bibliography

Baptism, Eucharist, and Ministry. Faith and Order Paper No. 111. Geneva: World Council of Churches, 1982.
"By-Laws of the WCC Commission on Faith and Order." Geneva: World Council of Churches, 2012.
"The Church: Towards a Common Vision." Faith and Order Paper No. 214. Geneva: World Council of Churches, 2013.
The Constitution of the Presbyterian Church (U.S.A.), Part II, Book of Order. Louisville: The Office of the General Assembly, 2013.
John Paul II. "Declaration 'Dominus Iesus' on the Unicity and Salvific Universality of Jesus Christ and the Church." http://www.vatican.va/roman_curia/congregations/cfaith/documents/rc_con_cfaith_doc_20000806_dominus-iesus_en.html.
"The Nature and Mission of the Church: A Stage on the Way to a Common Statement." Faith and Order Paper No. 198. Geneva: World Council of Churches, 2005.
"The Nature and Purpose of the Church: A Stage on the Way to a Common Statement." Faith and Order Paper No. 181. Geneva: World Council of Churches, 1998.

---

12. *Book of Order*, F-1.0302a.

Epilogue
Outside the (United) Church Is No Salvation

Edwin Chr. van Driel

I. "Liturgical-Missional" and the Problem of Protestant Ecclesiology

What does it mean to speak of a "liturgical-missional" vision for the church? I have to admit that when Neal Presa asked me to make a contribution to this conversation, it was not immediately clear to me what, in this context, these combined terms were meant to mean. But the advantage of participating in the third and last Moderator's Colloquium on Ecclesiology was that I had an opportunity to look back at how the conversation had developed so far; what themes had emerged, what arguments had been advanced, and what hopes and dreams had been expressed.

Looking over the presentations from previous colloquia, it seems that many participants were looking for a stronger, thicker relationship between the notions of "church" and "salvation"—church, that is, as the visible, tangible community of people gathered together, and "salvation" as the saving and transforming presence of Jesus Christ. For example, in his paper on the church as a missional community Darrell L. Guder spoke of the need for an ecclesiology which could counter ways of speaking about the church that reduce salvation to an individualistic and disembodied hope; that takes serious God's mission as the outworking of God's love for the entire creation; an ecclesiology that reclaims "the profoundly eschatological character of the church's calling"; and which acknowledges that "the divine strategy for the healing of the world is the calling, setting apart, formation, and sending of a particular people."[1] Corey J. Widmer, writing as the pastor of a multicultural church plant, called attention to the metaphor of "foretaste," the notion that the church, in all its diversity, "is called to be an anticipatory foretaste of a new and coming future."[2] Marney Wasserman, reflecting on our celebrations of the Lord's table, mourned that so many eucharistic services seem trapped in the past, remembering what Jesus did instead of being focused on the present, on "the thing that God is doing here with bread and wine, among us... with our eyes on the crucified Savior we miss the risen Lord."[3] Thomas E. Smith, also writing about communion, focused on the missional effect of the sacrament, because "the sacramental significance of the eucharist lies in it effecting what it signifies, namely, in effecting in the lives of its participants the saving grace of Jesus Christ, enabling them to go into the world in the strength of his love to incarnate the same."[4]

If this is indeed the focus of the liturgical-missional conversation, it touches on the sore spot of Reformed ecclesiology. While it is part of the Reformed confessional heritage to say, in the words of third-century church father Cyprian of Cartago, that "extra ecclesiam nulla salus" (outside the church is no salvation), over time this confessional stance has been gutted of real meaning.[5] Reformed theologians, wanting to combine Cyprian's saying with the dissenter roots of the Protestant movement, developed a set of concepts and distinctions that reinterpreted "church" as an *invisible*, spiritual community. As a result, Cyprian's saying became a kind of tautology: that is, outside the spiritual community of faith, the gathering of the elect, the invisible church, no one is saved. Simultaneously, the ties between the

---

1. Guder, "The Church," 118, 125, 127, 125.

2. Corey J. Widmer, "From Blueprint to Foretaste: Worship, Mission and Multiculturalism in Reformed Congregations," chapter 19 of the present volume.

3. Marney Wasserman, "Getting Out of the Past tense at the Lord's Table: Missional Implications of the Lord's Supper," chapter 11 of the present volume.

4. Thomas E. Smith, "The Centrality of Eucharist," chapter 10 of the present volume.

5. "Outside the Church of God there is no salvation. But we esteem fellowship with the true Church of Christ so highly that we deny that those can live before God who do not stand in fellowship with the true Church of God, but separate themselves from it" (*The Second Helvetic Confession*, XVII in *The Book of Confessions*, sec. 5.136, p. 87; "The visible Church, which is also catholic or universal under the gospel (not confined to one nation as before under the law), consists of all those throughout the world that profess the true religion, together with their children, and is the Kingdom of the Lord Jesus Christ; the house and family of God, through which men are ordinarily saved and union with which is essential to their best growth and service" (*The Westminster Confession of Faith*, XXVII in *The Book of Confessions* 6.141, p. 152). For Cyprian of Carthage, "Letter LXXII.21," 384.

visible church and salvation were loosened to the point of being accidental. Sure, most Christians will find Christ and salvation in the context of a visible ecclesial community, but this is not perceived as necessary. Listening to Christian talk-radio will do as well. Downgrading the place of the visible church in the story of salvation has left Reformed theology defenseless in the face of church schism and has crippled the development of a Reformed doctrine of ordination. If salvation is dependent on membership in the invisible, and not the visible church, there is no argument against breaking away from an existing church community. Moreover, if the visible church is accidental to salvation, so are ministers, whose ordinations happened in the context of public communities, not invisible ones.[6]

In this paper I wish to contribute to the "liturgical-missional" conversation by reflecting on the "*extra ecclesiam nulla salus.*" In the next section I will illustrate the history of Reformed re-interpretation of Cyprian's saying by a brief discussion of the ecclesiological position of three key Reformed thinkers: John Calvin (1509–64), Francis Turretin (1623–87), and Charles Hodge (1797–1878).[7] In the third section, I will propose an alternative Protestant reading of the relationship between church and salvation, which hangs on a reinterpretation of "salvation," rather than a redefinition of "church." I will make my proposal in conversation with a colloquium paper by David L. Stubbs,[8] in which he offers the most extensive theological reflection on the pair "liturgical-missional" to date. Finally, in a fourth section, I will make

---

6. Rather than expounding what it means to be "stewards of the mysteries of God" (1 Cor 4:1), Reformed accounts of ordained ministry have become functional and pragmatic. A perfect illustration thereof is the highly regrettable and hopefully short-lived decision of the PC(USA) to call its clergy "teaching elders"—as if ministers of Word and Sacrament are a kind of ecclesial educators. The liturgical acts of the minister—blessing and declaration of pardon, baptizing and breaking of bread, proclaiming the Word and yielding the keys of the kingdom, are in fact of a significantly different category than "teaching."

7. I use the word "illustrate" advisedly. My claim is not that these three theologians are themselves responsible for the shifting interpretation of the "extra ecclesiam nulla salus" among the Reformed, but rather that they embody three different phases in the development of Reformed ecclesiology. Turretin and Hodge are nonetheless pivotal figures given their central place in the history of education of North American Presbyterian candidates for ministry. In the nineteenth century, Turretin's three volume *Institutio Theologiae Elencticae* was the textbook for instruction in theology at several important North American Presbyterian theological schools (See Dennison, "The Life and Career of Francis Turretin," 639–48, esp. 648.) At Princeton Turretin's text was only replaced in 1872 at the appearance of Charles Hodge's three volumes of *Systematic Theology*. Hodge himself taught at Princeton for more than forty years and instructed more than three thousand students (On Hodge, see Gutjahr, *Charles Hodge*).

8. See chapter 2 of the present volume for David Stubbs' paper.

six suggestions about what such reclaimed relationship between church and salvation means for the common life in the denomination, in our congregations, and for the formation of candidates for ordination in our seminaries.

II. Extra ecclesiam nulla salus: Three Classical Reformed Interpretations

John Calvin

In the opening pages of the ecclesiological part of his *Institutes* John Calvin underscores his adherence to Cyprian's position: ". . . for those who have God as Father, the church is mother . . . For there is no other way to enter into life unless this mother conceive us in her womb, give us birth, nourish us at her breast, and lastly, unless she keep us under her care and guidance until, putting off mortal flesh, we become like the angels . . . Away from her bosom one cannot hope for any forgiveness of sins or any salvation."[9] If the church is our mother apart from whom no salvation is possible, how then can Protestants defend their leave of the parental home? To answer this question, Calvin makes use of two distinctions: one between the "visible" and the "invisible" church, and another distinction between a "true" and a "false" or "corrupted" church. The first distinction Calvin wields to underscore that when it comes to "the true church with which as a mother we must keep unity" it is the visible church of which he speaks.[10] This is in itself quite significant since, as we will see, later generations Reformed theologians solved the Protestant ecclesiological dilemmas by taking the invisible church as the focus of their ecclesiology. Not so Calvin. Scripture uses the notion of church in two ways, he says: as the community of all those who are truly "children of God by grace of adoption" (the invisible church) and "the whole multitude of men spread over the earth who profess to worship one God and Christ" (the visible church).[11] In this latter community, Calvin admits, we find "mingled many hypocrites who have nothing of Christ but the name and outward appearance."[12] Nonetheless, it is this latter, visible community that "we are commanded to revere and keep communion with" and that Calvin designates as "the mother of believers."[13] If we are then to

9. John Calvin, *Institutiones* IV.I.1, and IV.I.4; quoted according to the *Institutes of the Christian Religion*, 1:1012, 1016.

10. Ibid., IV.1., 1011.

11. Ibid, IV.I.7, 1021.

12. Ibid., IV.1.7, 1021.

13. Ibid., IV.1.7, 1022; IV.1.4, 1016.

keep communion with the visible church as the conduit of salvation, how can Calvin justify the schismatic roots of his own Genevan community? To answer this question Calvin introduces his second distinction, between the "true church" and the "false" or "corrupted" church. When it comes to the true church, we should "keep its communion scrupulously in all respects." False churches however are communities that have become "props of falsehood" and "receptacles of idols" from which one "must separate."[14] What distinguishes these two kinds of communities are certain "marks," that help us to identify where "a church of God exists."[15] Following earlier stipulations in the Lutheran tradition, Calvin then lifts up as marks "the Word of God purely preached and heard, and the sacraments administered according to Christ's institution."[16] Here Calvin left his followers with a real puzzle. How do we distinguish the pure from the impure preaching of the Word, and what makes the sacraments administered more or less according to Christ's institution? Calvin himself does not give us much to go on here. At some point in his exposition he even drops the qualifiers altogether.[17] The closest Calvin comes in unpacking these qualifiers is when he introduces the notion of necessary articles of faith. There is a sliding scale as to the 'purity' of preaching, Calvin says. Not all disagreements about doctrine should therefore lead to dissent. But some articles of faith are non-negotiable. "Such are: God is one; Christ is God and the Son of God; our salvation rests in God's mercy; and the like."[18] Then the question is: What falls under the category of "the like"? In suggesting we identify the true, visible church by looking for the marks of pure preaching and rightful sacramental administration Calvin opened the door for further fragmentation of the Protestant community, as different groups unpacked Calvin's qualifiers in different ways. Even more serious is a second problem: the marks which Calvin suggested are expressions of human and not divine agency. They are not acts of divine initiative but of human response: *faithful* preaching, *righty administered* sacraments. If these are the things which distinguish the true from the false church, and there is no salvation outside the true church, then salvation depends on whether or not humans form faithful, true churches. To say

14. Ibid., IV.II.10, 1051, 1050; cf. the discussion throughout the whole of chapter II (pp. 1041–53).

15. Ibid., IV.1.9, 1023.

16. Ibid., IV.1.9, 1023. For the Lutheran tradition, cf. *The Augsburg Confession*, VII: "The church is the assembly of saints in which the gospel is taught purely and the sacraments are administered rightly" (Kolb and Wengert, *Book of Concord*, 43).

17. "We have laid down as distinguishing marks of the church the preaching of the Word and the observance of the sacraments" (Calvin, *Institutes*, IV.1.10, 1024).

18. Ibid., IV.I.12, 1026.

this seems deeply problematic for a movement that had just discovered that salvation depends on *God's* acts and not ours. If what makes a church to be true depends on our faithfulness, on a Protestant account this therefore has to inevitably weaken the ties between church and salvation.

Francis Turretin

Turretin starts his ecclesiological discussion at the same place as Calvin: the church is necessary for salvation, and therefore it is crucial to know which church is true and which is not.[19] When he comes to discuss the distinction between the true and the false church, he again follows Calvin, lifting up two marks by which the true church can be recognized: "the pure preaching of the word with the lawful administration of the sacraments." Turretin does want to make a distinction in importance between these two: without "the pure preaching and profession of the word" the church cannot exist, but the administration of the sacraments does not have an equal degree of necessity.[20] The "marks of the church" continue to be understood in terms of human rather than divine agency. In his further unpacking of the "proper and essential mark" of the true church he describes its central characteristic as the correspondence between the church's doctrine and the word of God.[21]

However, between his opening paragraphs about the true church without there is no salvation, and the point where he discusses the marks that help us distinguish between true and false churches, Turretin offers about eighty pages of additional ecclesiological considerations—and in these pages he develops what can be read as an alternative strategy to understand the "extra ecclesiam nulla salus." The strategy is based on an identification between the *true* church and the *invisible* church. As I noted above, Calvin

---

19. "Since there is no salvation outside of the church (no more than out of the ark; nor does anyone have God as his Father in heaven whose church is not his mother on earth), nothing ought to be dearer to our hearts than that this mother may be known (in whose bosom God has willed us to be educated and to be nourished). It behooves us to be directed by her care until we grow up and arrive at the goal of faith. Also it behooves us to know what assembly is that true church with which (according to the command of God) we are bound to connect ourselves that we may obtain salvation" (Francis Turretin, *Institutio Theologiae Elencticae* XVIII.I.i; quoted according to the Dennison, *Institutes of Elenctic Theology*, 1). Cf. Turretin, *Institutio*, XVIII.XII.i, 86: "Since salvation cannot be obtained except in communion with the true church and many glory in this sacred name who are destitute of its truth, it is of great value to know its true marks that we may be able to distinguish the true fold of Christ from the dens of wolves."

20. Ibid., XVIII.XII.vii, 87.

21. Ibid., XVIII.XIV.iv, 121.

introduced the distinction between the true and the false church only after he had underscored that when it comes to the true, salvific church, he is speaking of the visible church. So not Turretin. Like Calvin, having staked his position on the essential importance of the church for salvation, he introduces the distinction between the invisible and visible church, but then says that the invisible church, "an assembly of elect persons, whom God by his word and Spirit calls out of the state of sin into the state of grace unto eternal glory," is the true church.[22] To underscore this point, Turretin argues that therefore "catechumens, the excommunicated and unbaptized... can be members of the true church, although they are not in the visible church."[23] In order to make this claim stick, Turretin builds on the distinction between invisible and visible church a dual ecclesiological structure, in which salvation is consistently connected with the invisible and not the visible church. For instance, Turretin makes a distinction between external and internal baptism, and argues that external baptism is not necessary for salvation.[24] External baptism is necessary for membership of the visible church only; internal baptism is necessary for membership of the invisible church.[25] Likewise, he makes a distinction between visible (or external) unity, and invisible (or internal) church unity: the former is only accidental, the latter essential to the church.[26] At this point, the "extra ecclesiam nolum salus" has become a tautology—be it at the expense of a place for the visible, tangible church community, for visible, tangible, acts like baptism, and for visible, tangible common life. But not only that. If obtaining salvation is a matter of being a member of the invisible and not the visible church, salvation itself cannot be visible. This is indeed what Turretin seems to hold. As part of his argument for identifying the true and the invisible church, he makes this comment: "The church is the kingdom of God. It does not come with observation . . . Because it is spiritual and internal, erected in the minds of men and occupied with things pertaining to the mind, not . . . in external and bodily things, but in righteousness, and peace, and joy in the Holy Ghost."[27] It is exactly here, I believe, that our theological suspicions should be raised. Is it true that the kingdom of God is spiritual and internal, only pertaining the things of the mind? Does that picture fit the ministry of Christ, who announces God's reign not only by forgiving sins and engages people in

---

22. Ibid., XVIII.II.x, 9; cf. the whole of ibid., XVIII.VII, 32–41.
23. Ibid., XVIII.II.xi, 10.
24. Ibid., XVIII.IV.iv, 24.
25. Ibid., XVIII.IV.vii, 24.
26. Ibid., XVIII.V.ii–iii, 27.
27. Ibid., XVIII.VII.xii, 37.

questions of the soul, but whose hands also feed real hunger, heal real bodies, and raise people from the dead? If it is not true that salvation concerns solely the mental and spiritual, would it not likewise be mistaken to think that the true church, as the gateway to salvation, is internal and invisible? A concept of a true, invisible church will only holds as much as a concept of invisible salvation will allow, and if salvation is too rich to be squeezed into the invisible, spiritual realm, the true church cannot be kept in the invisible either.

Charles Hodge

In Charles Hodge's work we find the final steps of the Reformed reinterpretation of the "extra ecclesiam nulla salus." Strikingly, in his three-volume *Systematic Theology* the church does not receive a chapter of its own. Hodge writes about the church in the context of a discourse about the difference between the Roman Catholic and Protestant views on the rule of faith and in a chapter on baptism.[28] In the first discussion Hodge deals with "the nature of the church." The idea that the church is essentially "an external, visible, organized society" is dismissed as a "Romish doctrine."[29] Rather, "the church as such, or in its essential nature, is not an external organization. All true believers, in whom the Spirit of God dwells, are members of that church which is the body of Christ, no matter with what ecclesiastical organization they may be connected, and even although they have no such connection . . . The condition of membership in the true church is not union with any organized society, but faith in Jesus Christ."[30] Hodge is so convinced that these are "the two opposing theories of the church, the Romish and the Protestant," that "it is unnecessary to cite authorities on either side."[31] If that is the case, then what to make of the claim of the *Westminster Confession* that outside the visible church there is no ordinary possibility of salvation?[32] Hodge does not deal with this in his *Systematic Theology*, but he does so elsewhere. It is very simple, he claims: "it is only saying that there is no salvation without the knowledge and profession of the gospel; that there is no the name by which we must be saved, but the name of Jesus Christ."[33] Here the Protestant strategy to gut the confessional stance of real meaning

---

28. Hodge, *Systematic Theology*, 1:129–39, and volume 3,
29. Ibid., 1:131.
30. Ibid., 1:134.
31. Ibid., 1:135.
32. See footnote 4.
33. Hodge, *Discussions in Church Polity*, 46.

has been completed: the visible church has been written out of salvation history.[34]

Even while membership of the visible church is thus not necessary for salvation, it is not the case that Hodge wants to deplete the visible ecclesial community of all importance. Rather, as a logical consequence of the Protestant reinterpretation strategy, the visible church is an expression of human response to the gospel, and membership thereof a sign of human obedience: "God has imposed duties upon his people which render it necessary for them thus to associate in a visible body."[35] What is not necessary, however, is that there is only one such visible body. In fact, the diversity of opinion that exists among the faithful about all sorts of things theologically, calls for a variety of ecclesial communities. While "diversity of opinion is indeed an evidence of imperfection," and therefore wrong, it is less problematic "than either hypocrisy or contention." It is "to be deplored, as every other evidence of . . . imperfection is to be regretted, yet the evil is not to be magnified above its just dimensions. So long as unity of faith, of love, and of obedience is preserved, the unity of the church is as to its essential principle safe . . . if the unity of the church arises from union with Christ and the indwelling of his Spirit, then all who are thus united to him, are members of the church, no matter what their external ecclesiastical connections may be, or whether they sustain any such relationship at all . . . It is plain therefore that the evangelical are the most truly catholic . . ."[36]

It is not difficult to recognize in these last comments by Hodge the practice of twenty-first-century North American Christians. Institutional unity is valued lowly; institutional loyalty sacrificed at the altar of church shopping and ecclesial strife. Denominational pluralism is either bemoaned

---

34. Hodge himself astutely formulates the classical Protestant strategy when he continues: "the proposition that 'out of the church there is no salvation' is true or false, liberal or illiberal, according to the latitude given to the word church . . . In the mouth of Protestants, it means there is no salvation without faith in Jesus Christ" (ibid., 46–47). Earlier in his argument he had spoken negatively spoken of those "Greek and Latin Churches" which made "salvation depend upon connection with a visible society" (ibid., 34). It is a sign of the success of the Protestant reinterpretation strategy that Hodge did not realize John Calvin sided with these "Greek and Latin churches."

35. Hodge, *Systematic Theology*, 3:547. One should not be misled by the title of this section of God's work: "The Visible Church is a Divine Institution" (ibid., 547). The upshot of Hodge's argument is not that God constituted the visible church, but that God commanded the church to be constituted. How this works out, one sees in Hodge's treatment of baptism. His preferred image for baptism is that of "a badge of Christian profession," alike to an oath taken by an office holder at his inauguration (ibid., 585). As such, it is an act of human obedience, not of divine initiative.

36. Hodge, *Discussions in Church Polity*, 44.

but seen as necessary consequence of religious diversity and authenticity, or even celebrated as a means to strengthen the religious marketplace. Visible church and salvation are disconnected; salvation is often perceived as a result of personal choice and faith. The question is, though: does this low esteem for visible ecclesial community do right by the narrative of Scripture? And if not, would this not call for a different interpretation of the "extra ecclesiam nulla salus?"

III. Extra ecclesiam nulla salus: An Alternative Interpretation

It is exactly at this point, I believe, that the "liturgical-missional" conversation offers important openings, because its participants are convinced that the church in its visible appearance is more than a voluntary organization and more than accidentally related to salvation. They are thus convinced because they believe the narrative of Scripture offers a richer, thicker account of the role of the visible church in the history of salvation. Based on these convictions, in this section I will offer an alternative interpretation of "outside the church is no salvation." Rather than trying to redefine "church," I will focus on the notion of "salvation." In the first half of this section I will gather the exegetical material that helps us recognize the close connections between church and salvation in the biblical narrative. I will do so in conversation with a paper presented at a previous colloquium by David L. Stubbs. In the second half I will offer an alternative account of Cyprian's saying which helps us turn away from the classical Protestant distinctions between true and false and visible and invisible church, but which nonetheless is rooted in a distinctive Protestant ecclesiology.

The Narrative of Scripture

Stubbs starts his presentation with a reflection on the notion of a "liturgical-missional vision" for the church. To say that the church is *missional* "is to claim that the church is a people who participate in the 'present reign of Christ' in such a way that 'the coming completed reign of God . . . is revealed and becomes effective in the present.'"[37] The word "missional," Stubbs argues, involves a series of claims about the church's relationship to the reign of God. The Kingdom of God is "at the center of Jesus' gospel." It is not

---

37. Stubbs, "Locating the Liturgical-Missional Church in the Bible's Story," chapter 2 in this present volume. Stubbs is here quoting from Guder, *Missional Church*, 87, who in turn quotes Küng, *The Church*, 126.

individual or spiritual, but embodied and relational: "a renewed state of the created world in which all relationships between God and humanity, humans and humans, and humans and the creation are set right." The church represents God's reign "by partially embodying it and also proclaiming the good news that in and through Christ, the reign of God has been inaugurated." Finally, this "task of representing the reign of God to the world" is the core on what the church is.[38] To say that the church is *liturgical* is to say that this community embodies God's reign particularly when it gathers in worship, because it is here that "God is present to God's people, molding and shaping them into the patterns of activity of the Kingdom of God."[39] The bulk of Stubbs' paper is then devoted to locating this understanding of the church in the context of the larger biblical narrative. The burden of this move is to show that the notion of a liturgical-missional community is at the heart of God's dealing with the world: a particular community is called to embody in its visible, common life God's intend for creation. Stubbs takes his readers on a journey through the Old Testament, pointing at God's dealing with the patriarchs, the covenant at Sinai, and the vision of the prophets. From there he moves to the story of Jesus, Pentecost and the church, and the new creation.

It seems to me that Stubbs has it exactly right: at the center of God's gracious dealing of creation are not primarily single individuals, nor an invisible, spiritual community, but a visible, embodied community, which is called in its common life to live into the reality of the inaugurated Kingdom of God. For the sake of my own argument, I would like to underscore three things.

First, this community is *covenantal*. At its core this community is constituted by God. God's covenantal actions call this community into existence. When God chose Israel, God did not elect an already existing nation but formed one out of a barren woman and a man who was as good as dead (Rom 4:19). One did not become part of Israel voluntarily but by birth and circumcision. Jesus' disciples did not choose him, but he chose them (John 15:16). One becomes a member of the Christian community by baptism—that is, by dying and being resurrected again (Rom 6:3–4). To be resurrected is not something we do, but something God does to us. The repeated pattern is not that of choosing, but of being chosen; not of gathering, but of being gathered; not of constituting, but of being constituted. This covenantal gathering starts with Israel and spreads from there to the nations, as they are incorporated into the community of the people of God.

---

38. Stubbs, "Locating the Liturgical-Missional," 18 above.

39. Ibid.

Second, this covenantal community is *eschatological*. In the biblical narrative, God relates to creation in two ways. Having called creation into being, God does not leave it to its own devices, but leads it to a final goal, what theologians call "eschatological consummation," and what Scripture calls the Kingdom of God. When humans wander away from God, God reaches out to God's creatures and draws them back in reconciliation. Each of these two ways of divine relating has its own logic and content. Eschatological consummation is about leading creation to fulfillment; reconciliation is about restoring that which is broken. Consummation is about human flourishing in intimacy with God; reconciliation is governed by the dynamic of sin and forgiveness. In the concrete narrative of Scripture, God's relating in reconciliation and eschatological consummation are intimately related, as a sinful humanity needs to be reconciled before it can be ushered into God's Kingdom. Nonetheless, these two ways of divine relating are still to be distinguished, as they relate to each other as means and goal. We are reconciled with God *so that* we may enter God's Kingdom. As God's covenantal community is thus concerned with anticipating and embodying the coming reign of God, it is therefore not simply concerned with the dynamics of sin and forgiveness. It is also, and maybe even primarily, concerned with living into God's eschatological consummation.

Third, this eschatological, covenantal community is *christocentric*. God's relating to creation in eschatological consummation is centered in Jesus Christ. Going through the hills of Galilee and Judea, Jesus announces that God's reign has come near: God is about to take on the powers-that-be, reclaim this creation, and usher in the abundance of God's Kingdom (Mark 1:15). When Jesus is arrested and killed by those very powers that be, and everything seems lost, it is Jesus' resurrection which vindicates him and shows that he was right after all. In Jesus' resurrection God is doing exactly that what Jesus said that was about to happen. After all, resurrection is an eschatological event. God is making good on the promises of a new creation, of a superabundant life under the reign of God. Jesus' resurrection is the "first fruits" (1 Cor 15:23) of the world to come. The new creation now has a foothold, right in the midst of our history. Upon Jesus' ascension he is seated at the right hand of God, the image of the place of power in the language of Scripture. Whereas Christ's resurrection implies that the Kingdom of God has been inaugurated, his ascension means that Christ is now the one in charge, the King of the kingdom. He is the one defeating the powers and leading creation to its eschatological consummation.

Of course, Christ is also the one who brings about reconciliation. Here the distinction between God's relating to creation in reconciliation and in eschatological consummation is crucial. In the narrative, Christ's reconciling work is completed on the cross. Christ died once for all (Heb 10:12). But his resurrection is only the *first* fruits of the new creation. The Kingdom has been inaugurated but not yet consummated. Christ's consummating work is still ongoing, and at the center of this ongoing, consummating work is the church. The church is the community of the baptized. To be baptized is to be united with Christ in his death and resurrection. As we go under in the water, we enter with him into the grave; when our head comes up again, we receive with him resurrection life (Rom 6:3–4; cf. Col 2:12). But as we participate in Christ's resurrection, we are already given to participate in the new creation (cf. Eph 2:5, 6). The church is therefore the only society on earth that is rooted in the future. Every other entity has its roots in what is already passed. We however have our roots in what, given Jesus' consummating work, is certain yet to come.[40]

I believe the fullest instantiation of this approach to ecclesiology is the letter to the Ephesians.[41] The letter's high emphasis on the visible church and its unity is well known:

> I . . . beg you to lead a life worthy of the calling to which you have been called, with all humility and gentleness, with patience, bearing with one another in love, making every effort to maintain the unity of the Spirit in the bond of peace. There is one body and one Spirit, just as you were called to the one hope of your calling, one Lord, one faith, one baptism, one God and Father of all, who is above all and through all and in all . . . (Eph 4:1–6)

---

40. Stubbs does underscore the Christocentric nature of the "liturgical-missional vision of God's people," but does not mention either Christ's resurrection or his ascension. He rather focuses on the "person" as the fulfillment of God's vision for creation: "What the temple symbolically represented—the place on earth where heaven and earth come together . . . is fulfilled in the two-natured person of Christ . . . He is the kingdom of God in himself. Unlike the covenant of Sinai, which was a blueprint for what the people of God was to be and do but was never completely put into practice by the people of Israel, in Jesus Christ this vision of human life under God's rule is fulfilled" ("Locating the Liturgical-Missional," 26 above). But it is not the fact that Christ is one person in two natures which in itself fulfill God's vision for creation; it is that he, because of his resurrection and ascension, has a still ongoing history, and that in this ongoing history and activity he leads the inaugurated, but not as yet completed reign of God to its consummation.

41. The Letter to the Ephesians has always received significant interests of those interested in ecclesiology, ecumenism, or church renewal. See, for instance, Barth, *The Broken Wall*; Newbigin, *The Household of God*; Peterson, *Practice Resurrection*. It is clear that Stubbs is attracted by the letter as well, as many of his expressions are drawn from this text.

But for our purposes it is of interest that the writer of the letter places the church in the context of a longer narrative; a narrative shaped by the three characteristics discussed above—covenantal, eschatological, and Christocentric. The church, the letter holds, is the outcome of a divine, eschatological "plan for the fullness of time" (Eph 1:10). The content of that plan was "to gather up all things in [Christ], things in heaven and things on earth" (1:9, 10). God brought this plan to execution in Christ's resurrection and ascension—by putting God's

> power to work in Christ when he raised him from the death and seated him at his right hand in the heavenly places, far above the rule and authority and power and dominion, and above every name that is named, not only in this age but also in the age to come. And he has put all things under his feet and has made him the head over all things for the church, which is his body, the fullness of him who fills all in all. (1:20–23)

This gathering of all things in Christ follows a particular pattern. It has started with Israel, but now also those who once were "aliens from the commonwealth of Israel, and strangers to the covenant of Israel" (2:12), have been "brought near" (2:13) so that the resurrected and ascended Christ "might create in himself a new humanity" (2:15), a new "household of God" (2:19), as both groups "grow together into a holy temple in the Lord" (2:19).[42] It was in particular Paul's calling, the writer of the Ephesians letter declares, to proclaim this eschatological intent for creation to the Gentiles, so that they may know themselves to be "fellow heirs, members of the same body, and sharers in the promise in Christ Jesus through the gospel" (3:5–8). As a result, this community formed out of both Jews and goyim, the church, "lets everyone

---

42. Earlier generations of exegetes were prone to understand the ecclesiological notions in Ephesians as shaped by either Hellenistic or Gnostic concepts about unity and community. But this ignores the fact that the notion of the "gathering up of all things" of chapter one is unpacked in chapter two as a "bringing near of those who once were far off," an incorporating into the "covenant of promise"—the promise being that in Abraham "all the families of the earth will be blessed" (Gen 12:3). In other words, the background is Jewish, not Hellenistic or Gnostic. An additional argument for such Jewish background is the writer's consistent speaking about "*the* Christ" in whom all things are gathered (see 1:10, 12, 20; 2:5, 14; 3:4, 8, 17, 19; 4:7, 12, 13, 20; 5:2, 5, 14, 23, 24, 29; 6:5). Ernest Best dismisses this as something "to which no significance should be attached to" (Best, *A Critical and Exegetical Commentary*, 143). But Markus Barth argues that these instances should consistently be translated as "the Messiah" rather than "Christ" (Barth, *Ephesians*, 66; to my mind appropriately so, given the notion of the incorporative Messiahship (see, e.g., most recently, Wright, *Paul and the Faithfulness of God*, 825–35, with reference to other literature.

see what is the plan of the mystery hidden for ages in God who created all things" and lets the powers-that-be know that their time is up (3:10).

It is exactly here that salvation is found: in this gathering activity of the resurrected and ascended Christ, in his knitting and fitting together of the scattered fragments of humanity into a new humanity, a new household of God. For the Ephesians writer "the gospel of salvation" concerns much more than reconciliation and atonement; it involves the very plan of God "to gather up all things in Christ." Salvation is, according to the Ephesians letter, that this fragments gathering, reuniting work of the resurrected Christ has now also reached *you;* that you too are being knitted into this new humanity, that in your baptism in the death and resurrection of Jesus Christ you have now become part of God's eschatological people (1:11–14). But this in turn means that the church is not accidental to salvation; that the church is not the place where you receive what you also could get on your own. Rather the opposite: *the church is the visible result of this gathering, reuniting work of the resurrected and ascended Christ.* Here this new humanity, this household of God receives form and shape. In other words: the church is not a means for salvation, no, being gathered to the church *is* your salvation.

The Theological Harvest

The theological narrative expounded above allows us to embrace Cyprian's saying in a new way: the church is indeed necessary for salvation—the church, that is, not as an invisible community of the elect, but the visible church, the concrete, embodied communities of which you and I are members. To be gathered to the church is one's salvation because in it Christ's eschatological work—his gathering of all things to himself—finds a concrete expression.

Everything here turns on the meaning of the term "salvation." At the heart of my proposed reinterpretation of Cyprian's saying lies the argument that salvation is more than being justified or forgiven, more than receiving eternal bliss. Salvation has a richer meaning because Christ's work has to do with more than reconciliation. Christ's work is twofold: reconciliation, completed once-for-all on the cross, and eschatological consummation, the ongoing leading of creation to its final goal. Both activities are, in biblical parlance, salvific. But "salvation" should not be narrowed to the former at the expense of the latter, lest we lose sight, among other things, of the result of the latter salvific work: the visible community of the church.[43]

---

43. In Stubbs, *The Open Table*, Stubbs makes a distinction between two kinds of ecclesiologies which seemingly line up with the two kinds of salvation I am

At the same time, it is because of this dual salvific work of Christ that Turretin can argue that catechumens, the excommunicated and unbaptized can be saved, even if they are not members of the visible church.[44] When Turretin speaks of "salvation," he is thinking of Christ's work of reconciliation; and, true to the insights of the Reformers, he wants to say that since we are reconciled with God unconditionally, by grace through faith, church membership should also not be seen as a condition for forgiveness of sins. In that sense, he is right. He errs, though, when he subsequently narrows salvation to reconciliation. Once we see that "salvation" not only includes reconciliation but also eschatological consummation, we have to say that

---

distinguishing here. Stubbs starts with making a point akin to the strategy utilized in his Colloquium paper, that the ways we think about the identity and role of the church go back to the ways we tell the gospel story. Stubbs then identifies a first way of conceiving of the church which he calls a "church as visible public" ecclesiology. It is rooted in a gospel narrative in which "God has planned to bring reconciliation to the world by healing it from the inside out," that is, "by revealing Godself to a particular people, calling them to a particular role and working with them." This plan starts with the calling of Israel and spreads because of God's action in Christ "through the calling of a renewed people of God, the church." While God's salvific actions involve "the forgiveness of sins," it is more fully focused on "the defect of sin and evil and the healing of humanity through the incorporation of all into this new community, this new household of God, this kingdom of Christ" (10, 11). Stubbs contrasts this with a telling of the gospel that is prevalent both in liberal and in conservative theological settings, in which it is emphasized that "in Jesus Christ, the sins of all are freely forgiven and walls are broken down between God and humanity," and in which people are invited to "break down walls between human beings, especially those among human beings that marginalize some because of race, gender, or class" (12; thus the liberal variant of this narrative) or "to put their trust in Jesus," as "salvation is understood in terms of a personal relationship with Jesus Christ, a relationship characterized above all by love and acceptance based on Christ's substitutionary death on the cross" (14; the evangelical variation). Both in the liberal and in the evangelical variation on this ecclesiology the church "is largely invisible rather than a public foretaste of and witness to the coming Kingdom of God" (14).

I sympathize with Stubbs' distinction, and the resonance between the first Gospel narrative and implied ecclesiology on the one hand, and the letter to the Ephesians, on the other, are obvious. The problem, however, is that both ecclesiologies which Stubbs here describes are what elsewhere I have called "infralapsarian," that is, part of the divine response to sin. But the salvation narrative in Ephesians is "supralapsarian," that is, it is concerned with God's eschatological, final goal for creation, a goal that is not contingent upon sin. As the church is part of this supralapsarian goal for creation, the church itself should, therefore, be conceived of as supralapsarian: to be gathered up into Christ is that for which we were created. For a brief discussion of the supralapsarian nature of Ephesians' account, see both van Driel, "Christ in Paul's Narrative"; van Driel, "Climax of the Covenant." For a discussion of the wider issues of supralapsarianism and infralapsarianism, see: van Driel, *Incarnation Anyway*.

44. See Dennison, *Institutes*, 6.

salvation in its full sense escapes the catechumens, the unbaptized, and the excommunicated, because the gathering work of Christ has not yet knitted them into the fabric of the new humanity, the new household of God.

If this is what is meant by salvation and church, the distinction between the "invisible" and "visible" church is not helpful. Salvation, Christ's eschatological work of drawing all things to himself, certainly engages both the visible and the invisible, the embodied and the spiritual. But his gathering activity is not said to establish two conceptually different, but only one, visible community.

Likewise, it will not do to speak of "true" and "false" churches. As I noticed above, this distinction differentiates visible ecclesial communities based on their response to Christ's gathering work: whether they preach the gospel faithfully and administer the sacraments rightly. If a visible ecclesial community does not respond to Christ's gathering work faithfully, it can become a "false" church. Over time, this strategy led some Reformed theologians conceive of the whole of the visible church as constituted by human response to the gospel. This is the prevailing ecclesiology in North America right now: churches as voluntary organizations one joins or leaves at will. However, the biblical narrative excludes such ecclesiological account. The church is an expression of Christ's gathering activity. It is thus not constituted by human response, but by divine initiative. Christ gathers people by uniting them to his death and resurrection through the waters of baptism, and knits them into the fabric of his new humanity. Of course, both individuals and communities can respond to this gathering activity by rejection. They can choose to live against the grain of their new baptismal identity. But even this does not undo the fact that they are baptized, marked with the cross of Christ forever. Seen in this way, a disobedient church is still a true church. It is only in the context of it being a true church, that is, a church established by Christ's gathering activity, that it makes sense to speak of a church's "disobedience."

Let's say it even more strongly: if "to be saved" means to be subject to Christ's gathering activity, then to leave the church, or to break the church, is to jeopardize salvation—because it goes against the grain of the gathering work of Christ. One jeopardizes salvation not in the sense that one cannot receive forgiveness and reconciliation but in the sense that one does not experience what it means to be "joined together and to grow into a holy temple in the Lord" (Eph 2:21).[45]

---

45. In an earlier essay I explored the problems with church schism from the perspective of "covenant." This current project offers the biblical-theological support for the arguments developed there: van Driel, "Church and Covenant," 449–61; reprinted in Thiessen, *Ecumenical Ecclesiology*, 62–75.

Finally: what does this reinterpreted "extra ecclesiam nulla salus" mean for the original problem that triggered so much Protestant ecclesiological reflection: the desire to adhere to Cyprian's saying while justifying the schism of Roman Catholics and Protestants? The traditional Protestant strategy was to argue that the Roman Catholic Church had become a "false" church and that departing a false church is not only justified but even demanded. On my alternative proposal there are no false churches: each church which is established by baptism is constituted by Jesus Christ and thereby a "true" church. An alternative Protestant justification would argue that while the Roman Catholic Church is a true church, it is nonetheless a disobedient church; and that disobedient churches should be left behind. It would go beyond the scope of this paper to explore this option, other than to say that, if my argument so far holds, it seems that schism itself is an expression of disobedience, and so it is questionable whether such alternative justification holds water.

But maybe it should not even be our goal to justify the schism. After all, the goal of the Reformers was not to split the church, but to reform the church. In that sense, the Reformation failed. The church split, and as a result, we jeopardized the salvation—"we," that is, both Protestants and Roman Catholics, because in our separation and divisions all of us went against the grain of Christ's gathering activity and thereby forfeited the change to experience what it means to live together as members of the household of God.

It is this last point that underscores that my alternative interpretation of the "outside the church is no salvation" is nonetheless an authentically *Protestant* interpretation. On the Roman Catholic interpretation of the "extra ecclesiam nulla salus" it is the Protestants, but not the Roman Catholics, who jeopardized their salvation in the Reformation schism, because they placed themselves outside of the community with Rome. There is no salvation outside of the Roman Catholic Church, because salvation comes to us through a visible community which is constituted by the historical act of Christ's calling and sending out of the apostles. Or, as the Second Vatican document *Lumen Gentium* formulates the argument: salvation cannot be found other than in the visible community with the church's bishops and the Roman pontiff, who together are the stewards of grace and "witnesses to divine and Catholic truth," gifted as they are "with a special outpouring of the Holy Spirit" that has passed down to them by the imposition of hands in episcopal consecration from the original recipients of this gift, Christ's apostles, onward.[46] A Roman Catholic interpretation of Cyprian's saying

---

46. *Lumen Gentium*, no. 25, 21, in *The Teachings of the Second Vatican Council*,

would suggest that the relationship between church and salvation is thus shaped by *Christ's acts in the past*. In contrast, my ecclesiological proposals hold that the relationship between church and salvation is founded upon *Christ's acts in the present*. There is no salvation outside of the church, because salvation comes to us through a visible community that is constituted by God's covenant with us in baptism. Salvation cannot be found elsewhere, because salvation is to be knitted into the new community called church. Churches are constituted not by episcopal ties to a past event, but by God's covenantal redefining of our lives in baptism. Where this happens, there is church. The result of these contrasting ecclesiological arguments is a different attitude towards Protestant churches. Roman Catholic ecclesiology asks Protestant churches to think *lower* of themselves. The Roman Catholic position holds that, given its historical heritage, there is a fullness to the Roman Catholic Church that Protestantism lacks. Protestant communities, even while they are made up of people who carry the name of "Christian," do not share in this historic apostolic succession, therefore miss a constitutive element of the church and so cannot be called "churches in the proper sense."[47] However, my ecclesiological proposals ask Protestant churches to think *higher* of themselves. I am asking them to think of themselves not as voluntary organizations, nor as communities constituted by human choice or action, but rather to see themselves as constituted by divine covenant, by the eschatological work of Jesus Christ. On my account, the Protestant problem is not our lacking of ecclesial fullness; our problem is that, in our divisions and ecclesial strife, we live against the grain of who we are.

IV. Church, Salvation, and Our Common Life: Six Proposals

The argument in the preceding paragraphs leads us to a fourth section of this essay. What would it be like for our own ecclesial community, the Presbyterian Church (USA), to live into this understanding of what it means to be church—as a place where the gathering, reuniting activity of the resurrected and ascended Christ receives form and shape, a place where he makes visible and tangible the salvation of the eschatological consummation? How would it help us imagine new possibilities for our common life?

108, 101.

    47. Thus the Congregation for the Doctrine of the Faith in their "Responses to some questions regarding certain aspects of the doctrine of the church," issued June 29, 2007. Available at: http://www.vatican.va/roman_curia/congregations/cfaith/documents/rc_con_cfaith_doc_20070629_responsa-quaestiones_en.html.

In this section I offer six proposals for the wider church, local congregations and mission plants, and, finally, our seminaries. In making these proposals I am mindful of our denomination's present difficulties. We are a body suffering from divisions and strife; hurting because of schisms that ripped apart presbyteries, congregations, and families. We are a church with dropping numbers, dwindling resources, and aging membership, and therefore even more prone to conflict, because, as every pastor knows, where anxiety rules conflict soon will follow. In this situation, what difference does a "liturgical-missional" understanding of the church make?

1. As a denomination we should stop trying to find unity among ourselves and start losing ourselves in the unity we have in Christ.

In 2012, the 220th General Assembly narrowly defeated a proposal to change the denomination's definition of marriage. Realizing that the issue would come back again during the 221st General Assembly (2014), the denomination was invited to engage in a study of "Christian marriage," guided by material prepared by the Office of Theology and Worship. The goal, without doubt, is for the denomination to find some common ground, some agreed upon approach, so as to steer away from further division when the General Assembly weighs proposals and takes its votes. Before the 220th General Assembly, the denomination engaged in similar studies and debates regarding the ordination of gays and lesbians. Several years before that there were the conversations stimulated by the report of the denominational Task Force on Peace, Unity, and Purity of the Church. In all likelihood, the years before the 222nd General Assembly (2016) will be occupied by similar rounds of conversations and debates.

All these conversations, taskforces, and reports, concern real, important theological issues. They stir up many emotions because deep-seated convictions are at stake. What I would like to call attention to, though, is the premise on which all these denominational efforts are based, a premise which, if the ecclesiology outlined above has any traction, is faulty. The premise is that our denominational unity is based on a common vision on theological and ethical agreement, and that in the absence of such common vision fracture and schism are inevitable.

It is no surprise that such premise is driving our denominational conversations. Most American mainline denominations function as if they are constituted by common confessional documents, liturgical practices, or polity agreements. In the PC(USA), the combined *Book of Confessions* and

Book of Order are even called "The Constitution" of the denomination. But if my argument so far holds, the church is not constituted by its common confessions, liturgical practices, or polity, but by the gathering work of its resurrected and ascended Lord. Our common ecclesial life is not based on our agreement with one another, but on Christ's reaching out to each one of us in the covenant of baptism, and calling us together into one community, knitting us into a new humanity. This is not to say that common confessions and practices and agreements on theological and ethical positions are not important. But they are nonetheless only *responses* to Christ's gathering, church-constituting work; they are not church constituting themselves. Even when we cannot come to theological or ethical agreement, even if we cannot come to a common confession, even if our liturgical practices lead us in different directions, we are still one church, because our communal church membership was not decided by us, but by the fact that Jesus Christ called us together in one body.

What would it mean for our denomination if, instead of moving from studies and debates about one "hot topic" after the other, we would focus our time and energy on living into this reality? What would it mean for us to learn practices, slowly, and sometimes painfully, of living together with people with whom we may strongly disagree, but with whom we nonetheless form the household of God? What would it mean for congregations to step away from developing one or the other specific theological identity, other than just the one given to us in baptism? What would it mean for presbyteries and General Assembly, to meet not to "settle" policy issues, but to bring rather our divisions at the foot of the cross?

Again, the issues that divide our denomination are real issues. I am not suggesting we smooth them over, deny the differences that exist among us. In fact, I believe the differences to be so serious, the fissures to be so deep, that, at least at this point, no compromise can bridge them and no "agreement" can forge a common mind. My point is that we already have a common mind: the mind of Christ. What kind of witness would it give to a culture accustomed to dividing itself up along partisan battle lines, if a Christian community would say: "We too disagree among ourselves; and we do not see a way forward to solve our differences. But nonetheless we will not let any of these issues divide us, because we know that our lives are not shaped by what we think or believe but by what Christ has done for each one of us"?[48]

48. This, by the way, is exactly the kind of thing the new Presbyterian Hymnal *Glory to God* wants to support the denomination in doing. The book's overarching theme is "salvation history," God's powerful acts of creation, redemption, and final transformation. It was a theme chosen because the hymnal committee believed that in

2. If this is what it means to be church, we need to rethink our understanding of church membership.

If a church is not a community based on common agreements or practices, but a community gathered together by Jesus Christ, this should have consequences for the way our polity conceives of membership in the church. It is here that the PC(USA)'s *Book of Order* expresses significant theological confusion. The section on "The Membership of a Congregation" starts with the notion of baptism: "In Jesus Christ, God calls people to faith and to membership in the Church, the body of Christ. Baptism is the visible sign of that call and claim on a human life and of entrance into the membership of the church."[49] This seems exactly right. The importance of this claim is that baptism is not something we do ourselves, but that is being done to us. In baptism we die and are resurrected (Rom 6:3–4; Col 2:12). Resurrection life is not something we can give ourselves; it is a gift we receive. In this way, we become part of the church. However, the *Book of Order* does not stop here. Two sections further, it suddenly introduces the notion of "active church membership."[50] There seems to be a higher level membership of the church than the one granted with baptism; and this higher level membership is dependent on choice. An active member "is a person who has made a profession of faith in Christ, has been baptized, has been received into membership of the church," and who "has voluntarily submitted to the government of this church, and participates in the church's work and worship."[51] The difference between the baptized member and the active member is that whereas the first one is subject to "pastoral care and instruction of the church, and may participate in the Sacrament of the Lord's Supper," the active member is also supposed to commit herself to a set of "disciplines and responsibilities" such as participating in worship, prayer, reading Scripture, giving offerings, and so on.[52] For some reason, the *Book of Order* seems to think that having been united with Christ in his resurrection life is not sufficient ground to engage in such practices. One first has to become an "active member."

---

this time of insecurity and anxiety our attention needs to be re-directed from ourselves to God; that we need to be reminded that the focus of history is not the rise or fall of empires or institutions but the certain future of God's inaugurated kingdom. See van Driel, "On the Theological Vision," 3–10.

49. *The Book of Order*, G-1.0301 (p. 20).

50. Ibid., G-1.0303 (p. 21).

51. Ibid., G-1.0402 (p. 22).

52. Compare ibid., G-1.0401 (p. 22), with G-1.042 (p. 22) and G-1.0304 (p. 21).

The *Book of Order* relies on two different notions: that of a "believers church" and a covenantal church, of an ecclesiology in which church membership is seen as expression of internal conviction and one in which it comes about through sacramental initiation. A believers church ecclesiology fits the North American cultural emphasis on freedom and choice.[53] But the gospel speaks about Christians "being rescued from the power of darkness and [being] transferred into the kingdom of [the Father's] beloved Son" (Col 1:13). That's very different imagery than a membership resulting from "voluntary submission to the government of this church." Therefore, I believe my colleague John P. Burgess is right when, in a contribution to an earlier Colloquium, he champions the abolishment of the "active membership" category in the *Book of Order*.[54]

3. To counter a culture of ecclesial schism and splintering, the PC(USA) ought to invest in the common life with other denominations.

We are not just a conflicted church; we are a church that is suffering schism. In the last couple of years we have dismissed several hundreds of congregations to other, dissenting denominations. The same has happened in other mainline churches. One of the poisons of schism is that it tends to shape the identity of ecclesial communities. That certainly is the case for "those who

---

53. There is, of course, one striking anomaly in this freedom and choice: that of the membership of this voluntaristic culture and its accompanying nationality itself. As Stanley Hauerwas comments: "We . . . have great difficulty passing on our faith in God to our children because we think they get to make up the kind of Christianity they will practice, which usually means after a time they quit practicing altogether. It is interesting to note that often parents who believe they should let their children make up their own minds about being a Christian (or a Jew) do not think their children can or should make up their minds about their loyalty to an entity called America" (Hauerwas, *Approaching the End*, 88).

54. John B. Burgess, "'Is There Any Good Reason to Join a Church?'—Baptism, Mission, and Life Together," chapter 9 in the present volume. The reader will notice that we differ in our argumentation however. Burgess's position is that the practices the *Book of Order* currently assigns to an active member actually come to one by baptism. Burgess's argument for this rests on the stories of Jesus' calling of the twelve disciples. I am not convinced of the validity of that argument, as these stories are simply not about baptism. I think the stronger argument for Burgess's specific claim would be to look at the Pauline notion of baptism as dying and being resurrected, and how Paul uses this notion to call his readers to a new way of life. But even so, these practices are not constitutive of one's church membership—baptism is. And it is here that the *Book of Order* notion of "active church membership" is wrong-footed.

leave." They often explicitly formulate an identity around the theme that caused the ecclesial strife. But it can happen no less with "those who stay." It can come through resentment of those who left, a sense of hurt and betrayal, a certain smugness about "having chosen the right side." It can also come through down playing of the importance of visible unity: the "real" church is the invisible church and the visible structures are only human constructs, not the church proper. So we speak in North American culture about the visible churches as "denominations," communities that posses only part of the Christian truth. We may even go so far as to defend denominational pluralism as good for the religious marketplace: Just like the competition of the marketplace forces companies to stay on their toes, could not the same be said about American churches?

I believe that the denomination needs to work consciously and explicitly not to let its identity be deformed by the poisons of schism. My first two suggestions could help with that effort. As many parting congregations are of a conservative bent it would be easy for those who stay now to identify as a more liberal denomination. If we do that, we fall in the trap of suggesting that our common life is held together by common practices and agreements. Instead, this is the moment to rather be focused on the identity we have in Jesus Christ. In addition, as a way to counter any down-playing of the visible nature of the church, I believe this is the moment for the PC(USA) to reinvest in the seeking of interdenominational unity. I suggest the PC(USA) turns to other American mainline denominations, beginning with its full-communion ecumenical partners—the ELCA, the RCA, and the UCC—and invite them to engage in an sustained conversation about the question: "*What do we lose by not sharing in a visible common life?*"

For a shrinking mainline denomination to seek closer institutional unity with another denomination could easily be interpreted as an economically motivated move. The economy of it all should in fact not easily be dismissed. What is lost—in terms of money, time, creativity—when we keep different but parallel ecclesial institutions running? The resources involved in church work are really God's resources. These economical issues are therefore simultaneously theological issues. Nonetheless, my main motivation is not economical, but ecclesiological. If my ecclesiological argument so far carries any water, then in being ecclesially divided we are jeopardizing our salvation, as we live against the grain of Christ's gathering activity. As continued splintering of our communities has led Protestant theologians to develop strategies that empty the visible nature of the church of any real meaning, we need to find ways to realize once again the evangelical connection between church and salvation.

Therefore I propose the formulation I offered above: What are we losing by not sharing in a visible common life? For one, I formulate the question in terms of "loss" instead of "gain." Conversations about the gain of church unification seem to easily steer up anxiety about what would be lost if churches united—specifically the loss of denominational identity. We rather need to find ways to face what is lost by staying separated. What is lost when on Sunday morning my family leaves our driveway to go to church and turn right, while our neighbors simultaneously leave their house to go to church and turn left? And for another, I try to find a different term for what traditionally was called "institutional unity." Esteem for institutions is low. The "institutional church" is associated with committees and subcommittees, with Robert's Rules and church bureaucracy. In reality though, "institutional life" has to do with "common life." Institutional life concerns a group of people engaged in a common effort to reach out to the neighborhood. It is people filling the shelves of the food bank. It is people gathering around the table, stretching out their hands, and receiving bread and wine. All of that is an expression of people gathered together in the common life of an institution. I believe that, *exactly* at this point of conflict, schism, and low investment in "institutions," the denomination should reach out to its sister churches and ask: What is lost, when there are two, three, or four of such tables in the same street, but in different buildings? What is lost when there are two, three, or four of such groups of people wanting to reach out to the same town with the good news of Jesus Christ? Not just what is lost economically, but what is lost to the gospel that they are proclaiming, and what is lost to themselves? Are they still able to "let everyone see what is the plan of the mystery hidden for ages in God who created all things;" are they letting the powers-that-be know that their time is up (Eph 3:10)? Or does the very thing they do, suggest that the powers have won after all?

4. Struggling local congregations should be lead to join forces with a local ecumenical partner.

The gospel is a story of an empty grave. As Christians we believe that the natural flow of things does not have the last word, but that God can call forth a people out of a man who was as good as dead (Rom 4:19). I believe the key to rediscovering the visible church may lie exactly with small, struggling congregations whom seemingly do not have a future.

American mainline churches consist mostly of small congregations. Research from the end of the last century indicate that more than half of all mainline Protestant congregations have one hundred or fewer members.

This corresponds with the situation in the PC(USA): in 2009, 50 percent of all its congregations had a membership under one hundred. Not even half of these congregations has an installed pastor, and a bit less than a third has no pastoral leadership whatsoever.[55] Small churches simply do not have the resources to support a pastor's salary, health insurance, and other costs, especially when this comes on top of the costs of building maintenance, some sort of ministry and outreach, et cetera.

Mainline denominations stimulate their small churches to do one of three things: to call a part-time pastor, to yoke with neighboring congregations within the denomination, or to make use of the services of a trained lay person. Each of these three "solutions" has significant drawbacks. A part-time call often puts significant financial burdens on pastors. A yoked congregation significantly compromises the pastor's pastoral presence: not only will the pastor spend significant time on the road moving between the points of her parish, but also because the pastor will live in only one of the communities in which her churches are located. Trained lay leaders, such as the PC(USA) commissioned lay pastors, are hardly equipped for their task, having on average received a training the equivalent of less than one semester of introductory level college education.[56]

A much better solution is, I propose, for congregations to join forces with other mainline churches. Given the nature of the American religious landscape, most of these small, struggling mainline congregations are located in townships that also house similarly small, struggling mainline churches with different denominational affiliations. What if these congregations, rather than choosing one of the solutions mentioned above, would call a pastor together? Politywise, this is possible. The PC(USA) is in full communion with the ELCA, the UCC, and the RCA.[57] "Full communion" means, among other things, that a local congregation affiliated with one of these denominations can call an ordained minister affiliated with one of the other partnering denominations. In addition, there is precedent for cooperation between Presbyterian and United Methodist churches. The ELCA in turn is in full communion with the Episcopal Church and the United Methodist Church.[58] This means that a wide variety of combinations is possible. The Protestant churches that are in full communion could call together one pastor from any of the partnering denominations. In a town where there is

55. "PC(USA) Comparative Statistics 2009."
56. Wheeler, *Preparation*, 7.
57. Cf. "A Formula of Agreement."
58. For the former, cf. "Called to Common Mission." For the latter, see "Confessing Our Faith Together."

a Presbyterian Church, a Lutheran Church, and an Episcopal Church, the three congregations could call an ELCA pastor that serves all three congregations because, while Presbyterians and Episcopalians are not in full communion with each other, the Lutherans are in partnership with each. I am not suggesting that congregations would merge, nor even that they would worship together—although, in the long run, that would be most desirable. They would not even have to give up their separate church buildings—although that too, given the pressure that real estate puts on church budgets, would be worth serious consideration. They could all keep their own church plant and church services, but one pastor could serve them all. They could certainly combine church programs: adult education, as well as confirmation classes, Bible studies, and missional and outreach work. The advantages are numerous, starting with the fact that under this model congregations would once again have a fully trained minister of Word and Sacrament living in their own town. Thus, a minister would now have ample opportunity to get to know the local community in which she serves, including the many personal relationships that will tie these different church communities together, and would not lose time in traveling from one town to another. Churches will save significant amount of money, certainly if they would go beyond the sharing of the pastor in sharing ministries and buildings. But maybe most importantly: from being locked into the depressing spiral of lack of money, lack of leadership, and anxiety for the future, churches may find themselves once again be viable communities, whose cooperation is a visible witness to the gathering and reuniting work of Jesus Christ.[59]

What would need to happen for this proposal to be implemented? As for church polity, all requirements are in place. What I am advocating is legally already possible. Some practical measures would help, though. First of all, in most mainline denominations congregations have enough autonomy that they cannot be forced to work together. Ecclesial authorities however could certainly stimulate trans-denominational congregational cooperation. Regional authorities—Presbyteries, synods, dioceses—could identify congregations that would profit from these arrangements and initiate conversations. They could also propose arrangements for clergy called to these cooperations. For example, no clergy person serving congregations from two or three denominations should be expected to visit regional meetings of two or three denominational structures. Seminaries could prepare candidates for multi-denominational service by teaching theology and worship from more than one denominational perspective. They could, preferably in

---

59. For a very similar suggestion, based on the experience of cooperation between a PC(USA) and a UMC congregation, see Wheeler, "Ready to Lead?"

cooperation with regional ecclesial authorities, offer special continuing education trainings for clergy serving in these multi-denominational services. Most importantly, both local congregations and denominations will have to give up their denominational idolatry in forsaking the idea that proper ministry only takes place in one denominational context. For that, awareness of the eschatological nature of the church and of its calling to be a visible witness of the gathering work of Jesus Christ, could be a great help.

5. We should reclaim the notion of missional comity.

The missional-liturgical conversation opens up new perspectives for mission and evangelism. For one, it emphasizes the ecclesial nature of mission. Over the last two decades or so the missional church movement has argued that the church is by its very nature missional. And rightly so: after all, Christ's eschatological work, which constitutes the church, "missional": gathering the scattered fragments of humanity, drawing them out from under the authority of the powers that have governed them so far, and knitting them together into a new people. But because of this, the mission of the church is intrinsically ecclesial: the salvation that is offered in mission takes the form of being gathered into the church.[60] For another: On my propos-

60. *Contra* the popular book by Frost and Hirsch, *The Shape of Things to Come*. For Frost and Hirsch, the church has become completely instrumental, a means to evangelism. In fact, on close reading of this book for Frost and Hirsch the "church," as agent of mission, can as much be an individual or a group of friends rather than a body sacramentally united and with its own meaning as the place where salvation is found. Coming from a very different perspective, Teresa Lockhart Stricklen, "Worship as the Missional Church's Whence and Whither: A Liturgical Missional Ecclesiology," chapter 3 in the present volume, shows the same lack of appreciation of the ecclesial shape of mission when she argues, with Clark Cowden, that "the institution of a missional church functions like an airport that helps people get to their destinations for service to the world in Christ's Spirit. No one wants to live, or even stay long, in an airport." The church is much more than a transit place: it *is* the destination, be it not the destination in its completed form. I wonder whether Stricklen's position is the result of a lack of appreciation of the particularity of the work of Christ and the Spirit. Earlier she had argued, this time quoting John Dally, that "God's Reign 'is present on earth whenever life accurately reflects the will and sovereignty of God. It is the way life and society would be if a compassionate God were in charge or imitated instead of' human powers that lord over others . . . Preaching the Realm of God is difficult, though, because there is no *there* to point to, for God's Reign is not a place, but a way of being under God's Rule in Christ through the power of the Holy Spirit" (quoting from Dally, *Choosing the Kingdom*, 50). On the account of the Ephesians Letter the universality expressed in this line of thought is to be applauded; but what seems lacking is its particular center. God's reign is not *wherever* life reflects the will of God, but wherever *Christ gathers all things to himself*. And as such, there is a place one could point to if

als, missional churches will be internally conflicted churches. After all, my suggestions contain a strong emphasis on church unity, even in times of deep theological turmoil. Can such conflicted churches be missionally effective? What will their witness be, if they are internally so divided about the content of the Gospel? I believe the missional-liturgical response needs to be that the missional strength of an internally divided church can lie exactly in its weakness, if by holding on to unity, even while deeply disagreeing, its members are a living witness to their Christ-given baptismal identity, which shapes them deeper than their own theological divisions are strong.

My main suggestion is however that mainline churches, as they rediscover their missional identity, should also re-engage the notion of missional comity. "Comity" refers to the late nineteenth-century agreements among Protestant mission boards to a division of territory and assignment of spheres of mission. The idea was not to waste resources by competing in the same territory with missionaries from another ecclesial tradition, and to support one another's efforts by mutual agreement on employment of workers, their salaries, standards of membership for the churches, transfer of membership, the adoption of similar standards of discipline, and respect of each other's disciplinary process.[61] According to Lesslie Newbigin, the spiritual father of the North-American mission church movement, the notion of comity shaped the way the newly founded churches related. "The acceptance of this principle . . . means that in any one place—town or village—there is *normally* but one Christian congregation, and upon this congregation rests the responsibility for the evangelization of the area allotted to it under the principle of comity."[62] Following this comity principle, the Church in South India, Newbigin's church, "has refused to accept the necessity to cater for varieties of tradition, caste and class by setting up a variety of congregations in each place. The principle of comity has meant this, that the typical congregation in a South Indian country town consists of men and women who have nothing in common save the redemption in Christ. That means, as has been said, strain and stress within the congregation . . . But it also does mean that men are driven back to Christ and compelled to ask themselves again and again how much it matters to them that Christ died for them."[63] Comity however not only had a strong influence on the internal relationship in the churches; it also had a profound influence on

---

one wants to find God's kingdom: the place where God's reign becomes visible, in the community of the church.

61. See Beaver, *Ecumenical Beginnings*.
62. Newbigin, *The Reunion of the Church*, 12.
63. Ibid., 13.

how these churches thought about mission: "Where there is only one Christian congregation in a town or village or district, its members can never forget the fact that the responsibility for making known the Gospel in that area rests upon them alone. If they do not do it, no one else will. Where, on the other hand, there is a multitude of competing congregations it is well-nigh impossible for their members to feel resting upon themselves the full responsibility for their neighbours. Inevitably each congregation becomes more concerned with the maintenance of its own distinctive life."[64]

The notion of comity became part of American church life in the late forties and early fifties of the twentieth century, when the suburbs were built and American mainline denominations coordinated their church planting efforts.[65] Since then, "comity" has virtually dropped out of the missiological conversation. But now that the mainline churches are reclaiming their missional identity, and a church like the PC(USA) wishes to support 1001 new worshiping communities, should the church not also reclaim the notion of comity? Assuming the goal is not so much to strengthen our own tribe, but to be in the service of Christ's gathering activity, how can we assure that these new worshipping communities do really engage those areas where the church does not have a place yet, instead of competing with existing church communities? In fact, would this not be extraordinary chance to found communities who are not tied to just one denomination, but who are cooperative efforts of several ecclesial communities? Doing so will raise whole new questions, and create extra difficulties. But it would also be a much better reflection of the salvation given to us in Jesus Christ.

6. Seminaries ought to pay more attention to the ecclesial formation of candidates for ordination.

Protestant seminaries are good at intellectual formation, training their students in the classical academic theological disciplines of exegesis, history, and theology. They are also good at professional formation; for decades now they have thought of themselves as "professional schools." They are becoming good at personal and spiritual formation, as the recent attention to seminary education as a form of *paideia* and formation starts to shape their educational practice. But what about ecclesial formation? By "ecclesial formation" I mean the creation of a disposition to understand our engagement with and sharing of the treasures of the gospel as fundamentally a catholic

---

64. Ibid., 15.

65. See, for instance, "Protestants Plan Comity Program," 718; "Southwest Ohio Has a Comity Plan," 1286–87.

project.⁶⁶ By being ordained one becomes a representative on the ministry of Word and sacrament as entrusted by Jesus Christ to the wider, visible church. Through his ministers Christ enacts his gathering work, as he gives them "to equip the saints for the work of ministry, for building up the body of Christ, until all of us come the unity of the faith" (Eph 4:12–13). While as a minister one works in a particular place, in that place one represents the wider church, and, in the end, of Christ himself. This is why ordination to Word and Sacrament is not performed by a local congregation, but it is "an act of the whole church carried out by the presbytery."⁶⁷ It is also why, in the PC(USA), in her ordination service a candidate makes promises concerning her relationship to the wider church, not a local congregation.⁶⁸ Finally, this is why, in the PC(USA) upon one's ordination one is no longer a member of a congregation, but instead becomes a member of Presbytery.⁶⁹

If my argument holds, awareness of this wider ecclesial context of one's ordination is of utmost importance, because in representing the unity of the wider, visible church to a congregation, the pastor represents that what is salvific: Christ gathering all things into himself. Seminary is the place *par excellence* to be prepared for this aspect of ordained ministry because it is a microcosm of that wider, visible church. Students who may know only one, or a few, local congregations, are brought together with fellow Christians coming from very different locations—geographically, socioeconomically, racially, and theologically. And not just in the class room, but in all aspects of life. By going to chapel together, eating in the common room, living communally in the dorms, in family play dates and sharing of personal joys and woes, students of very different backgrounds learn what it will mean to serve together in one church.

I doubt that this aspect of seminary training receives much explicit attention. Not only is the formational role of places like chapel, the refectory, and a school's living quarters highly under theorized, but I believe ecclesial formation plays hardly a role in the way seminaries reflect on the purposes and desired outcomes of their education. When we train students for church

---

66. I owe this formulation to Sheldon W. Sorge, the Pastor to Pittsburgh Presbytery.

67. *The Book of Order*, G-2.0701 (p. 36).

68. For example, she promises to be instructed by the confessions of the church, to be governed by the church's polity, to abide by its discipline, to be a friend to her colleagues, to further the peace, unity, and purity of the church (not *a congregation*, but *the church*), to serve the people with energy, intelligence, imagination, and love (not *a particular* people, but *the* people that are part of the church), to be active in government and discipline, and to serve on the governing bodies of the church. See ibid., W-4.4003 (pp. 122–23).

69. Ibid., G.2.0704 (p. 36).

ministry, the implicit understanding of "church" is usually either local or global. We train them in the things they will do in a local congregation: to lead worship, to preach, to teach and to offer pastoral care. We give them a sense of the worldwide Christian community by courses in global Christianity and mission and by sponsoring trips to ecumenical organizations and Christian communities oversees. But other than offering an obligatory polity class, where in our seminary teaching do we give our students a sense of the wider visible church as the primary context of their future ordination? And in that case, can we be surprised if pastors see themselves primarily in the service of a local congregation, and feel free to take that congregation to another denominational community if they feel so compelled?[70]

If "to be saved," however, means for one to be folded into Christ's gathering work, for one knitted into the fabric of the new humanity, the new household of God, then seminaries ought to reflect explicitly upon that extraordinary gift that is given to them, to be a place where people can experience what it means, even for a season, to live and eat and pray together as "citizens with the saints and members of the household of God" (Eph 2:19).[71]

V. Conclusion

Reformed ecclesiology has always suffered from opposing intuitions. Reformed theologians inherited from Calvin on the one hand a high appreciation for the church, and on the other hand a need to defend the schism of the Reformation and a strong sense that God's forgiveness is unconditional, and therefore also not bound to church membership. The strategies the Reformed developed over time to combine these different theological desiderata let to a significant erosion of the role of the visible church in salvation history.

---

70. One question that needs to be asked in this context is this: is ecclesial formation even under more pressure at seminaries that are theologically rather than ecclesially aligned? It is my observation that in my own presbytery, of the pastors who led their congregations out of the denomination without adherence to the denomination's ordering of dismissal of congregations or the presbytery's separation procedures, in overall majority were trained at non-denominational seminaries.

71. An explicit reflection on the formational aspects of a seminary's chapel, common room, and living quarters should have consequences for how we evaluate the pros and cons of online theological education. It is telling that in the discussions about this phenomenon there is much attention to the ways in which online learning may facilitate spiritual formation of seminarians, but there is no reflection at all on the relationship between ecclesial formation and online education.

The way forward is to rediscover the richness of the notion of "salvation" in the biblical parlance. Salvation is not just concerned with forgiveness and reconciliation, but also with eschatological consummation. The goal of creation is for all things to be gathered up in Christ, and the visible church is the place where Christ's salvific, gathering activity already shapes our lives. Once we rediscover that, we may not only have found a way of solving the dilemma of Reformed ecclesiology, but we may also be able to develop richer relationships within the denomination and among the still divided Christian churches.

Bibliography

Barth, Markus. *The Broken Wall: A Study of the Epistle to the Ephesians.* Chicago: Judson, 1959.

———. *Ephesians 1–3.* Anchor Study Bible 34. Garden City, NY: Doubleday, 1974.

Beaver, R. Pierce. *Ecumenical Beginnings in Protestant World Mission: A History of Comity.* New York: Thomas Nelson, 1962.

Best, Ernest. *A Critical and Exegetical Commentary on Ephesians.* Edinburgh: T. & T. Clark, 1998.

"Called to Common Mission." 1999. http://www.elca.org/Who-We-Are/Our-Three-Expressions/Churchwide-Organization/Ecumenical-and-Inter-Religious-Relations/Full-Communion-Partners/The-Episcopal-Church/Called-to-Common-Mission.aspx.

Calvin, John. *Institutes of the Christian Religion.* Edited by John T. McNeill. Translated by Ford Lewis Battles. Library of Christian Classics. Philadelphia: Westminster, 1960.

"Confessing Our Faith Together." 2009. http://www.gccuic-umc.org/dmdocuments/Confessing_Our_Faith_Together.pdf.

The Constitution of the Presbyterian Church (U.S.A.), Part I, Book of Confessions. Louisville: The Office of the General Assembly, 1999.

The Constitution of the Presbyterian Church (U.S.A.), Part II, Book of Order. Louisville: The Office of the General Assembly, 2013.

Cyprian of Carthage. "Letter LXXII.21." *Ante-Nicene Fathers* 5. Edited by Alexander Roberts and James Donaldson. Peabody, MA: Hendrickson, 2004.

Dally, John. *Choosing the Kingdom: Missional Preaching for the Household of God.* Herndon, VA: Alban, 2008.

Dennison, James T., Jr. "The Life and Career of Francis Turretin." In *Institutes of Elenctic Theology*, edited by Francis Turretin, 3:639–58. Translated by George Musgrave Giger. Phillipsburg, NJ: P&R, 1992.

"A Formula of Agreement between the Evangelical Lutheran Church in America, The Presbyterian Church (U.S.A.), the Reformed Church in America, and the United Church of Christ." 1997. http://oga.pcusa.org/ecumenicalrelations/resources/formula.pdf.

Frost, Michael, and Alan Hirsch. *The Shape of Things to Come: Innovation and Mission for the 21st Century Church.* Peabody, MA: Hendrickson, 2003.

Guder, Darrell L. "The Church as Missional Community." In *The Community of the Word: Toward and Evangelical Ecclesiology*, edited by Mark Husbands and Daniel J. Treiter, 114–30. Downers Grove, IL: InterVarsity, 2005.

———, ed. *Missional Church: A Vision for the Sending of the Church in North America*. Grand Rapids: Eerdmans, 1998.

Gutjahr, Paul C. *Charles Hodge: Guardian of Orthodoxy*. Oxford: Oxford University Press, 2014.

Hauerwas, Stanley. *Approaching the End: Eschatological Reflections on Church, Politics, and Life*. Grand Rapids: Eerdmans, 2013.

Hodge, Charles. *Discussions in Church Polity: From the Contributions to the* Princeton Review. Selected and arranged by William Durant. New York: Scribner's, 1878.

———. *Systematic Theology* [1871–73]. Vols. 1 and 3. Grand Rapids: Eerdmans, 1997.

Kolb, Robert, and Timothy J. Wengert, eds. *The Book of Concord: The Confessions of the Evangelical Lutheran Church*. Minneapolis: Fortress, 2000.

Küng, Hans. *The Church*. Garden City, NY: Image, 1967.

Newbigin, Lesslie. *The Household of God: Lectures on the Nature of the Church*. 1954. Repr., Eugene, OR: Wipf & Stock, 2008.

———. *The Reunion of the Church: A Defence of the South India Scheme*. London: SCM, 1960.

Peterson, Eugene H. *Practice Resurrection: A Conversation on Growing Up in Christ*. Grand Rapids: Eerdmans, 2010.

"Presbyterian Church (USA) Comparative Statistics 2009." Louisville: PC(USA) Research Services, 2009. http://www.pcusa.org/media/uploads/research/pdfs/2009_table_15.pdf.

"Protestants Plan Comity Program." *The Christian Century* 66/23 (June 8, 1949) 718.

"Southwest Ohio Has a Comity Plan: Church Leaders Propose Coordinated Effort in Cities and Rapidly Growing Areas Between." *The Christian Century* 72 (1955) 1286–87.

Stubbs, David L. *The Open Table: What Gospel Do We Practice*. Theology and Worship Occasional Paper No. 22. Louisville: PC(USA) Office of Theology and Worship, 2011.

The Teachings of the Second Vatican Council. Introduction by Gregory Baum. Westminster, MD: Newman, 1966.

Thiessen, Gesa, ed. *Ecumenical Ecclesiology: Unity, Diversity and Otherness in a Fragmented World*. London: Continuum, 2009.

van Driel, Edwin Chr. "Christ in Paul's Narrative: Salvation History, Apocalyptic Invasion, and Supralapsarian Theology." In *Galatians and Christian Theology: Justification, the Gospel, and Ethics in Paul's Letter*, edited by Mark W. Elliott et al., 230–38. Grand Rapids: Baker Academic, 2014.

———. "Climax of the Covenant vs. Apocalyptic Invasion: A Theological Analysis of a Contemporary Debate in Pauline Exegesis." *International Journal of Systematic Theology* 17 (2015) 6–25.

———. "Church and Covenant: Theological Resources for Divided Denominations." *Theology Today* 65 (2009) 449–61.

———. *Incarnation Anyway: Arguments for Supralapsarian Christology*. New York: Oxford University Press, 2008.

———. "On the Theological Vision that Shaped *Glory to God*." *Call to Worship* 47 (2014) 3–10.

Wheeler, Barbara G. *Preparation of Commissioned Lay Pastors: A Study of Representative Features.* New York: Auburn Center for the Study of Theological Education, 2008.

———. "Ready to Lead? The Problems with Lay Pastors." *The Christian Century* (June 13, 2010). http://www.auburnseminary.org/ready-lead-problems-lay-pastors.

Wright, N. T. *Paul and the Faithfulness of God.* London: SPCK, 2013.

www.ingramcontent.com/pod-product-compliance
Lightning Source LLC
Chambersburg PA
CBHW071238230426

43668CB00011B/1497